Financial Control for
Your Hotel

Financial Control for Your Hotel

Michael M. Coltman

VNR VAN NOSTRAND REINHOLD
New York

Library of Congress Catalog Card Number 91-3263
ISBN 0-442-00731-1

Printed in the United States of America.

Figures in chapters 4, 12, and 15 are reprinted with permission from Coltman, M., *Hospitality Management Accounting, Fourth Edition* (New York: Van Nostrand Reinhold, 1991).

Figures in chapters 6, 7, 8, and figures 9-2, 9-5, 9-6, and 9-7 are reprinted with permission from Coltman, M., *Cost Control for the Hospitality Industry* (New York: Van Nostrand Reinhold, 1988).

Figures 7-2, 7-3, and 7-5 are reprinted with permission from Coltman, M., *Hospitality Industry Purchasing* (New York: Van Nostrand Reinhold, 1990).

Van Nostrand Reinhold
115 Fifth Avenue
New York, New York 10003

Chapman and Hall
2-6 Boundary Row
London, SE1 8HN, England

Thomas Nelson Australia
102 Dodds Street
South Melbourne 3205
Victoria, Australia

Nelson Canada
1120 Birchmount Road
Scarborough, Ontario MIK 5G4, Canada

16 15 14 13 12 11 10 9 8 7 6 5 4 3 2 1

Library of Congress Cataloging-in-Publication Data

Coltman, Michael M., 1930-
    Financial control for your hotel / Michael M. Coltman.
      p. cm.
    Includes index.
    ISBN (invalid) 0-442-00731-1
    1. Hotels, taverns, etc.—Finance. I. Title.
TX911.3.F5C634VJ   1991
647.94′068′1—dc20
                                    91-3263
                                     CIP

Contents

Preface

The last ten years have seen far-reaching changes in the hospitality industry, particularly in those operations that comprise about 80 percent of all properties: the small hotel or motel of 50 rooms or less. As a result of these changes, the nature of the industry has altered from one in which anyone could make a profit without really trying to one where a more professional approach from entrepreneurs entering the industry is required.

Operating a small hotel is not as easy as it may sometimes appear. In the middle of the tourist season when the traveler without a reservation finds it difficult to obtain a room, it must seem that the accommodation operators spend all their time ringing up the cash register and carrying their deposits to the bank. But the cash registers that ring so loudly in August usually do not make the same happy sound in the doldrums of December.

There are many different types of small accommodation property, including tourist cabins, campgrounds, trailer parks, roadside or highway motels, resort hotels and motels, suburban motels and motor hotels, and city motels, motor hotels, and hotels. For the sake of simplicity in this book we shall simply use the word *hotel* to cover all of these different accommodation types, with reference to a particular type only where it is deemed necessary.

Each type of hotel is unique in its own way. Nevertheless, with reference to financial control, most of the same principles apply. Even though this book is entitled *Financial Control for Your Hotel*, and even though it is primarily concerned with the financial aspects of your business, it should be emphasized that financial controls alone are not sufficient to ensure a successful business.

Before financial control can be practised, you must have effective management of your operation. The term *management* in this context covers all aspects of your business, such as operational control, employee relations, public relations, and marketing. In other words, financial control is only one function of management.

The title of this book might lead you to believe that you must be an accountant to understand and practice financial control. You do not have to be an accountant, become an accountant, or have an accounting background to understand and put into practice the principles, procedures, and techniques outlined throughout this book.

Further, although this book provides you with many different tools to use, you should not try to use all of them. In other words, you must be selective with the book's "menu" and choose the techniques that fit your needs and can be applied in your operation.

Finally, this book does not discuss financial control for foodservice operations within a hotel. For detailed information on this topic the reader is referred to *Financial Control for Your Foodservice Operation*, published by Van Nostrand Reinhold.

ONE

Introduction

MANAGING MONEY

Running a hotel, just like running any business, is about managing money. Without managing money, no business can be successfully operated and will probably eventually fail.

To generate and manage money, you must have enough profit to stay in business and ensure that this profit produces enough cash to make all payments when they are due. Thus, it is just as important to plan for cash as it is for profit. Note that profit and cash are *not* the same thing, as you will discover as you read this book.

What Does Financial Control Mean?

Profit and cash availability will result only if you have good financial control. Financial control means

- Knowing where you are at any time from a profit and cash perspective. (This is really the basis of all financial control.)
- Planning where you are going through the use of budgets and other tools.
- Ensuring you reach where you plan to go through regular financial reports that monitor your progress.

Knowledge of Accounting

In order to exercise any form of financial control, you must know something about accounting. You can obtain this knowledge without becoming an accountant. If you are the owner or operator of a hotel you probably question why you need to understand accounting because you employ an accountant with whom you can have regular meetings and discussions.

Even if your hotel is not large enough to employ a full-time accountant, it is likely that you have an "outside" accountant who handles your books, prepares your accounts, and looks after regulatory requirements such as filing annual income tax returns. He or she can also meet with you regularly to discuss your business. Indeed, this accountant probably knows a lot about many different businesses, such as small manufacturing firms, retail stores, and restaurants, and can compare your results with those of other businesses. But those other businesses are not like the hotel business, and comparison of your results with theirs is meaningless. Further, an external accountant cannot possibly know everything about each of these different businesses, cannot be a specialist at each of them, and can thus only discuss your business with you in general terms.

Knowledge of Hotel Problems

For example, does an external accountant know anything about managing labor cost in a hotel operation, about room pricing, and about the problems inherent in operating a seven-day-a-week business? The answer is: probably not. You, however, know about these day-to-day problems, but probably know little about accounting. Therefore, this book has been written to:

- Discuss hotel operations and relate them to what your accountant does so that *you* can better understand what your financial statements tell you about your business.

- Explain how you can interpret accounting information to improve the effectiveness of your hotel's operations and maximize its profits and cash flows.

Inadequate Records

Unfortunately, many small hotel owners fail to keep adequate records and make no attempt to understand the basics of accounting. As a result, they often do not know whether the business made a profit or a loss until weeks after the end of each financial period (month, quarter, half year, or year) because they have not provided their accountant with sufficient information to prepare proper financial statements. Although these "official" financial statements are important (and necessary in such matters as filing income tax returns), there is no reason why any hotel owner, given adequate accounting records, cannot prepare interim financial statements that will give at least some indication of how the hotel is doing on a monthly basis.

As various methods, tools, and techniques of financial control are explained throughout this book, you will probably wonder why your accountant does not do all this for you. If your accountant is a full-time employee, it is likely that he or she either does not know how to do this or does not have the time. If the individual does not know, then a little investment of your time in explaining what you want produced (in addition to the regular financial statements) will provide the needed information. If your accountant does not have the time, then you will either have to invest your own time to do the work, or hire somebody else (such as an outside accountant) to produce the information desired.

If you presently use an outside accountant (because your hotel is not large enough to require a full-time accounting employee), you will be paying that accountant a fee based on the time involved each month to produce your financial statements. That accountant probably has the knowledge to produce a great deal of other information if instructed to do so. But since that will entail more time, there will be an additional cost, unless you again do the work yourself.

Regardless of the situation, there is going to have to be an extra investment of time (and thus money) by *someone* to produce the desired additional financial information. However, that investment is sure to result in improved profits and cash flow, and therefore generate a higher return on your investment in your hotel.

BASIC ACCOUNTING INFORMATION

Accounting was developed to identify and record financial information about a business. It provides information about a company's assets, liabilities (debts), owners' investment, sales (revenue), and expenses. An accounting system allows you or your accountant to prepare basic financial statements (balance sheet and income statement), and other financial reports and analyses that will help you in decision making and in running an efficient, effective, and profitable business. Basic information that any hotel needs to have records of include:

- Sales (sometimes called revenue) by day, week, month, or quarter, and further broken down into cash or credit sales (by type of credit card, if necessary). Electronic or computerized front office sales equipment can readily provide much of the required sales detail without requiring extensive paperwork.
- Operating expenses by type (for example, purchases, labor, supplies, and other operating costs) in total by month, and by department in a large operation. Payroll (labor cost) is a major expense for most hotels and there are legal requirements concerning the detail that you must record. In particular, payroll withholdings (for unemployment insurance, income tax, and others) must be properly documented.

It is important that you keep documents supporting all transactions. Documents include guest account folios, purchase invoices, cancelled checks for all purchases, and receipts or memos for cash payments not otherwise supported by an invoice or cancelled check.

Decision Making

Hotel managers are constantly making decisions. These decisions can be improved by using various kinds of accounting information. Promptly produced accounting information can be used to:

- Measure your current performance against established objectives, such as achieving a desired percentage of labor cost relative to sales.
- Provide answers to questions such as: How much money is in the bank? What payments are due to lenders in the next year? How much can the operation afford to spend on needed new furnishings or equipment?
- Analyze sales and cost trends to make more effective plans about future trends of sales and costs.
- Help in producing forecast accounting information (such as budgets) to chart the strategies that you can use in future periods to meet your financial objectives. In other words, financial forecasts can provide a profit plan for the future.

Decision Principles

In your hotel, effective decisions based on financial information can only be made if this information is gathered and presented using certain basic principles. The most important principles are:

- *Accuracy.* For accounting information to have any validity, it must be as accurate as possible. This accuracy, however, must be balanced with practicality. For certain types of information, the more accurate it is the more time it takes to gather—and time costs money. There is a point beyond which the extra cost of accuracy is not worth the benefit. For example, it takes considerable time to take inventory and cost it accurately. Therefore, it makes sense in the case of certain inventory products to estimate their value rather than spend valuable time trying to be too accurate. For example, consider a resort hotel that operates an adjacent golf driving range as part of its recreational facilities. It makes sense to estimate the value of thousands of used golf balls on hand in various stages of wear and tear rather than spend an excessive amount of time trying to put a value on each individual golf ball.

- *Timeliness.* Information must also be timely. For example, if labor cost is measured each month against a desired standard, then the actual labor cost must be prepared within a few days of each month end so that you can make a timely comparison with the standard. If the actual labor cost is not available until, let us say, 30 days after the end of the month, and comparison with your standard shows that corrective action should have been taken, then an entire month's time has been lost. You must recognize this timeliness limitation (as many hotel operators do) and organize your information-gathering system accordingly. Indeed, so important is timeliness of labor cost information that many hotel operators calculate labor cost at the end of each day in order to compare it with their operation's standard.

- *Consistency.* For reasons of comparability of financial information from one accounting period to the next, consistency should prevail. In other words, the method of recording accounting information should not be changed without good reason. For example, if your hotel operates a gift shop, at each month-end a value must be placed on the inventory of unsold products. There are a number of different methods for pricing (valuing) this inventory. The method selected should be used consistently unless there is a good reason to change it.

Routine Decisions

Two broad types of decisions made by most hotel operators can be identified. The first is a routine decision made on a day-to-day basis and related to ongoing operations. An example of this type of decision concerns how many housekeeping employees to have on duty each day to cope with anticipated volume of business. Historic information concerning past occupancies combined with reservations already made can help in this type of routine decision making. For these routine decisions, you need to establish systems that allow the necessary decision-making information to be provided promptly and accurately.

Nonroutine Decisions

The second type of decision is a nonroutine (or infrequent) one. This type of decision concerns questions such as:

- Should I invest in redecorating the guest rooms?
- Should room rates be revised?
- Should I start a second hotel operation?

This type of decision is much more difficult to make than a routine one, and involves a far more serious situation if the wrong decision is made. For example, if you make a routine decision to have more employees on duty than were actually needed for a particular day, labor cost will be higher than it should be — but it only affects that day (so long as the same mistake is not continuously made). In contrast, if you decide to change your room rates and later discover that regular customers do not like the change and stay away, business will decline, and if the rates are changed back to the way they were before, it may take a long time before the "lost" customers are persuaded to return.

FINANCIAL STATEMENTS

Regularly each month you should prepare, or have prepared, a set of financial statements to monitor your operation's progress. The basic documents in this set of financial statements are an income statement (also known as a profit and loss statement) and a balance sheet.

The income statement shows revenues (sales) less expenses to arrive at profit. The profit (or loss, if expenses exceed revenues) is transferred to the balance sheet and becomes part of the owners' equity. If all accounting entries have been made correctly, the balance sheet will then *balance*. The balance sheet equation, as it is known, is:

$$\text{Assets} = \text{Liabilities} + \text{Owners' equity}$$

Assets are items owned by your hotel (for example cash, inventory, and furniture and equipment). Liabilities (debts or obligations) are items owed by your hotel such as unpaid accounts, bank loans, or other payments due in the future. Owners' equity (also sometimes referred to as *net worth*) is the difference between the assets and the liabilities. It is comprised of the money you — and any other owners — have invested in the hotel, plus the profits (less any losses) since the business began.

It perhaps makes more sense, from an owner's perspective, to state the balance sheet equation as:

$$\text{Assets} - \text{Liabilities} = \text{Owners' equity}$$

because, if the hotel were liquidated, the assets would be sold for cash, the cash used to pay off liabilities, and the owner(s) would receive whatever remained. Logical as this view of the balance sheet is, however, accountants prefer to express the equation in the traditional way since an even balance is then maintained.

Transactions

A balance sheet is prepared from accounts in which business transactions are recorded. A business transaction is an exchange of goods or services (for example, renting a room to a guest). In accounting, each transaction affects two or more accounts (this is why it is frequently referred to as double-entry accounting). No transaction can affect only one account. In this way, the balance sheet is always kept in balance (and your accountant eternally happy). This is illustrated very simply by considering what happens if you start a new small hotel by investing $25,000 in it. The balance sheet would look like this:

Assets		Owner's Equity	
Cash	$25,000	Investment	$25,000

If you then purchase from a supplier $5,000 of linen inventory on credit, the balance sheet now reflects the fact that assets have increased (because of the inventory) and so have liabilities (because the supplier must be paid for the linen) and looks like this:

Assets		Liability	
Cash	$25,000	Accounts payable	$ 5,000
Inventory	5,000		
		Owner's Equity	
		Investment	25,000
Totals	$30,000		$30,000

The balance sheet balances because the left-hand side (totaling $30,000) equals the right-hand side (also totaling $30,000).

Let us now assume that you make cash sales of $5,000 (increasing the cash account by that amount) during the first week and spend $3,000 for cash wages (reducing the cash account by that amount). As a result, you make a profit of $2,000 ($5,000 sales less $3,000 labor cost) causing your equity to increase by $2,000. The balance sheet now looks like this:

Assets		Liability	
Cash	$27,000	Accounts payable	$ 5,000
Inventory	5,000		

Owner's Equity

		Investment	25,000
		Profit	2,000
Totals	$32,000		$32,000

In practice, transactions such as making sales or incurring expenses are not recorded immediately on the balance sheet (because the balance sheet just would not have enough room on it and would be continuously changing). Instead, they are entered into accounting records called journals and then into accounts in a ledger, or (in a small business with fewer transactions) directly into the accounts in the ledger. It is the ledger, supported by the journals, that is commonly called the "books of account." Only at the end of an accounting period (such as the end of the month) is a new balance sheet created.

Further, when it is time to prepare the balance sheet, all the transactions relating to sales and expenses are first summarized on the income statement. As a result, even though the income statement is a separate document, it can be considered as an extension of the balance sheet's owners' equity section, and the balance sheet equation can be illustrated as follows to reflect this:

$$\text{Assets} = \text{Liabilities} + \text{Owners' Equity}$$

Income Statement
(Sales less expenses)

Accounts

In a business's ledger, there is usually one account for each type of asset, liability, owners' equity, sale (revenue), and expense. At the end of each accounting period only the account balances at that time are transferred to the balance sheet or to the income statement then to the balance sheet.

In accounting, each account is considered to have a left-hand side and a right-hand side. The left-hand side is where debit (usually abbreviated to Dr) entries are made, and the right-hand side is where credit (Cr) entries are made:

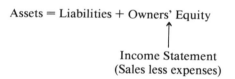

Debit (Dr)   Credit (Cr)

Because of their shape, these simply illustrated types of account are referred to as "T" accounts. In practice, you will never see accounts that look like this, but they are very useful for understanding and learning the basic rules of accounting.

When transactions are entered in the accounts, the entries in the debit side of the accounts must always equal the entries in the credit side. If this does not occur, the balance sheet will not balance. As the accounts are closed (totaled up) at the end of each accounting period, the difference between the debit and credit entries in each account provides the balance figure for that account.

You should not view debits as increases in the balance of accounts, and credits as decreases. Debits can either increase or decrease the balance, and credits can also either increase or decrease the balance. The rules for this are illustrated in the following "T" accounts:

Assets		Liabilities		Owners' Equity	
Debits	Credits	Debits	Credits	Debits	Credits
increase	decrease	decrease	increase	decrease	increase
balance	balance	balance	balance	balance	balance

Because sales increase owners' equity, sales account entries have the same effect as those for the owners' equity account, and because expenses decrease owners' equity, expense account entries are the reverse of those for sales. This is illustrated as follows:

Sales		Expenses	
Debits	Credits	Debits	Credits
decrease	increase	increase	decrease
balance	balance	balance	balance

The normal account balance for each of the five types of account would be:

Account	Normal Balance
Asset	Debit
Liability	Credit
Owners' Equity	Credit
Sales	Credit
Expenses	Debit

and an example of each would be:

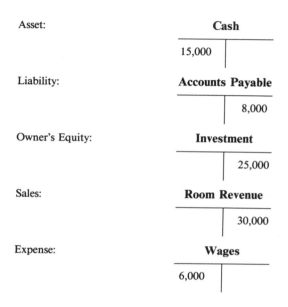

	Asset:	**Cash**
		15,000

	Liability:	**Accounts Payable**
		8,000

	Owner's Equity:	**Investment**
		25,000

	Sales:	**Room Revenue**
		30,000

	Expense:	**Wages**
	6,000	

IMPORTANCE OF MATCHING PRINCIPLE

For most hotels there are hundreds, if not thousands, of individual sales transactions (and often as many expense transactions) each month. At the end of each period when financial statements are desired, it is likely that some transactions have not yet been recorded. If they are not recorded, then the income statement will not reflect the hotel's true profit.

In order for the profit to be correct, any unrecorded transactions must be adjusted for by using an important concept in accounting known as the matching principle. The matching principle simply states that transactions should be recorded at the time they occur and not necessarily at the time cash is exchanged. For example, consider the following situation.

- Assume a regular customer of your hotel is allowed to charge his room rent to an account that is mailed out at the end of the month. Under the matching principle, the sales to that customer are shown as revenue for the month even though you may not receive the cash for several weeks. Similarly, a customer might pay an account by using a credit card. At that time the sale is still recorded as revenue, even though payment is not received from the credit card company until two weeks or more after the customer's credit card voucher is mailed to it.

• Purchases may be delivered to your hotel by suppliers without your having to pay cash on delivery. In other words, suppliers sell to you on credit. At each month-end, all purchases made must be recorded even though you may not make payment to suppliers until several weeks later.

• Assume you pay the insurance premium on your hotel's premises for the entire year in January. If you show this full payment as an expense on the January income statement, that statement will be distorted (the insurance expense will be higher than it should be) and the income statements of the other 11 months in the year will also be wrong (because they will show zero for insurance). Therefore, when the insurance is paid in January, the full amount is recorded as "prepaid insurance" (and shown as an asset on the balance sheet), and one-twelfth of that expense is transferred each month from the prepaid account to the expense account. Other expenses that are prepaid (such as rent) are handled in the same way.

• Assume that you normally pay your employees each Friday for time worked up to that Friday, and that the last day of a particular month falls on the following Monday. In the three days (Saturday, Sunday, and Monday) since payday, the employees who have worked will have earned money that you will not be paying them until the following Friday. Nevertheless, in order for your income statement to reflect the correct labor cost for that month, the wages earned must be recorded in a liability account (such as "accrued wages" or "wages payable") and also as a labor expense that appears on that month's income statement.

Adjustments

When your accountant prepares your month-end financial statements, he or she makes sure that all these types of transactions are adjusted for. The correct recording of these adjustments (and likely many others in most hotels) at each month-end will match all sales with all expenses incurred to generate those sales. It is not necessary that you understand the mechanics of adjustments, but it is important that you understand the need for them in order that your stated monthly profit is as accurate as possible. Using adjustments to match sales and expenses is known as *accrual accounting* —as opposed to *cash accounting*, under which entries are made in the books only when cash is received or paid out.

This does not suggest that cash-based accounting is never used. In fact, it might be quite a good idea to use it in some situations. For example, a small hotel that rents rooms only on a cash basis and pays cash for all wages and supplies might well use a cash-based accounting system, or a combined cash/accrual system. However, because most hotels usually have some purchases and sales (as well as other transactions) that are not on a cash basis, the matching concept of accrual accounting is assumed to be used throughout this book.

TWO

Understanding Your Balance Sheet

In order to understand financial statements, you do not have to be able to prepare them. However, if you understand how financial statements are put together, you have the advantage of being able to analyze the information they present in greater depth.

INCOME STATEMENT VERSUS BALANCE SHEET

The two major financial statements are the balance sheet and the income statement. Although the balance sheet and the income statement are prepared as separate documents, you must keep in mind the close relationship between them. This is clear when you compare the definitions of the two statements.

The balance sheet gives a picture of the financial position of a business *at a particular point* in time.

The income statement shows the operating results of the business *over a period* of time.

The period of time referred to for the income statement usually ends on the date of the balance sheet:

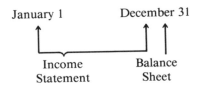

The balance sheet is discussed in this chapter, and the income statement in Chapter 3.

THE BALANCE SHEET

On the left-hand (or debit) side of the balance sheet are listed the assets or resources that your hotel has. On the right-hand (or credit) side are listed its liabilities (or debts) and the owners' equity. Total assets always equal total liabilities plus owners' equity (this is the balance sheet equation discussed in Chapter 1).

The asset side of the balance sheet is generally broken down into three categories: current assets, fixed or long-term assets, and other assets. The breakdown of assets into these categories is not for balancing reasons, but for the sake of convenience when analyzing the balance sheet.

Current Assets

Current assets are cash or items that can or will be converted into cash within a short period of time (usually a year or less). The following accounts for a hotel generally appear under current assets.

Cash.   Cash includes not only cash in various bank accounts (such as a general checking account and a payroll account), but also cash on hand in sales register cash drawers, cash not yet deposited in the bank, and cash held as a basic on-site fund for change-making purposes and paying for cash-on-delivery purchases.

Accounts Receivable.   Accounts receivable include any amounts due from customers. If your hotel operates on a cash-only basis, then it will have no accounts receivable. However, most hotels accept credit cards that allow customers to charge their accounts. These credit card sales are accounts receivable until payment is received.

Another example of an account receivable might be a hotel that leases out part of its premises to another business (for example, a gift shop or newsstand) and receives rent for that space and/or commissions on sales of merchandise. Any unpaid rent and/or commissions are accounts receivable.

Allowance for Doubtful Accounts.   If your hotel includes in accounts receivable any accounts that may not be collectible, an allowance for doubtful accounts should be established for the total amount of these doubtful accounts. This amount is shown as a separate item on the balance sheet and is *deducted* from the accounts receivable total to arrive at the net realizable amount. Some small hotels who have only nominal amounts of accounts receivable do not bother with setting up an allowance for doubtful accounts.

Marketable Securities.   At times your hotel may have excess cash on hand. Instead of leaving these excess funds in the bank at little or no interest, it is usually a good idea to place them in short-term investments (such as government bonds that pay better-than-bank interest) that can be quickly sold and converted back into cash when needed. Because these investments are readily convertible to cash, they are known as marketable securities.

Inventory.   Most hotels carry little or no inventory, other than nominal amounts of stationery, guest supplies, cleaning supplies, and similar items. At each balance sheet date it may be necessary to physically count and cost these inventories to provide a total value for all unused products on hand. This value appears as an asset on the balance sheet.

Prepaid Expenses.   Many hotels prepay certain expenses at the beginning of the year. These expenses might include rent, licenses, property taxes, and insurance. In each case at each balance sheet date the amount that is still prepaid should be included on the balance sheet.

For example, if your hotel's annual insurance premium of $4,800 is prepaid at the beginning of each year, and a balance sheet is prepared halfway through the year, the balance sheet's prepaid expense account should show at that time $2,400 for insurance along with any other prepaid amounts for any other expenses.

Fixed (Long-term) Assets

Fixed (or long-term) assets are those of a relatively permanent nature, not intended for sale, that are used in generating revenue. This category of assets might include the following:

Land.   If your business owns the land on which the hotel sits, the land account will reflect the cost of this land. Cost includes expenditures such as legal costs and title fees for purchasing it and the cost of clearing it to make it usable. This cost is reduced by any cash recovered subsequent to the purchase, such as the salvage value of any materials sold from a building that was previously there and torn down to prepare the site for your hotel.

Building.   A hotel that owns its own building records that building's cost in this account. Cost includes all expenditures to construct the building if it were a new one, or the cost of purchase (including renovations) of an existing building. Cost also includes all items such as materials, labor, architect and designer fees, building permits, construction or renovation financing expenses, and taxes during the construction or renovation period.

Note that, if land and an existing building were purchased as a package for your operation, at the time of purchase the total purchase cost must be realistically allocated to the land account and the building account. The purchase contract may show this breakdown. If not, a professional appraisal may be required. This cost allocation is needed for income tax purposes because building costs can be depreciated, while land costs cannot be.

Furniture, Fixtures, and Equipment.   The furniture, fixtures, and equipment (FFE) account includes all furniture in guest rooms and other areas (such as reception and office), fixtures (such as carpets, drapes, and lamps), and all equipment (such as cleaning and office equipment). Cost of these items includes actual purchase price including taxes, import duties, freight, shipping insurance charges, and installation. If your hotel owns any automotive equipment (for example, some hotels have vehicles that they use to provide transportation to the property for guests arriving at the local airport), that equipment may be included with FFE, or may be shown in a separate fixed asset account.

Accumulated Depreciation.   Long-term assets are shown on the balance sheet at their cost. From the cost figures for building and FFE (but not land) is deducted accumulated depreciation. Accumulated depreciation reflects the estimated decline in value of the assets due to wear and tear, the passage of time, changed economic conditions, or other factors. (Depreciation will be discussed in more detail in the next chapter.)

The difference between the asset cost figure and the accumulated depreciation is referred to as net book value. Net book value does not necessarily accurately reflect the current market or replacement value of the assets in question. For example, if your hotel building is in good condition and you planned to sell your business and move on to some other endeavor, the building might be worth far more to a purchaser than its depreciated value on your balance sheet.

Linen and Uniforms.   The value of linen and uniforms either in reserve in inventory or in actual use at the balance sheet date is shown in this account. Items in reserve are valued at their cost, while those in use are valued at less than cost because usage reduces their value below cost.

Other Assets

If your hotel has any other assets that do not fit into either the current or fixed categories they are included in a separate asset category. Some examples are:

Leasehold Improvements.   Some hotel operations do not own land or a building. Instead they operate in leased (rented) premises. If your hotel is in leased premises that you have spent money on to improve or renovate to make them operable for your style of hotel, the cost of those improvements is recorded in the leasehold improvements account.

Leasehold improvements might include redesign of the lobby (for example, installation of additional walls or partitions) or paving of a parking lot. These improvements are of benefit during the life of the business or the remaining life of the lease. The costs should be spread over this life. This spreading of costs is much like depreciation for building and FFE, except that in the case of leasehold property it is generally called amortization.

Deposits.   Many leased hotels are required to pay a deposit equivalent to one or more months' normal rent. This deposit is held by the landlord and is allocated to the last month or months of the lease contract. Another type of deposit might be one paid to a gas, electricity, or other utility company. Such deposits are assets, but not current ones because they cannot be readily converted into cash.

Goodwill.   Goodwill is the price you pay in excess of the value of the tangible assets (land, building, FFE) when you purchase an existing hotel. Goodwill is shown on the balance sheet at cost and is then amortized (written off) over the hotel's life or 40 years (whichever is shorter).

Franchise Fees.   Many hotels today are franchised operations. If your hotel is franchised, you have probably had to pay a fee to the franchisor for that franchise right. This fee (including any legal and other costs to obtain the right to the franchise) is shown on the balance sheet and is amortized over the franchise life.

License Fees.   Hotels sometimes have to pay a fee to a local government to obtain a license to operate. The license cost should be shown on the balance sheet and be amortized over a reasonable number of years.

Investments.   Investments are differentiated from some other assets (such as marketable securities) because they cannot be readily converted into cash and thus cannot be used in the day-to-day operations of your hotel. For example, you may have invested in a piece of land adjacent to your hotel for future expansion, or in a piece of land in another location to start a second hotel some time in the future. Investments are normally shown on the balance sheet at their cost.

Total Assets

The total of all the asset categories (current, fixed, and other) gives the total asset value, or total resources, of your hotel.

Liabilities and Owners' Equity

On the right-hand side of the balance sheet are the liabilities and owners' equity sections. The liabilities and equity show how your assets (resources) have been financed or paid for. The liability section is comprised of current liabilities and long-term liabilities.

Current Liabilities

Current liabilities are those debts that must be paid or are expected to be paid in less than a year. On a hotel balance sheet, you are likely to see the following current liabilities:

Accounts Payable — Trade.   Trade accounts payable include liabilities (unpaid accounts) for goods (for example, supplies) and services (for example, a contracted piped-in music service) incurred in the normal course of your business.

Accounts Payable — Other.   The other accounts payable account is used for amounts payable other than for day-to-day purchases of goods and services. For example, if equipment had been purchased, any amount still due and payable to the equipment supplier is recorded here.

Notes Payable.   Sometimes amounts are due and formalized by a document known as a note. This might occur when equipment is purchased or when a bank loan is received. Any unpaid amounts (including interest) on the note(s) are recorded in this account.

Taxes Payable.   The taxes payable account includes amounts due for such items as income taxes, federal and state payroll withholding taxes (including any matching amount your hotel must pay), and sales taxes due to a taxing authority and collected from customers as an extra charge on the room rate. On the balance sheets of large hotels, each type of tax payable may be shown as a separate account.

Accrued Expenses. Accrued expenses are those amounts due for expenses incurred but not yet paid at the balance sheet date. For example, assume that employees are paid on every second Friday and that the month-end balance sheet is prepared on the Monday following a payday. Even though employees have not been paid for three days of work at the balance sheet date, that amount is still due to them and is recorded as a liability under accrued expenses on the balance sheet. Other common accrued expenses are unpaid interest, rent, and utilities. In large hotels, the balance sheet may show accrued salaries and wages as an account separate from other accrued expenses.

Deposits on Group Business. Your hotel may handle group business such as bus tours. It is common practice when a customer books group business for a deposit to be collected at the time the contract is signed by the customer. If any deposits are still being held at the balance sheet date for future group business, the total of these deposits is recorded as a liability because, if the business is cancelled within a reasonable time prior to the event, the deposit amount is likely refundable to the customer. If the business does occur, at that time the deposit amount is taken out of the liability account and shown as sales revenue.

Dividends Payable. If your hotel business is operated as an incorporated company it may have declared (decided to pay) dividends but not yet paid them out at the balance sheet date. If so, they are recorded as a liability (just like unpaid employee salaries and wages).

Current Portion of Long-term Debt. If your hotel has arranged a mortgage from a lender to buy the land and/or build the hotel, that mortgage is probably repayable year by year over a long number of years and is shown as a long-term liability. However, any amount of that long-term debt payable within the next twelve months is shown as a current liability.

Long-term Liabilities

Long-term liabilities are the debts of your hotel that are payable more than one year beyond the balance sheet date. Included in this category are mortgages and similar long-term loans such as notes or bonds—less the current portion shown under current liabilities. In a large hotel, each type of long-term liability might be shown separately on the balance sheet.

Owners' Equity

In general terms, the owners' equity section of your balance sheet is the difference between total assets and total liabilities. It represents the equity, or the net worth, of the owner(s) of the hotel. From a legal point of view, there are three ways for any business to operate: as an incorporated company, as a proprietorship, and as a partnership.

Incorporated Company. If you are operating your hotel as an incorporated company, the owners' equity is comprised of two main items: capital (shares) and retained earnings.

An incorporated company is limited by law to a maximum number of shares it can issue, known as the authorized number of shares. Shares generally have a par or stated value. It is this par value multiplied by the number of shares actually issued up to the authorized quantity that provides the total value of capital on the balance sheet.

Most small hotels that operate as incorporated companies issue *common shares*. However, some hotels also issue another type known as *preferred shares*. Preferred shares rank ahead of common shares, up to certain limits, as far as dividends are concerned. Preferred shareholders may also have special voting rights, and they normally rank ahead of common shareholders in the event that you liquidate the hotel.

The other part of the owners' equity section of the balance sheet for an incorporated business is retained earnings. Retained earnings are the link between the income statement and the balance sheet. For that reason, the retained earnings part of the owners' equity section of the balance sheet is covered in the next chapter where the income statement is discussed.

Proprietorship. If your hotel is a proprietorship where you are the sole owner, the owner equity section of the balance sheet will normally have a single line on it as follows:

Owner capital $xxx.xx

showing the value of your equity (net worth) in the business at the balance sheet date. This capital is the total of the amount originally invested in the business, plus any profits (less any losses) since it began, less any funds withdrawn by you from the business.

Partnership. If your business is a partnership (two or more owners), there will be a line in the owner equity section showing the owner capital for each partner. For example:

Partner A, capital $xxx.xx
Partner B, capital $yyy.yy
Partner C, capital $zzz.zz

Each partner's capital amount at the balance sheet date is calculated in the same way as for a proprietorship, with each partner's share of profits (or losses) allocated to his or her capital account according to the agreement drawn up when the partnership was formed.

Balance Sheet Presentation

The amount of detail shown on your hotel's balance sheet depends on the amount of information desired, the size and complexity of the hotel, and whether the business is a proprietorship, partnership, or incorporated company. For example, a large hotel's balance sheet might show each type of cash account as a separate item, while a small hotel's balance sheet might combine all the various cash accounts into a single figure on the balance sheet.

Some operators want their balance sheets simplified as much as possible because this makes them easier to "read" at first glance. Where more detail about an account is needed, this might then be shown as an addendum or footnote on an adjoining page.

The balance sheet is sometimes presented with assets on the left and liabilities and capital on the right. This method of presentation is known as the account form or method and is the one most commonly used.

Another common method is the report form. This method is vertical rather than horizontal as in the account form. In the report form, the balance sheet is considered to have a top half and a bottom half. The top half is for the assets and the bottom half for liabilities and owners' equity, as illustrated in the balance sheet in Figure 2.1.

IMPORTANCE OF BALANCE SHEET

The balance sheet is important because it can provide information such as

- Your hotel's liquidity or ability to pay its debts when they have to be paid.
- How much of your hotel's past profits have been retained in the business to help it expand and/or reduce the amount of outside money (debt) that has had to be borrowed.
- The breakdown of your hotel's assets into current, fixed, and other, with details about the amount of assets within each of these broad categories.
- Your hotel's debt (liabilities) relative to owners' equity. In general, the greater the amount of debt relative to equity the higher is your hotel's financial risk.

BALANCE SHEET AS OF DECEMBER 31, 19X1		
ASSETS		
Current Assets		
Cash	$ 25,400	
Accounts receivable	15,200	
Marketable securities	42,000	
Supplies inventory	4,700	
Prepaid expense	4,900	$ 92,200
Fixed Assets		
Land	$ 60,500	
Building	882,400	
Furniture and equipment	227,900	
	$1,170,800	
Less: Accumulated depreciation	(422,000)	
	$ 748,800	
Linen and uniforms	18,300	767,100
Total Assets		$859,300
LIABILITIES AND OWNERS' EQUITY		
Current Liabilities		
Accounts payable	$ 16,500	
Accrued expenses	4,200	
Income taxes payable	20,900	
Credit balances	800	
Current portion of mortgage	26,000	$ 68,400
Long-term Liability		
Mortgage payable		486,800
Total Liabilities		$555,200
OWNERS' EQUITY		
Common shares	$ 200,000	
Retained earnings	104,100	304,100
Total Liabilities and Owners' Equity		$859,300

Figure 2.1   Sample balance sheet.

Balance Sheet Limitations

There are some aspects of your hotel's business that the balance sheet may not disclose. For example:

- Because transactions are recorded in the value of the dollar at the time the transaction occurs, the true value of some assets on the balance sheet may not be apparent. Suppose your hotel owned the land on which the building sits and that the land was purchased several years ago. Because of inflation and demand for limited land, it is likely that the land today is worth far more than was paid for it. This may also be true of some other assets. The balance sheet normally does not show these assets at today's market value.

- If you purchased your hotel from a previous owner who had built up a successful business, and if you paid an amount for that business above the actual market value of the purchased assets, that amount would have been recorded on the balance sheet at the time of purchase as "goodwill." Goodwill that a hotel has is normally recorded only at the time a business is purchased. Therefore, if you started your hotel from scratch, have a good location compared to your competitors, and/or have a good reputation and faithful clientele, and/or have a superior work force with a good morale, your hotel is probably worth far more than the balance sheet assets show, simply because the goodwill you have built up is not reflected on the balance sheet.

- Another value similar to goodwill that is not shown on the balance sheet is your hotel's investment in its employees. This investment takes the form of time and money spent on recruiting, training, evaluating, and promoting motivated employees. Obviously, it is difficult to assign a value to these human resources, but they are, nevertheless, an asset to your hotel.

- Many items recorded on balance sheets are a matter of judgment or estimate. For example, in recording depreciation for assets such as equipment and furniture, a number of different depreciation methods may be used. What is the best depreciation method to use? Similarly, which is the best method to use of several available for the valuation of linen inventories? Because you must thus use judgments or estimates to decide, your balance sheet may not reflect correct values for all assets. If the judgments or estimates used are wrong, then the balance sheet is incorrect.

- Balance sheets also reflect the financial position of your hotel at only one moment in time. After that moment passes, the balance sheet continues to change as further transactions occur, yet these changes are not reflected until another balance sheet is produced a month or more later. If your current balance sheet showed a healthy cash position at that time, and a week later you spend most of that cash on new furniture, the balance sheet tells nothing about the impending use of most of the cash available.

THREE

Understanding Your Income Statement

INTRODUCTION TO THE INCOME STATEMENT

There are a number of different names used for what in this book will be referred to as the *income statement*. Some of the alternatives are income and expense statement, profit and loss statement, statement of operations, and earnings statement.

The income statement shows the operating results (sales less expenses) of your hotel for a period of time (month, quarter, half-year, or year). Many hotel operators consider the income statement to be more valuable than the balance sheet. However, in order to have complete understanding of your hotel's operations you should be able to understand both the income statement and the balance sheet, along with any supporting statements and/or schedules that might be useful for your particular operation.

No single statement or schedule alone can provide complete information. For example, an income statement can show that your hotel made a profit for the year (always a good idea), but the related balance sheet may show there is insufficient cash in the bank to pay current liabilities (not a good idea).

Questions the Income Statement Can Answer

The income statement, nevertheless, can provide answers to some important questions such as:

- What were the sales last month? How does that compare with the month before and with the same month last year?
- Did last month's sales keep pace with the increased cost of labor and other expenses?
- What were the sales by department for the operating period?
- Which department is operating most effectively?

- Is there a limit to maximum potential sales? Have we reached that limit? If so, can we increase sales in the short run by increasing room rates or in the long run by expanding the premises?
- What was the labor cost percentage? Did it meet our objective?
- Were operating costs (such as for supplies) in line with what they should be for the sales level achieved?
- How did the operating results for the period compare with budget forecasts?

SALES (REVENUE)

Sales can be defined as increases in assets (cash or accounts receivable) from selling goods and/or providing services as part of your hotel's normal operations. Thus, renting rooms either for cash or on credit produces sales or revenue. On the other hand, a bank lending your hotel money to be used for landscaping may be temporarily increasing your hotel's bank account, but is not producing any revenue.

Similarly, if a deposit is received by your hotel for a future reservation, that deposit is not recorded as a sale until the guest actually arrives and uses the room. In the interim it is recorded on the balance sheet as a liability: *deposits payable.*

In other words, revenue is only recorded at the time an exchange of goods or services for "money" takes place. That money can be in the form of cash (renting a room with the customer paying cash), a credit card voucher that a customer signs at the end of the stay, or a promise to pay money (a tour bus company manager signing an invoice at the end of a group stay and agreeing to pay the invoice within 30 days). In the latter two cases, the hotel receives money (in the form of accounts receivable) and revenue is earned even though no cash has yet been exchanged.

Revenue Detail

Most hotels separate rooms sales or revenue accounts from those for other departments (such as a newsstand/gift shop). The main reason for separating sales by department is so that sales trends for each can be followed and statistics for each calculated and analyzed.

Separate revenue accounts will also be required for interest income (such as interest earned on a bank savings account), commission income (for example, from vending machines), and for any other type of revenue that is not directly related to rooms sales.

EXPENSES

The amount of detail concerning expenses shown on your income statement depends on the type and size of your business and your need for more or less information.

Expenses are defined as the use of cash or the incurrence of liabilities —or a combination of both—to purchase goods or services in the normal course of your hotel's operation. Clearly, paying cash for employee labor is an expense, as is the cash purchase of operating supplies. In the case of other items, however, the point at which a purchase becomes an expense is not as clear.

For example, when products to be sold in your gift shop are purchased, these purchases are placed in inventory (a balance sheet asset) and only become income statement expenses as the goods are taken out of storage and sold.

Similarly, the purchase of an item of furniture or equipment is not recorded as an expense at the time of purchase. For example, when a new item of office equipment is purchased, it is recorded at that time on the balance sheet as a fixed or long-term asset. As the equipment is used over its useful life, its value declines (depreciates). Only as that value declines is the amount of decrease recorded as depreciation expense on the income statement.

Cost of Sales

In your rooms department there is no cost of sales expense because you are selling space and not a tangible product that the customer consumes (such as food in a restaurant) or uses (such as toiletry items from your gift shop).

If you operate a gift shop in your hotel, products to be sold are placed in inventory until they are sold. As they are sold, the cost of products sold is transferred from the inventory account and becomes an expense on the income statement called *cost of sales*. On your income statement the cost of sales is deducted from sales to give *gross profit*, from which other expenses are then deducted:

Sales	$10,000	100%
Cost of sales	4,000	40
Gross profit	$ 6,000	60%
Other expenses	5,000	50
Profit	$ 1,000	10%

Gross Profit

Gross profit is important. If you do not have the right gross profit, you cannot then achieve an adequate net profit. Suppose gross profit is 60 percent of sales and net profit 10 percent as illustrated above. If gross profit drops to 59 percent, net profit declines to 9 percent as follows:

Sales	$10,000	100%
Cost of sales	4,100	41
Gross profit	$ 5,900	59%
Other expenses	5,000	50
Profit	$ 900	9%

In other words, a $100 reduction in gross profit from $6,000 to $5,900 represents about 2 percent of gross profit:

$$\frac{\$100}{\$6,000} \times 100 = 1.7\%$$

but the $100 reduction in net profit (from $1,000 to $900) represents a 10 percent decline in that profit:

$$\frac{\$100}{\$1,000} \times 100 = 10\%$$

This demonstrates how a small change in gross profit (through control of cost of sales) can have a significant impact on a department's profitability.

A change in sales can also have a significant impact on your rooms department's profit. The reason is that most of its expenses are fixed (that is, they do not change with a change in sales). Of course, this is only true up to a certain level of sales increase. At some point labor cost is likely to increase to cope with the additional sales volume.

Direct Expenses

After sales (and cost of sales and gross profit where applicable) are listed on the income statement, the direct operating expenses are listed, totaled, and then deducted from sales (or gross profit) to produce profit before indirect or undistributed expenses.

Direct expenses are defined as those that are controllable by and are the responsibility of a department manager. For example, the rooms department manager is responsible for direct expenses of the rooms department, and the gift shop department manager for direct expenses of the gift shop department. These expenses will increase or decrease to a greater or lesser degree as sales increase or decrease. Typical direct expenses for a hotel's rooms department are:

Salaries and wages

Employee benefits

Travel agent commissions

Contract cleaning

Laundry

Linen and uniforms

Operating supplies

Indirect Expenses

The next category of expenses to be listed, totaled, and deducted are the indirect or undistributed ones. These generally vary little regardless of the sales volume. They are not normally controllable by or the responsibility of an operating department head, and are often described as overhead costs. Typical of these are:

Administration and general

Marketing

Property operation and maintenance

Energy

Transportation

Fixed Charges

After the undistributed expenses have been deducted, this produces income before fixed charges. The fixed charges generally include:

Rent, property taxes, and insurance

Interest

Depreciation

(Because depreciation is a special kind of fixed expense, a more detailed discussion of it is given later in the chapter.)

Income Tax

After the fixed charges have been deducted on the income statement, this provides the amount of profit before income tax. Income tax is then deducted to arrive at net profit. Income tax includes taxes for all levels of government (federal, state, and city).

Income tax is only shown on your income statement if your hotel is an incorporated business. Proprietorship and partnership hotels will not show any income tax because any profits of the business are taxable and payable by the individual owner(s)—and not by the organization—at personal tax rates.

A sample income statement for a hotel operating as an incorporated company is illustrated in Figure 3.1.

RETAINED EARNINGS

Usually the balance sheet and the income statement for an incorporated company are accompanied by a statement of retained earnings. The statement of retained earnings lists the net profit of the business (from the income statement) for a period (let us say a year). The net profit is added to the preceding year's figure of retained earnings to give the new total. If any dividends were paid out during the year, these are deducted to arrive at end-of-year retained earnings. In other words, the retained earnings are the accumulated net profits (less any losses) sustained by the business since it began, less any dividends.

A completed statement of retained earnings is illustrated as follows:

Statement of Retained Earnings for Year Ending December 31, 19x1

Retained earnings December 31, 19x0	$ 63,900
Profit for year 19x1	40,200
Retained earnings December 31, 19x1	$104,100

Note how the $40,200 of net profit from the income statement (Figure 3.1) has been transferred to the statement of retained earnings and the year-end retained earnings figure of $104,100 transferred to the balance sheet (see Figure 2.1).

Note that the retained earnings are not necessarily represented by cash in the bank because the money may have been used for other purposes such as purchasing new equipment or expanding the size of the building.

INCOME STATEMENT FOR YEAR ENDING DECEMBER 31, 19X1		
Room revenue		$359,400
Direct expenses		
Salaries and wages	$55,600	
Employee benefits	3,300	
	$58,900	
Commissions	500	
Contract cleaning	1,200	
Laundry	2,900	
Linen and uniforms	7,600	
Operating supplies	8,100	79,200
Income before undistributed expenses		$280,200
Undistributed expenses		
Administration and general	$16,200	
Marketing	11,700	
Property operation & maintenance	11,500	
Energy	13,200	
Transportation	6,200	58,800
Income before fixed charges		$221,400
Fixed charges		
Rent, property taxes, insurance	$12,600	
Interest	85,800	
Depreciation	70,400	168,800
Income before income tax		$ 52,600
Income tax		12,400
Net income		$ 40,200

Figure 3.1 Sample income statement.

Proprietorship or Partnership

For a proprietorship or a partnership, a statement of retained earnings is not used. Instead, there is a statement of capital similar to a statement of retained earnings but using different terminology. For example, the statement of capital for a proprietorship might show the following:

Capital January 1, 19x0	$ 83,900
Net profit for year	40,200
	$124,100
Withdrawals	(20,000)
Capital December 31, 19x1	$104,100

Withdrawals are funds taken out of the business by the proprietor for personal use (similar to dividends for an incorporated company). The closing capital figure is then transferred to the balance sheet. Alternatively, all the information from the statement of capital could be shown directly on the balance sheet, thus eliminating the need for a separate statement of capital.

In the case of a partnership, the statement of capital is similar to that for a proprietorship, except that for each partner the beginning of the year capital is shown, and his or her share of net profit is added and withdrawals deducted to arrive at end of the year capital, which is then transferred to the balance sheet. Again, if space permits, the full information for each partner can be shown directly on the balance sheet, eliminating the need for a separate partnership statement of capital.

DEPRECIATION

When long-life assets (such as building and equipment) are purchased by your hotel, they are recorded on the balance sheet as assets at their original cost price. If at the time of purchase these assets were shown as expenses on the income statement, that income statement and all future ones would show a distorted net profit because they would not be conforming to the matching principle (discussed in Chapter 1).

To avoid these distortions, in each accounting period that benefits from the use of a long-life asset a portion of the cost of that asset is recorded on the income statement, and at the same time deducted from the balance sheet asset by way of accumulated depreciation as discussed in Chapter 2.

The portion of the asset's cost recorded on the income statement is known as depreciation expense and reduces profit for that period. This has cash flow advantages because depreciation is not a cash expense. That is, it does not require an outlay of cash at the time you record the depreciation expense. It simply reduces on your books the value of the related asset(s). However, by recording it as an expense you reduce taxable profits and save income tax, which means you save cash and increase your cash flow. For that reason, most businesses claim the maximum depreciation allowable for tax purposes.

Asset Life

What is the useful life of an asset for depreciation purposes? This is often a matter of opinion influenced by such factors as inadequacy, obsolescence, and economic changes. In the case of a building, useful life could be 30, 40, or 50 years or more. In the case of a piece of equipment, it could be as much as ten years or as short as a couple of years if a new and better piece of equipment becomes available.

There are a number of different methods for calculating depreciation. Some of these are discussed.

Straight-line Method

Straight-line depreciation is probably the simplest of all depreciation methods because it spreads the cost of the asset, less any estimated trade-in or scrap value at the end of its useful life, equally over each year of the asset's life. The equation for calculating the annual amount of depreciation is:

$$\frac{\text{Cost of asset} - \text{Trade-in value}}{\text{Service life of asset in years}}$$

In this equation, note that cost is a known and exact figure. The other two figures are estimates, but through experience and discussion with suppliers they can be fairly realistically estimated, thus making the depreciation expense calculation reasonably accurate. Let us assume the following concerning the purchase of a piece of equipment: initial cost $32,000 and trade-in value $2,000 at the end of its five-year life. Annual depreciation will be:

$$\frac{\$32,000 - \$2,000}{5 \text{ years}} = \frac{\$30,000}{5} = \$6,000 \text{ per year}$$

To obtain the monthly depreciation expense, you simply divide the annual rate by 12.

Declining Balance Method

With the straight-line method (assuming a five-year life) one-fifth (or 20 percent) of the cost of the asset less its trade-in value was the annual depreciation. Using the same facts, with the declining balance method the straight-line depreciation rate of 20 percent is doubled to 40 percent and 40 percent is then multiplied by the undepreciated balance (book value) of the asset each year to obtain the depreciation expense for that year. With this method, you ignore any trade-in or scrap value.

In other words, in year one the depreciation expense is 40% × $32,000 (the cost of the asset) = $12,800. The book value of the asset is now $32,000 − $12,800 = $19,200. Year two depreciation expense is 40% × $19,200 = $7,680. If this information is set up in the form of a schedule for all five years, it would appear as follows:

Declining Balance Depreciation

Year	Annual Depreciation	Net Book Value
	Initial cost	$32,000
1	40% × $32,000 = $12,800	19,200
2	40 × 19,200 = 7,680	11,520
3	40 × 11,520 = 4,608	6,912
4	40 × 6,912 = 2,765	4,147
5	40 × 4,147 = 1,659	2,488

The declining balance method of depreciation is sometimes referred to as an accelerated method. You will note that the depreciation expense is high in the early years and decreases as the years go by. The reasoning behind this accelerated method is that maintenance costs are low in the earlier years of an asset's life, but increase with age. Therefore, in theory, the sum of depreciation plus maintenance should be approximately the same each year.

There are also tax advantages to using accelerated depreciation. Because depreciation expense is higher in the early years, your taxable profit will be lower and thus income taxes reduced. Over the long run the total tax will be the same, but, by reducing income taxes in the early years, you can increase cash flow in those years.

Units-of-Production Method

The equation for the units-of-production depreciation method is:

$$\frac{\text{Cost of asset} - \text{Trade-in value}}{\text{Estimated units of production during asset's life}}$$

To illustrate, assume a hotel purchases a vehicle for $8,000. It is estimated that this vehicle will be driven for 50,000 miles before it is traded in for $800 at the end of its useful life. The cost of depreciation per unit of production (mile) is:

$$\frac{\$8,000 - \$800}{50,000} = \frac{\$7,200}{50,000} = \$0.144$$

Annual depreciation expense is based on the mileage driven in each year. Assuming 10,000 miles in year one, annual depreciation is 10,000 × $0.144 = $1,440. Subsequent years' depreciation is calculated in a similar manner.

The units-of-production depreciation method has the advantage of equitably spreading total depreciation over each period of the asset's useful life. Disadvantages are that it does not easily allow calculation of each period's depreciation expense in advance (useful, for example, in budgeting, to be discussed in Chapter 16); nor is it likely to give higher depreciation amounts in the early years of the asset's life which, as mentioned earlier, is useful for reducing income taxes and increasing cash flow.

Depreciation and Income Tax in the United States

A number of times in this chapter the topic of depreciation in relation to income tax has been mentioned. Some additional comments about depreciation and income tax are now in order.

Generally, the U.S. Internal Revenue Service (IRS) regulates the amount of depreciation that may be claimed for tax purposes for depreciable assets purchased after 1980. The concept of depreciation, according to the Economic Recovery Tax Act of 1981, was replaced with the concept of cost recovery (referred to as the accelerated cost recovery system or ACRS). Under the ACRS, the useful life of an asset and its salvage value are no longer relevant. The cost of an asset can be recovered (depreciated) over an allowed period of time, regardless of the asset's life.

Four time periods are allowed: 3, 5, 10, and 15 years depending on the type of asset. In general, the cost recovery amount allowed for depreciation expense is based on statutory percentages that are similar to declining balance depreciation.

As long as you are in business for a full year, it does not matter when you purchase an asset during that year. A full year's cost recovery (depreciation) may be claimed. In other words, if you purchased a new item of lobby furniture on the last day of your accounting year, you may still claim a full year's cost recovery. This is useful to know, because if you were planning to buy a new fixed asset early next year, it might be a good idea to advance the purchase to the end of the current year to benefit now from that additional depreciation allowance.

Depreciation and Income Tax in Canada

In Canada, the Income Tax Act states that declining balance depreciation must be used and stipulates the maximum percentage rate of depreciation (called Capital Cost Allowance — or CCA — by the tax department) that may be used for each class or type of asset (for example, 5 percent on buildings, 20 percent on most items of equipment, 30 percent on automotive equipment).

As long as you are in business for a full 12 months (which would be the normal situation unless your business is just starting up), it does not matter when you buy an asset during the current fiscal year; you may only claim a half-year's depreciation in the asset's year of purchase. In other words, even if you bought an asset on the last day of your fiscal year you may still claim a half-year's depreciation. Thus, if you intend buying an asset next year, by buying it late in the current year you will be able to reduce the current year's tax payable by claiming the equivalent of a half-year's depreciation.

Which Depreciation Method to Use?

Generally, it is wise to show on your income statement the maximum depreciation that can be claimed to minimize income tax. Even though for tax filing purposes you may only claim depreciation using allowable rates, this does not mean that you cannot use a different method or different rate of depreciation on your books. However, when you file your annual tax return you cannot deduct on your income statement for tax reduction purposes any depreciation in excess of the allowable amount.

Note also that it is possible to use one depreciation method for one type of asset, and a different method for another. However, once a particular method has been selected for an asset, you should use it consistently during that asset's life.

A difficult decision for the hotel operator is the choice of depreciation method to use. Regardless of the method selected, one fact is quite clear — you can never record more depreciation for an asset than its cost. Whether the asset is depreciated by an accelerated method or not, total depreciation expense cannot exceed the investment in that asset.

Also, if you eventually sell all your assets and receive more for them than their written down or net book value, you run into a recapture of depreciation situation. This means that you now pay tax on the excess amount of depreciation you previously claimed. For example, if you had a vehicle with a book value of $4,000 that you sold for $5,000, you are likely to be liable for tax on the recaptured depreciation of $1,000.

Finally, note that in no case can you claim any depreciation on land that your hotel owns. Land is a nondepreciable asset so far as the tax department is concerned.

Because the subject of depreciation can be quite complex, and the regulations concerning it are changed by the government from time to time, it is best to consult with your accountant in any matters concerning depreciation. This is particularly true if you are expanding your operation by buying the assets of another hotel and you wish to maximize the total depreciation that you can claim in future years on those purchased assets.

FOUR

Internal Control

In a very small hotel very few internal controls are required because the owner/operator usually handles all the cash coming in and going out and, by being present, ensures a smooth and efficient operation. In large hotels, one-person control is no longer possible and it is necessary for the owner/operator to implement a system of internal control.

PRINCIPLES OF INTERNAL CONTROL

A good system of internal control incorporates the following two broad requirements:

1. Methods and procedures for employees in the various jobs to follow to ensure they
   - Act according to your policies
   - Achieve operational efficiency
   - Protect assets (such as cash and inventory) from waste, theft, or fraud.
2. Reliable forms and reports that measure the efficiency and effectiveness of the hotel and provide accounting and other information that, when analyzed, indicates problem areas. This information must be accurate and timely if it is to be useful. It must also be cost-effective; in other words, the benefits (cost savings) of your internal control system must be greater than its cost. Information produced must also be useful. If the information is not used then you have wasted effort and money.

Management Attitude

Most employees are honest by nature but, because of a poor internal control system or (worse still) complete absence of controls, are sometimes tempted to be dishonest. If you do not care, why should your employees?

Management Supervision

By themselves, control systems solve no problems. They do not guarantee protection against fraud or theft. Even with a good control system, collusion (two or more employees working together for dishonest purposes) may go undetected for a long time. For this and other reasons, your control system must be supervised by you or a delegated manager.

Employee Selection

An important aspect of effective internal control is employee competence, trustworthiness, and training. This means that you should have a good system of screening job applicants, selecting employees, employee orientation and on-the-job training, and periodic employee evaluation.

Obviously, supervisory personnel must also be competent, with skills in maintaining your operation's standards, motivating employees they supervise, preparing staffing schedules, maintaining employee morale (to reduce the cost of employee turnover), and implementing procedures to control labor and other costs. A poor supervisor will fail to extract the full potential from employees and will thus add to your hotel's operating costs.

Job Responsibilities

One of the requirements for good internal control is a clear definition of job responsibilities. For example, in the case of deliveries who will do the receiving? Will it be a clerk/receiver, the maintenance man, or you? And once that is determined, how is receiving to be handled?

Defined job responsibilities are needed so that, if errors occur, the person responsible can be held accountable. This does not imply penalizing employees, but rather that if the employee involved needs and receives further training future similar errors will not occur.

Written Procedures

Once job responsibilities have been determined, you should establish written job procedures so that employees responsible will know what the procedures are. Written procedures are particularly important where employee turnover is high (often the case in the hotel industry) and continuous employee training to support the internal control system is required.

It is impossible in this chapter to provide procedures that will fit every possible hotel situation because of the wide variety of types, sizes, and styles of hotels and their differing needs. Even in two hotels of similar type and size, the procedures for any specific control area may differ due to management policy, type of customer, layout of the establishment, or numerous other reasons. However, as an example, the following could be a set of procedures for front office staff for handling credit cards:

1. When a guest checks in, ask if payment will be by credit card or some other method.
2. If it is to be by credit card ask to see the card.
3. Verify that the card is one acceptable to this hotel (such as American Express, Diners Club, Carte Blanche, Visa, or Mastercard).
4. If acceptable, check the date on the card to make sure it has not expired.
5. Run the credit card through the imprinter and attach the blank credit card voucher to the guest's account folio.
6. As you return the card, remind the guest to see the front office cashier before departing to verify the accuracy of the account and sign the credit card voucher for the charge.
7. Before filing the account folio with the cashier, check the credit card number to make sure it is not on the credit card company's cancellation list. If it is, advise the front office manager of the situation.
8. Initial the top right-hand corner of the credit card voucher to show that the card has been checked against the cancellation list and is not listed.

When the guest checks out:

9. Check the credit card voucher attached to the guest's account folio to ensure the credit card number has been verified.
10. If it has not been, check the cancellation list and advise the front office manager if it is listed. Do not process the account any further.
11. Provide the guest with the account so that he or she can verify that it is correct.
12. When the guest approves the account, transfer the total amount to the credit card voucher and have the guest sign the voucher.
13. Provide the guest with his or her copy of the account and the guest's copy of the credit card voucher.

Standards and Results

Once procedures have been established and the employees given detailed written guidelines about how to perform tasks, you need to establish standards of performance. This requires designing forms and reports to provide information about all your hotel's operations. Without good records and reporting systems, employees will be less concerned about doing a good job. The forms, reports, and other records that are part of the internal control system will depend entirely on the size and type of your establishment.

Properly designed forms and reports provide you with the information you need to determine if standards are being met. They also allow you to make decisions that will improve the standards, increase productivity, and ultimately produce higher profits.

For example, one of the many benchmarks used in a hotel to measure its effectiveness is the rooms occupancy percentage. You need to know if the occupancy percentage you actually achieved is close to the standard desired. In a later chapter you will see how cost control standards can be established and actual results evaluated for labor.

Many of the operating statistics that are useful for analyzing and monitoring the ongoing progress of your hotel can be calculated daily. Favorable and unfavorable trends can be determined as they occur rather than too late for effective action to be taken.

As an example, Figure 4.1 illustrates a type of report that could be used by a hotel for monitoring daily operations.

Use Machines

Whenever possible machines should be used for control. Although machines cannot prevent all possibilities of theft or fraud, they can considerably reduce these possibilities. For example, the installation of front office guest account equipment makes daily rooms revenue control easier and will probably eliminate the need to produce a manual hand transcript (to be discussed in the next chapter) and may mean a night auditor is no longer required. Also, the saving in labor will contribute toward the cost of the equipment.

System Supervision and Review

One of your major responsibilities in internal control is continuous system supervision and review. This supervision and review is necessary because any system becomes obsolete as business conditions change. Also, without continuous supervision your control system can break down.

In small hotels, the supervision and review of the internal control system is the owner/operator's responsibility. In a larger hotel, the supervision and review responsibility may be delegated to a manager.

SALES

	TODAY	MONTH TO DATE	FORECAST MONTH TO DATE	LAST MONTH TO DATE	LAST YEAR MONTH TO DATE
ROOMS					
FOOD					
BEVERAGE					
TELEPHONE/TELEGRAM					
VALET					
LAUNDRY					
OTHER					
TOTAL REVENUE					

STATISTICS

	TODAY	MONTH TO DATE	FORECAST MONTH TO DATE	LAST MONTH TO DATE	LAST YEAR MONTH TO DATE	BANK REPORT	
TOTAL ROOMS OCC.						BALANCE YESTERDAY	
COMP. & HOUSE USE						RECEIPTS	
VACANT ROOMS						DISBURSEMENTS	
TOTAL ROOMS AVAIL.						BALANCE TODAY	
AVERAGE ROOM RATE						ACCOUNTS RECEIVABLE	
% OF OCCUPANCY							
NO. OF DOUBLES						BALANCE YESTERDAY	
% OF DOUBLE OCC.						CHARGES	
% OF FOOD COST						CREDITS	
% OF BEVERAGE COST						BALANCE TODAY	

PAYROLL AND RELATED EXPENSES

	TODAY		MONTH TO DATE		FORECAST MONTH TO DATE		LAST MONTH TO DATE		LAST YEAR MONTH TO DATE	
	AMOUNT	%	AMOUNT	%	AMOUNT	%	AMOUNT	%	AMOUNT	%
ROOM										
FOOD & BEVERAGE										
OVERHEAD DEPTS.										

Date _____

Day _____

Weather _____

Figure 4.1 Manager's daily report.

CONTROL OF CASH RECEIPTS

Good cash handling and internal control procedures are not only important to you as owner, but also to the employees involved because a good cash control system will show that employees have handled their responsibilities correctly and honestly.

All cash receipts should be deposited intact each day in the bank. A deposit slip (receipt) stamped by the bank should be retained by you. If all cash received each day is deposited daily, no one who handles it will be tempted to "borrow" cash for a few days for personal use.

Employees who handle cash (and other assets such as inventories) should be bonded. In this way, losses are less likely to occur because the employee knows he or she will have to answer to the insurance company if shortages arise.

Separate Recordkeeping and Asset Control

One of the most important principles of good cash control is to separate the functions of recording information about cash and actual cash handling.

Consider the accounts of guests to whom you have rented rooms on credit with invoices mailed out to these people at the end of each month. These accounts are an asset (accounts receivable). Checks received in payment are given to the bookkeeper who records the payments on the accounts. These checks, along with other cash and checks received from customers, are deposited each day in the bank. There is nothing wrong with this procedure so long as the bookkeeper is honest.

A dishonest bookkeeper could practice a procedure known as *lapping*. Guest A owes you $150 on account. When he receives his statement at the month-end he sends in a check for $150. The bookkeeper does not record the payment on Guests A's account. Instead, the check is simply put in the cash drawer and $150 in cash is removed for personal use by the bookkeeper. The bookkeeper's remittance at the end of the shift will balance, but Guest A's account will still show an unpaid amount of $150.

When Guest B with an account for $170 sends in her payment, the bookkeeper records $150 as a payment on Guest A's account, puts the $170 check in the cash drawer, and removes a further $20 in cash for personal use.

A few days later Guest C's payment of $200 on his account is received. The bookkeeper records $170 on Guest B's account, puts the $200 check in the cash drawer and takes out $30 more in cash.

This lapping of accounts will eventually increase to the point where the bookkeeper can no longer cover a particular account and the fraud will be discovered. However, the outstanding account may be so large that the misappropriated cash cannot be recovered from the dishonest book-keeper.

To aid in preventing this type of loss, separation of cash receiving and recording on accounts should be instituted. Checks or cash received in the mail in payment of accounts should be deposited directly in the bank by you or a responsible employee. The employee looking after the accounts receivable is simply given a list of account names and amounts received, and the appropriate accounts can be credited without that person handling any money. In other words, the responsibilities for handling cash and recording payments on accounts are separated.

CONTROL OF CASH DISBURSEMENTS

For minor disbursements that have to be handled by cash, you should establish a petty cash fund. You should put enough cash into this fund to take care of about one month's transactions. The fund should be the responsibility of one person only. Payments out of it must be supported by a receipt, voucher, or memorandum explaining the purpose of the disbursement.

When the cash fund is almost used up, the supporting receipts, vouchers, and memoranda can be turned in and the fund replenished with cash up to the original amount. Receipts, vouchers, or memoranda turned in should be stamped "paid," or cancelled in some similar way, so that they cannot be reused.

All other disbursements should be made by check and supported by an approved invoice. All checks should be numbered sequentially and be used in sequence. Checks should be prepared by you or a responsible person, but that other person should have no authority to sign the checks. As checks are prepared, the related invoices should be cancelled in some way so that there is no possibility of their being fraudulently reused. Any checks spoiled in preparation should be voided so that they cannot be reused.

Bank Reconciliation

One control that is necessary in a good internal control system is a monthly bank reconciliation. This reconciliation should be handled by you or your accountant. At each month-end, you should obtain a statement from your bank showing each daily deposit, the amount of each check paid, and other items added to or subtracted from the bank balance. The cancelled (paid) checks should accompany this statement. The steps in the reconciliation are:

1. Compare each cancelled check amount with the amount on the bank statement. Make a note of any differences so that the bank can be notified to make the necessary correction.

2. Arrange your cancelled (paid) checks in number sequence.

3. Verify the amount of each cancelled check with the amount on your check register or journal. Make a note of any outstanding checks. An outstanding check is one made out by you but not yet paid by the bank.

4. To the bank statement balance, add deposits made by you and not yet recorded by the bank, and subtract any outstanding checks.

5. To your bank balance amount add any amounts added by the bank on its statement but not yet recorded by you (for example, bank interest earned on deposits) and subtract any deductions made by the bank (such as automatic payments on loans and interest or service charges).

6. Once steps 1 to 5 have been completed, the two balances should agree. If they do not the work should be rechecked. If the figures still do not agree, then errors have been made either by the bank or on your books. These errors should be discovered and corrected.

To illustrate how a reconciliation is carried out, consider the following hypothetical figures:

Bank statement balance	$4,456
Company bank balance	6,848
Deposit in transit	2,896
Outstanding checks—#355	372
#372	40
Interest earned on deposits	98
Bank service charge	6

The reconciliation is as follows:

Bank Balance	Your Balance
$4,456	$6,848
2,896	98
(372)	(6)
(40)	
$6,940	$6,940

METHODS OF THEFT OR FRAUD

The remainder of this chapter lists ways in which theft or fraud has happened in hotels. These lists are not exhaustive. They include the more common ways in which misappropriations of assets have occurred. The lists can never be complete because, regardless of the improvements that you make to your internal control system, there is always a method of circumventing the system (particularly if there is collusion between employees).

Deliveries

Methods that suppliers or delivery drivers can use to defraud a hotel when they observe that effective control procedures for receiving are not being used include the following:

- Invoicing for high quality merchandise when poor quality has been delivered.
- Putting correct quality items on the top of a box or case with subquality items underneath.
- Opening boxes or cases, removing some of the items, resealing the boxes or cases, and charging for full ones.
- Putting delivered items directly into storage areas and charging for more than was actually delivered.
- Taking back unacceptable merchandise without issuing an appropriate credit invoice.

Receiving and Inventory

The people working in and around your receiving and storage areas, if these are not properly controlled, could defraud by:

- Working with a supplier's delivery driver by approving invoices for deliveries not actually made to your hotel.
- Working with a supplier's delivery driver by approving invoices for high quality merchandise when poor quality merchandise has been delivered.
- Pocketing items and walking out with them at the end of the shift.
- Using garbage cans to smuggle items out the back door.
- Removing items from a controlled storeroom and changing inventory records to hide the fact.

Cash Funds

Cash funds include general reserve cash under your control, the petty cash fund, and banks or change funds established for cashiers for making change. Persons handling cash can cheat by:

- Removing cash and showing it as a shortage.
- Using personal expenditure receipts and recording them as paid-outs for business purposes.
- Removing cash for personal use and covering it with an IOU or post-dated check.
- Underadding cash sheet columns and removing cash.
- Failing to record cash income from sundry sales such as vending machines or empty returnable containers.

Accounts Payable and Payroll

The person(s) handling accounts payable and/or payroll can practice fraud by:

- Setting up a dummy company and making out checks on false invoices in the name of this company.
- Working in collusion with a supplier and having the supplier send padded or dummy invoices directly to the accounts payable clerk.
- Making out checks for invoices already paid.
- Padding the payroll with fictitious employees.
- Padding the gross pay amount on employee(s) checks in collusion with the employee(s).
- Carrying employees on the payroll beyond their termination date.

Front Office

The front office area can also be a source of extra income for dishonest employees. A dishonest desk clerk could practice fraud and pocket extra cash by:

- Registering a late arriving guest who is also checking out early, collecting payment in advance, destroying the registration card, and failing to record the revenue on a guest account folio. This may require collusion between the desk clerk and the maid who cleans the room.

- Keeping cash from day-rate guests under similar circumstances to the preceding situation.
- Registering the guest, collecting in advance, and subsequently cancelling the registration card and blank guest folio as a "did not stay." Again this may require collusion between desk clerk and maid.
- Charging a high rate on the guest's copy of the account and recording a lower rate on the hotel's copy where the accounting system is a manual one.
- Changing the hotel's copy of the account to a lower amount after the guest has paid and gone.
- Making a false allowance/rebate voucher with a forged signature after a guest has paid and gone and using this voucher to authenticate a reduction of the hotel's copy of the guest folio.
- Creating false paid-outs for fictitious purchases for the hotel, or using personal expenditure receipts to justify the paid-out.
- Charging cash-paid guest accounts to fictitious companies.
- Using credit cards from authentic charge accounts to subsequently convert cash-paid accounts to fictitious charge ones.
- Lapping payments received on city ledger accounts (see earlier section in this chapter where this was discussed).
- Collecting cash from an account receivable thought to be uncollectible, pocketing the cash, and writing the account off as a bad debt.
- Collecting cash from an account receivable previously considered to be a bad debt and not recording the cash credit to the account.
- Recording the guest account as a "skip" (a guest who intentionally leaves without paying) after the guest has actually paid the account.
- Receiving deposits for room reservations in advance of the guest's arrival and failing to set up a guest account with the deposit credited.
- In collusion with the guest, not charging for an extra person in the room in order to receive a tip.
- Selling deposit box or room keys to thieves or burglars.

In the following chapters, methods and procedures that will prevent or at least minimize many of these fraud possibilities will be detailed.

FIVE

Guest Account Control

Even though a manual system of guest account control is described in this chapter, it is recognized that many hotels today use machines (and even computers) for this purpose. By understanding how a manual system operates, however, you will also understand how a machine or computer system works because the same principles apply.

In small transient hotels where guests seldom, if ever, stay more than a night, and where no charges other than the room rate are made to accounts by guests, the registration card can serve as the guest account. In other words, front office employees simply write the room charge on the card after the guest has registered, and the guest usually pays the room rate in advance, in cash or by credit card. The guest may be given a perforated stub of the registration card as a receipt (see Figure 5.1). If the guest pays by credit card, the guest's copy of the credit card voucher also serves as a receipt.

At the end of the day, you only need to run an adding machine tape of the registration card/account figures to determine total revenue or income for the day. The total should then agree with the total cash and credit card vouchers in the cash drawer.

GUEST ACCOUNTS

In larger hotels where the guests may stay more than one night and where accounting records must be more formalized, you have to use accounts that provide space to record the room rate for more than one night.

If charges or additions to accounts for items other than the room rate are allowed (for example, for telephone calls or for the hotel's restaurant or gift shop), then the account must provide space for this. The accounts can still be combined with the registration card and are generally designed in duplicate with the top copy having a carbon backing. In this way, when guests check out they can be given either the original or the duplicate copy

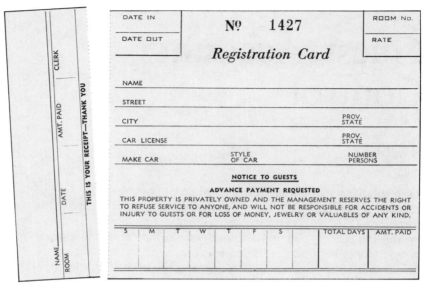

Figure 5.1   Registration card.

of this account/registration card as a receipt providing full details of all charges for the stay. Figure 5.2 illustrates a duplicate combined guest account/registration card.

Weekly Accounts

In hotels where guests may stay for a week or more (for example, in resort operations), it is recommended that the account be designed with seven columns. More than seven columns are not necessary because it is a good idea, even if guests stay for longer periods, to present them with a copy of the account at the end of the seventh day. This serves two purposes. First, it allows the guest to review the account and to question any charges he or she thinks are incorrect. Second, the guest can be asked to pay the account at the end of each week.

Account Completion

In some hotels the account is completed as soon as the guest registers and prepays the room rate for the night. This occurs where it is the operation's policy to request payment in advance, or if guests indicate they wish to pay in advance.

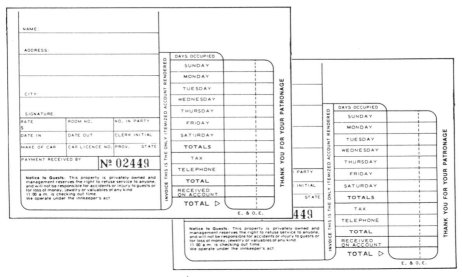

Figure 5.2 Registration card/guest account.

In such cases, the room rate and tax (if applicable) are recorded in the appropriate places and the amount paid is recorded on the Cash line to bring the account to a zero balance as illustrated in Figure 5.3. At that time the guest can be given a copy of the account as a receipt.

In other cases, particularly where the guest is likely to have other charges posted or added to the account, it is left open for the one or more nights that he or she is staying, and the total amount paid will be recorded on the cash line on the day of departure.

Deposits

Note that, if a deposit has been sent in prior to the guest's arrival, it is a good idea to prepare an account for the guest at that time and record the deposit amount on the cash line. The account can then be held with this prepaid amount, or credit balance, until the guest arrives and registers. An example of this is illustrated in Figure 5.4. Note also that the closing balance figure is in parentheses to indicate it is a credit balance.

Telephone Charges

In most hotels the only charges in addition to the room rate that are posted to guests' accounts are for the use of the room telephone.

Telephone charges are of two types: local and long distance. In some

	GUEST ACCOUNT															
Room no. _107_				Name _MR. J. BIDWELL_												
Arrival _Apr. 22_				Departure _Apr. 23_ Rate $ _32.00_												

Date	Apr. 22															
Opening balance																
Room	32	00														
Tax	1	60														
Local phone																
Long distance																
Restaurant																
Paid out																
Miscellaneous																
Total	33	60														
Cash	33	60														
Closing balance	0															

Figure 5.3   Guest account.

hotels, it is the policy to allow the guest to make "free" local calls. This reduces the amount of accounting paperwork and is a service that is valued by guests, particularly if they are business travelers who have to make considerable use of the telephone.

In other cases, there is a charge for each local call made. Local calls should be metered automatically by room number at the front office. As a guest checks out, the meter reading showing the number of calls made from that room is simply multiplied by the appropriate charge per call. The total local telephone call amount is then added to the account before it is totalled and paid.

With automatic switchboards it is also possible for guests to directly dial long distance calls from their rooms. After the call is completed, the telephone company operator contacts the hotel front desk and provides the necessary information such as where the call was placed, the number of

GUEST ACCOUNT																

Room no. 121   Name Ms. D. Scott

Arrival May 11   Departure May 14   Rate $30 00

Date	May 11															
Opening balance																
Room																
Tax																
Local phone																
Long distance																
Restaurant																
Paid out																
Miscellaneous																
Total																
Cash	30	00														
Closing balance	(30	00)														

Figure 5.4   Guest account showing deposit.

minutes, the total telephone company charge for the call, and the room number from which the call originated. Most hotels add a service charge to the telephone company amount to help pay for the telephone equipment.

It is a good idea to record all information about each long distance call on a voucher. A completed voucher for a long distance call is illustrated in Figure 5.5. These vouchers serve several purposes. For example, they

- Allow the front desk cashier to give the guest details about long distance charges if they are questioned when the account is presented for payment.
- Aid in carrying out a daily telephone call control, as you will see later in this chapter in the section on the transcript.
- Permit a double check against the telephone company's monthly billing of long distance calls against your hotel's own records.

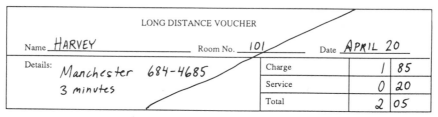

Figure 5.5 Cancelled voucher.

In some hotels, after the long distance voucher is completed, the total charge information is recorded on the guest account. In other cases, because some guests make several long distance calls a day, and because the guest account may have only sufficient space to record one amount for long distance charges, it is necessary to file all the vouchers by room number until the end of each day. At the end of the day, for each room, the vouchers can be added and the total charge recorded on the guest account as a lump sum.

When the long distance voucher total or totals are recorded on (posted to) the account, each voucher should have a line drawn through it (as illustrated in Figure 5.5). This shows that it has been posted and prevents double charging the guest for the same call.

An alternative to using long distance vouchers, particularly if there are not too many calls each day, is to list the information about each call on a long distance daily sheet such as that illustrated in Figure 5.6. The use of this sheet reduces the amount of paperwork and achieves the same control purpose as vouchers.

Restaurant Charges

If your hotel has a restaurant that a guest may use and have the charge added to the room account, the restaurant sales check serves as the voucher. After it is signed by the guest and the room number recorded on it, the restaurant must ensure that the sales check is sent to the front office as soon as possible so that it can be posted to the guest account in a similar way to the posting of long distance charges.

Other Charges

If your hotel offers other services such as laundry or dry cleaning, vouchers should be prepared for these services in a similar way to those for long distance calls.

LONG DISTANCE DAILY SHEET								Date _APRIL 20_			
Name	Room No.	Place called	Number	Charge		Service		Total			
HARVEY	101	Manchester	684-4685	1	85	0	20	2	05		
WILSON	110	Concord	692-7111	3	25	0	30	3	55		
JORDAN	103	Amherst	681-2880	4	00	0	40	4	40		
DEVLIN	109	Lakeside	724-1021	2	40	0	25	2	65		
RIVERS	104	Manchester	688-8432	2	90	0	30	3	20		
STEELMAN	106	Churchville	398-1654	1	90	0	20	2	10		
CHURSKI	107	Stanton	724-6880	2	45	0	25	2	70		
			Totals	18	75	1	90	20	65		

Figure 5.6 Long distance daily sheet.

Paid-Outs

In some hotels, particularly those of a nontransient nature, you may allow guest "paid-outs." A paid-out transaction can occur, for example, when a guest telephones a local shop to have a purchase delivered. At the time of the delivery to the hotel the guest may not be in the room. Your front office employees may be given the authority to accept delivery on behalf of the guest and pay the shop. In this situation, the front office cashier should complete a paid-out voucher, attach it to the delivery invoice, and post the paid-out charge to the guest's account.

Note that if cash has been paid out for such a transaction, the voucher is the equivalent of cash, and should be handled as if it were cash so that the cash can be balanced at the end of the day.

Coding Vouchers

In larger hotels, with a variety of vouchers for different types of transactions, it might be a good idea to color code them (for example, white for long distance, pink for laundry/dry cleaning, green for paid-outs). In this way, the voucher can be more easily identified by type of transaction.

Balancing Accounts

Figure 5.7 is an illustration of a guest account completed for a stay of several days with various voucher postings to it.

Note that at the end of each day the closing balance figure at the bottom of the account becomes the opening balance amount at the top of

GUEST ACCOUNT

Room no. __101__   Name __MR S. SKULSKI__

Arrival __Apr/20__   Departure __Apr. 23__ Rate $__35.00__

Date	Apr. 20		Apr. 21		Apr. 22		Apr. 23	
Opening balance			41	00	82	50	138	95
Room	35	00	35	00	35	00		
Tax	1	75	1	75	1	75		
Local phone	0	30			1	50	0	50
Long distance			4	75				
Restaurant	3	95			15	10		
Paid out					3	10		
Miscellaneous								
Total	41	00	82	50	138	95	139	45
Cash							139	45
Closing balance	41	00	82	50	138	95	0	

Figure 5.7 Completed guest account.

the next day's column. If all vouchers are posted to their correct guest accounts as the vouchers are handled, or at the least at the end of each day, the account can be kept up to date at all times with a running balance ready for the guest to pay it the moment he or she wishes to check out.

Guest Account Control

Note that the account illustrated in Figure 5.2 has a preprinted, sequential number on it. It is a good idea to number your guest accounts. This is useful for accounting control purposes. If a guest is staying for more than a week the account number should be cross-referenced to the account number for the following week, and vice versa. This makes it easier to trace back all the accounts for a guest's entire stay should this be necessary.

In addition, guest account usage can be controlled by filing the accounts in number sequence after they are paid. This sequence can then be checked from time to time (let us say, once a week) and any missing account numbers identified. The reason for missing accounts should then be checked. For example, an account may not yet be filed because it is being held as an account receivable. On the other hand, fraud occurs if a cashier destroys the account after it is paid and pockets the cash.

CASH SHEETS

Each day a cash sheet should be prepared by the front office cashier. Any payments received for reservation deposits and part or full payments on account should be listed immediately on this sheet. If there are any guest cash disbursements or paid-outs, they should also be recorded on this sheet.

House Paid-Outs

In addition, there might be "house" cash disbursements or paid-outs that should also be recorded on the cash sheet. House paid-outs are simply minor purchases, such as office supplies, that are paid with cash from the front office cash drawer at the time the purchase is made.

To authenticate these transactions, the cashier should have in the cash drawer the invoice or cash register slip from the supplier from whom the purchase was made. If the transaction is one for which there is no invoice or register slip, then a memo or house paid-out to record the facts should be prepared identifying the transaction as a house paid-out.

You should verify each day that each house paid-out is an authentic one to prevent a dishonest cashier from preparing fictitious entries and pocketing the cash.

Balancing the Cash Sheet

At the end of each day, the various sections of the cash sheet should be totaled by the cashier, the recapitulation section completed, and the deposit figure balanced with the amount of cash in the cash drawer. The cash should then be deposited intact each day in the bank. A completed cash sheet showing how the bank deposit amount is calculated is illustrated in Figure 5.8.

An alternative cash form is illustrated in Figure 5.9. This form of cash accounting breaks down the payments received by guests into their departmental elements, providing more detailed information for income statement purposes.

| | | | | DATE _APRIL 20_ | | | |

FRONT OFFICE CASH SHEET

CASH RECEIPTS				CASH DISBURSEMENTS—GUESTS			
ROOM NO.	NAME	AMOUNT		ROOM NO.	NAME	ITEM	AMOUNT
108	PARDIN	35	55	102	MASTIN	DRY CL.	3	10
107	CHURSKI	105	10	109	DEVLIN	DRY CL	4	00
103	JORDAN	38	40				
102	JASON	36	85				7	10
	VISA (CITY LEDGER)	91	90				
		307	80				

CASH DISBURSEMENTS—HOUSE

Office Supplies 4 85

4 85

RECAPITULATION

TOTAL RECEIPTS			307	80
DISBURSEMENTS—GUESTS	7	10		
DISBURSEMENTS—HOUSE	4	85		
TOTAL DISBURSEMENTS			11	95
DEPOSIT			295	85

Figure 5.8 Front office cash sheet.

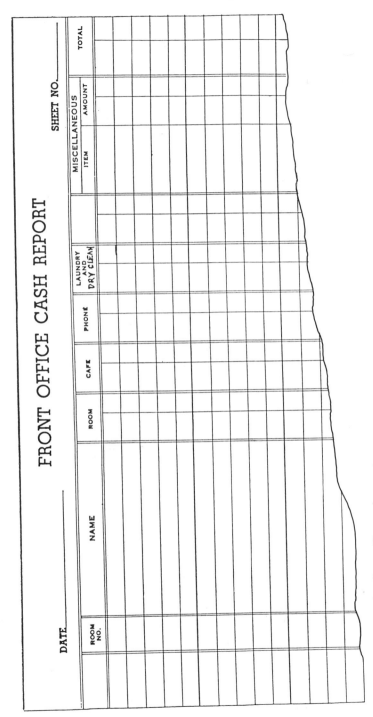

Figure 5.9 Alternative front office cash report.

Cash-based Accounting

In small hotels, the system of guest accounts and the daily cash sheet explained so far are adequate for control purposes. Such hotels operate on what is referred to as a cash basis.

In larger operations, and particularly where there are a variety of charges to guest accounts and where the hotel is not dealing with guests who arrive one day and depart the next, it is useful to complete a *transcript* each day.

THE TRANSCRIPT

The transcript has two basic purposes:

- To summarize all the guest-account transactions for the day and to show the current balance of each account.
- To balance all the accounts and prove the accuracy of all the transactions that occurred on guest accounts that day.

The transcript is normally completed at the end of each day when there are unlikely to be any more guest arrivals or charges to guest accounts. In very busy hotels with late arrivals, this work is frequently carried out by the person on the midnight to 8 A.M. shift, who is frequently given the title of night auditor as the transcript provides an audit of each 24-hour transcript cycle.

The transcript is a columnar sheet, with column headings paralleling the wording on guest accounts. One line on the transcript is used for each guest account as illustrated in Figure 5.10.

Preliminary Steps

You should instruct the night auditor to perform the following preliminary steps before completing the daily transcript:

1. Make sure all vouchers are assembled.
2. Check each voucher to see that it has a cancellation mark showing it has been posted to an account.
3. Record any unposted vouchers on the appropriate guest account.
4. Separate and total all vouchers by department.
5. Check that each cash sheet entry has been posted to its proper account.

TRANSCRIPT

Date APRIL 20

GUEST'S NAME	Room No	Account No	No. Guests	Opening Balance	Room	Tax	Local Phone	Charges Long Distance	Rest't	Guest Pd Out	Misc	TOTAL	Cash	Closing Balance	City Ledger
HARVEY	101	3707	3		34.00	1.70		2.05				37.75		37.75	
JASON	102	3662		35.60			1.25					36.85	36.85		
MASTIN	102	3706	1		32.00	1.60				3.10		36.70		36.70	
JORDAN	103	3652		33.50			0.50	4.40				38.40	38.40		
NARVADO	103	3704	2		30.00	1.50			12.40			43.90		43.90	
RIVERS	104	3701	2	58.20	28.00	1.40		3.20				90.80		90.80	
KRAFT	105	3716		52.40								52.40			52.40 Visa
LIVITZ	106	3700		43.20								43.20			43.20 M'card
STEELMAN	106	3699	1		37.00	1.85		2.10				40.95		40.95	
CHURSKI	107	3719		98.50			0.25	2.70	3.65			105.10	105.10		
PARDIN	108	3715		34.80			0.75					35.55	35.55		
JONES	108	3703	2		38.00	1.90						39.90		39.90	
DEVLIN	109	3698	1		38.00	1.90		2.65		4.00		46.55		46.55	
LONG	109	3702		38.15			0.75		4.30			43.20			43.20 Visa
WILSON	110	3721	3		42.00	2.10		3.55	26.20			73.85		73.85	
CITY LEDGER				415.20								415.20	91.90		323.30
TOTALS			15	809.55	279.00	13.95	3.50	20.65	46.55	7.10		1180.30	307.80	410.40	462.10

Figure 5.10 Transcript.

61

6. Ensure that no cash entries appear on accounts that do not appear on the cash sheet.

7. Add up the cash sheet to obtain separate totals for cash receipts and guest paid-outs.

8. Record room rates and, where applicable, tax on each account.

9. Total the day's charges and credits on each guest account and calculate each account's closing balance.

10. Record today's closing balance figure as the following day's opening balance on each account.

Completing the Transcript

The following are procedures for completing and balancing the transcript:

1. Take one account at a time (preferably in room number sequence) and record today's information from the account in the appropriate transcript columns. Note that for some room numbers there may be two accounts, and therefore two lines are required on the transcript — one for the guest who checked out of the room on that day, and the other for the account of the newly arrived guest in that room.

2. Add up each column on the transcript after all account information has been recorded. The figure in the Opening Balance column should be the same as the total of the figures in the Closing Balance and City Ledger columns of yesterday's transcript (City Ledger accounts will be discussed later in the chapter).

3. The total figure in the tax column should be the appropriate tax percent in your jurisdiction. In our case it is 5 percent of room revenue.

4. The total figure in the Long Distance column should be the same as the total on the adding machine tape of all the long distance vouchers for that date. Alternatively, the column total should be balanced against the Long Distance Daily Sheet (Figure 5.6).

5. The total in the Restaurant column should be balanced in the same way as for Long Distance.

6. The total in the Guest Paid-Out column should be similarly balanced. In addition, this column should agree with the Cash Disbursements–Guests section of the Cash Sheet (Figure 5.8).

7. The Cash column total should also agree with the Cash Receipts section of the Cash Sheet (Figure 5.8).

8. Once all column totals have been checked (and corrections made if necessary), the transcript can be crosstotalled as follows:

Opening Balance + Room + Tax + Local phone + Long distance
+ Restaurant + Guest paid-out + Miscellaneous = TOTAL

In our case, the figures are:

$$\begin{array}{r} \$ \ \ 809.55 \\ 279.00 \\ 13.95 \\ 3.50 \\ 20.65 \\ 46.55 \\ \underline{\quad 7.10} \\ \$1,180.30 \end{array}$$

9. Finally, the TOTAL column total less the Cash column total must agree with the sum of the final two transcript columns: Closing Balance + City Ledger, or in our case:

$$\$1,180.30 - \$307.80 = \$872.50$$

and

$$\$410.40 + \$462.10 = \$872.50$$

Deposits on Accounts

When a guest sends in a deposit prior to arrival, an account is prepared in advance. The deposit amount is recorded on the account and the account showing a credit balance held until arrival. On the date the deposit is received this amount will be shown on the cash sheet and in the Cash column of the transcript.

The credit balance is carried forward on the transcript each day until the date of arrival, when the credit will be offset by room and other charges incurred by the guest. Credit amounts are usually recorded in parentheses —for example, ($25.00). When adding up the transcript columns, these amounts are deducted to arrive at the correct column total.

Locating Errors

Errors may be discovered in completing and balancing the transcript. For example, if the Restaurant column total added up to $46.55 and restaurant vouchers on hand or the daily restaurant sheet total added up to $51.55, it is likely that a restaurant charge has not been recorded on the account or on the transcript.

A process of elimination will show which charge was missed and the error can be corrected. If the guest has already left the hotel, you must then decide if the charge will be forgotten, or if a bill for the restaurant charge will be sent to the departed guest. All errors of this type must be corrected before the transcript can be balanced.

Other types of error include transposition of figures, posting to the wrong guest account, and compensating errors.

Transposition of Figures.   This occurs when an amount such as $43.40 is recorded as $34.40. Transpositions frequently occur in carrying forward yesterday's Closing Balance figures to today's Opening Balance column.

Posting to the Wrong Account.   This type of error can often go unnoticed until the wrongly charged guest complains. The guest account to which the charge has been wrongly posted can easily be credited to correct the error. However, if the guest to whose account the charge should have been posted has already left the hotel, the revenue may be lost unless a bill for the amount is sent to that guest.

Compensating Errors.   A compensating error occurs when two mistakes are made, one offsetting the other. For example, a long distance charge may be overposted to one guest's account by one dollar and underposted to another guest's account by the same amount. This type of error can go undetected unless the guest who is overcharged complains.

ACCOUNTS RECEIVABLE

At any time, the totals of the Closing Balance column and the City Ledger column of the transcript are your hotel's accounts receivable. The accounts receivable are made up of house accounts (the accounts of guests still registered and staying in the hotel—or the total of the Closing Balance column) and the City Ledger accounts (the accounts of guests who have left the hotel but whose accounts have not yet been paid).

City Ledger Accounts

City Ledger accounts generally include the accounts of guests who have charged the account balance to a credit card or to a company, the accounts of individuals or companies who have rented meeting rooms in your hotel, and the accounts of "skips" (those who left and "forgot" to pay their bills).

The simplest way to handle City Ledger accounts on the transcript is to list them, on the day of departure, in a separate column of the transcript as illustrated in Figure 5.10. This temporarily separates them from the house accounts (those in the Closing Balance column).

For example, with reference to Figure 5.10, note that there were three City Ledger accounts on this day. To arrive at the City Ledger transcript column total, these three amounts were simply added to the balance of all other City Ledger accounts of $323.30. On the following day the City Ledger column total of $462.10 is carried forward and recorded in the Opening Balance column. This method makes it easy to keep a running balance of the total accounts in the City Ledger.

If your hotel does not have many City Ledger accounts, they could be listed individually on the transcript (just as the other house accounts are listed individually) until payment is received. However, when you have many City Ledger accounts, copying them from transcript to transcript each day can create unnecessary work. The method shown in Figure 5.10 is a useful shortcut. Note also on this figure how a City Ledger payment is handled on the transcript and on the cash sheet (Figure. 5.8).

Other Situations

As the transcript is completed it can signal two possible situations with accounts receivable: weekly accounts and large account balances.

It is common practice when guests stay for more than seven nights to present them with a copy of the bill at the end of each seven-day period. In such a situation, the person who completes the transcript should start a new guest account (cross-referencing the two account numbers). In this way, the guest can be presented with a copy of the weekly account. This will give the guest an opportunity to check the account and question it if necessary. It will also remind the guest to make a payment on the account.

Another value of the transcript is to indicate any accounts that have unusually large balances on them (whether the guest has been there for a week or not). Some hotels have a limit on the amount a guest may have on an account (for example, $500) before he or she is requested to make payment).

Guest Count

Finally, note on the transcript the column headed Number of Guests. The total figure in this column indicates the number of guests staying in the hotel overnight. A guest count figure is recorded on each line only where there is a room charge for that night. This guest count figure can be used to provide useful statistical information to be discussed in Chapter 10.

Housekeeping Control

Control of front office guest accounts can be achieved by having the head housekeeper complete a rooms occupancy form each day. On this form in the left-hand column will be preprinted the number of each room in your hotel. To the right of that column are other columns in which can be recorded each day by the head housekeeper the status of each room such as occupied, unoccupied, and out of order. There can be an additional column showing the number of people in each occupied room.

Each day you, or a delegated responsible individual, can compare the head housekeeper's record of rooms occupied with the transcript record and investigate any differences.

Rebates (Discounts)

In your hotel you may allow front office employees to give guests a rebate or discount off the quoted room rate in certain circumstances. For example, after an overnight stay a guest may complain about being placed in a room where the television set did not work. In that case, a front office employee may be authorized to reduce the room charge by $5. To authenticate this reduction to the room rate already posted to the guest account, a rebate voucher should be completed explaining the reason for the discount. The guest should be asked to sign the voucher.

It is possible for a dishonest employee to create a fictitious voucher after a guest has paid the account in full, forge the guest's signature, and pocket cash equivalent to the voucher's amount.

Obviously, it would be preferable that you, as hotel owner or manager, authorize each rebate voucher in the presence of the guest. However, as this may not be practical, you should take whatever steps are necessary to authenticate each rebate voucher, since such a voucher (just like a paid-out voucher) is the equivalent of cash.

Rebate vouchers can be recorded on the daily cash sheet in the same way that paid-outs are so that the front office cashier's cash remittance will still balance.

GUEST CHECK-OUT

Guests may pay their accounts in a variety of ways when checking out, such as cash, personal check, credit card, traveler's check, or charge to a company.

Cash

Front office cashiers should be instructed in proper cash handling procedures such as:

- Be neat and tidy with cash.
- When unwrapping rolls of coins, count them before putting them away and report any shortages.
- If a guest presents bills, do not put them in the cash drawer until change has been made and the guest has accepted it.
- Always count aloud the change as it is being handed over.
- Avoid becoming confused when handling cash, particularly with people who seem intent on creating confusion in the hope that a mistake will be made in their favor.
- Learn to recognize counterfeit money and be aware of any counterfeit money or stolen checks in circulation.
- When one employee hands over money to another employee (for example, at the change of a shift), both employees should count the money so there is no disagreement about the amount handed over.
- Never leave the cash drawer unlocked in an unattended front office.
- No payments should be made out of the front office cash (for example for wages, petty purchases, COD items) unless a receipt is put in the cash drawer or a paid-out voucher completed.
- When handwriting figures relating to cash amounts (on guest accounts, for example), ensure that these figures are clear and legible.

Personal Checks

Many hotels will not accept personal checks from guests unless the person is well known to the hotel and stays there frequently. The reason for not cashing checks, or accepting them in payment of accounts, is that if a personal check is accepted from a guest and is subsequently returned from the bank marked "not sufficient funds" (NSF) it may be very difficult to recover the amount from the departed guest.

If your operation accepts personal checks from guests in payment of accounts, the check should be made out for the exact amount of the account — and not for $20 or $30 more that the guest receives back in cash. Some suggested procedures for accepting personal checks are:

- Ask for one or two pieces of identification if the guest is not known to the hotel. Identification should include an item (such as a driver's license) where the photograph and signature of the person appear. Compare the photograph with the guest, and the signature with that on the check.

- Record identification information on the reverse of the check.

- Check the date on the check to make sure it is current.

- Look for erasures or changes on the check. Anything that has been changed (for example, a date or an amount) should be initialed by the guest.

- Look for a difference between the amount figures and the amount numbers. For example, it is easy to write the figures $45.00 and write the amount as "Fifty-four."

- Do not accept pre- or postdated checks, or checks made payable to a company.

- Do not accept any two-party checks. A two-party check is one signed by a person other than the person cashing it.

- Once a check is accepted, endorse it immediately with the hotel's "For Deposit Only" stamp. This prevents forged endorsements if the check is lost or stolen prior to depositing it in the bank.

Credit Cards

Most hotels accept nationally recognized credit cards in payment of guest accounts. In order to minimize losses from credit cards, procedures should be established so that those at the front desk know exactly what to do when presented with a credit card. A set of procedures for handling guests' credit cards was provided in Chapter 4.

Some credit card issuing companies allow the card to be used by the guest to receive cash or to cash personal checks up to a limited amount. In this situation, you should be aware of any special procedures that the card company requires if such a request is made by a guest. Use all necessary identification precautions in such cases, and be aware of the maximum amounts of cash or personal check limits that are in effect for each individual credit card company.

Commissions paid on credit card revenue can range as high as 6 percent. Chain hotel operations with their high volume can usually benefit from lower commission costs. Bank credit cards (such as Visa and Master-Card) entail charges that are also lower. You should, therefore, train employees to encourage guests to use the card (if the guest offers a choice) that minimizes commission costs. In particular, since accounts charged to bank credit cards can be converted within a day or so into cash, it is wise to encourage the use of these cards rather than those from organizations that may not pay as promptly.

Traveler's Checks

Many people who travel on vacation prefer to carry traveler's checks rather than cash. A traveler's check is like a certified check as far as you are concerned. When a guest wishes to cash a traveler's check, or use one to pay the account, ensure that the guest signs the check in front of you, and that this second signature compares with the original signature placed on the check when it was purchased.

If the guest signs a second time without the signature's being witnessed, ask the guest to sign the check on the back and compare this endorsement with the original signature. Do not hesitate to ask for some form of identification if in doubt.

If large amounts of traveler's checks are cashed, it might be a good idea to ask the issuing companies to put your hotel on their mailing list so they can advise you of the serial numbers of checks that have been lost or stolen and may be in circulation in your area. Some issuing companies also have ways of identifying forged traveler's checks. The local police fraud squad can also frequently provide helpful information in this regard.

Charge to a Company

Company representatives and salespeople of businesses in your area may provide you with a great deal of business. Many of these travelers have their accounts paid directly by their company. If a guest requests this service, you should first check with the office of the company concerned to authenticate that the charge is legitimate.

Many companies provide lists of their representatives who are entitled to charge their accounts. This, of course, makes it easier for you. Once it is ascertained that an account can be charged to a company, have the guest sign the account and provide details of the company name and address.

With company charge accounts, it is not necessary to give the guest his or her copy of the account. In fact, if this were done there would be no copy available to send to the company unless your accounts were printed in triplicate. Since this is costly, it is not recommended.

One other possibility is that a departing guest's account is to be paid by someone else still in your hotel. If this is so, check with the guest still registered to be sure this is acceptable, and have the departing guest sign the account before attaching it for payment to the account of the guest still registered.

Preparation of Account for Payment

It was mentioned earlier that accounts should be kept up to date so that they are ready whenever a guest leaves. However, there may be charges that have to be added to the account just prior to finalizing it. For example, if local telephone calls are metered, the meter reading may need to be translated into a dollar amount at the time of check-out so that the amount can be posted to the guest account.

Also, if your hotel has a restaurant and guests are allowed to charge restaurant meals to their accounts, you should check with the restaurant to see if there is a restaurant voucher (sales check) still to be processed for a guest checking out. This is particularly important where guests check out immediately after breakfast.

SIX

Purchasing

To many small hotel operators, purchasing is simply a matter of telephoning suppliers who can provide needed products, placing an order, and having it delivered as soon as possible. In other situations, a supplier's representative may arrive at the premises and write up an order without the hotel operator's having any record of products and quantities ordered or their prices.

With these unorganized methods of order placing (rather than effective purchasing) there is no attempt to contact alternative suppliers, or compare product qualities and prices. In fact, some purchasers do not even ask about prices!

As a result of these "informal" purchasing methods, the supplier is acting primarily as a warehouse for the purchaser and is used as the supplier because it will make emergency deliveries—a service that is offered because it knows it is the sole or main supplier and charges high prices because it has little or no competition.

Unfortunately, this and similar purchasing practices that focus only on the short-run situation can cost from 10 to 20 percent more than if systematic procedures are followed. A hotel that is dependent on and loyal to only one supplier may be overlooking quality and price advantages available from alternate suppliers.

SPECIFICATIONS

Effective purchasing requires that you complete purchasing specifications for major expenditure items such as guest room furniture and linen. Obviously, for many items you purchase specifications may not be practical or necessary. This might apply in the purchase of items required on an everyday basis, such as cleaning and paper supplies.

Depending on the circumstances, a specification can be quite short and informal and may include only the brand name and quantity desired of a needed product. In the case of other purchases (for example, equipment) a specification can be several pages long.

Who Prepares Them?

Specifications may be prepared by you or by a department head who has the authority to purchase the item. In other cases, specifications may need to be prepared jointly by two or more people, such as the user in conjunction with the general manager.

Factors to Consider Before Preparing Specifications

What actually appears on a specification can be influenced by any or all of the following:

- Your hotel's objectives with particular reference to quality standards. For example, is your operation a high-quality resort or an economy-priced motor hotel?
- The budget available. This is particularly true for major capital items such as equipment. In other cases, competition from other hotels may force you to reduce room rates which, in turn, reduces the funds available for purchasing certain items or reduces the quality you can afford in needed products.
- Time and resources (personnel) available for preparing detailed specifications.
- Distance to the supplier's source of supply (because this can affect delivery schedules).

How Many Copies?

You should produce sufficient copies of specifications so that one copy may be sent to each potential supplier and copies distributed to appropriate personnel such as the purchasing manager (in a large hotel), the department head involved, and the person responsible for receiving the products.

Advantages of Specifications

The main advantages of specifications are that they

- Require those who prepare them to think carefully and document exactly what their product requirements are.
- Serve as a standard for quality.
- Leave no doubt in suppliers' minds about what they are quoting on, thus reducing or eliminating misunderstandings between your hotel and the supplier.

- Eliminate, for frequently purchased items, the time that would otherwise have to be spent repeating descriptions over the telephone or directly to salespersons each time the product is needed.
- May reduce purchasing costs because you are not paying for a higher quality than is needed.
- Permit competitive bidding where this method of purchasing is used, and may increase competitive bidding if generic products are specified.
- Make it much easier to complete purchase orders. (Specifications define the products required. Purchase orders are contractual obligations to make a purchase and will be discussed later in this chapter).
- Allow the person responsible for receiving to check the quality of delivered goods against a written specification of the quality standard desired.

PURCHASING METHODS

Before considering which suppliers to purchase from, you should first be familiar with all possible purchasing methods. There are many different purchasing methods available, and you cannot select the right supplier without first considering the type of purchasing method that is best for your hotel and the products that it needs.

Many purchasers will select only one of the many arrangements to be discussed in the following sections, and stick with it without considering other methods. Again, this can be an approach that unnecessarily adds to purchase costs. In other words, it is rare that a single purchasing method is best. You need to select the most appropriate one for each type of product and change that method when necessary to meet market conditions.

Single-source Buying

In some situations single-source buying is necessary. This could occur when the product required is unique, and there is only one manufacturer or supplier. In such cases, you may have little control over the cost of the item. For example, if you wanted a particular item of guest room furniture made by only one manufacturer, then your purchasing options are limited.

Competitive Buying

Competitive buying is also known as open market buying, quotation buying, market quote buying, call sheet buying, or riding the market. This method entails waiting until the goods are needed, then taking bids from suppliers to fulfill those needs. Probably the majority of day-to-day purchases made by the typical hotel are bought through competitive buying.

Under competitive buying, quotations are received by telephone, in person directly from a salesperson, or in writing through the mail from suppliers. Quotations are often recorded on an in-house quotation sheet. After this is complete and the supplier(s) selected, the quotation sheet is given to the receiver to check prices on invoices received when goods are delivered.

Traditionally, purchasers in small hotels use competitive buying and purchase products from the supplier who offers the lowest price for each product. This is not necessarily the most viable method of purchasing because it means that a supplier is frequently required to deliver only one or two items out of, let us say, 20 that were quoted on. It costs no less for a supplier to deliver one case of a product than 10 cases. If the cost of a delivery is $50, and 10 cases are delivered, the delivery cost is only $5 per case. If one case is delivered, the delivery cost is $50 per case. Either way, you end up paying this delivery cost in the price of the product.

Further, when suppliers make bids in this type of competitive buying situation, they have no way of knowing if they will receive an order, or how many items out of a list they are quoting on they will receive an order for. In this uncertainty, and because of the cost of delivery, suppliers tend to bid higher than would be the case if they knew they would receive the complete order so long as the total overall cost of all items in a list were lower.

Therefore, if you need a variety of products, the best strategy usually is to buy from the supplier who offers the lowest overall cost (even though the cost on some individual items might be higher than from other suppliers), and advise all suppliers that this policy is in effect. This should result in lower overall prices in the long run.

Competitive buying also works well as long as you understand that all suppliers are not equal in the services they offer. For example, the supplier with the lowest overall prices may not offer the best delivery schedule.

In some situations, because of the time and cost involved in competitive buying, you may want to select only one or two suppliers and stick with them without requesting quotations from others. In this situation, the important consideration is that these suppliers must be carefully selected on the basis of their reputation for reasonable prices and dependable services.

Competitive buying is not popular with suppliers whose product prices appear higher, but whose services (such as extending a longer credit period) make the total value a better purchase. Also, because suppliers offering better services generally have higher prices, suppliers without comparable services may raise their prices to just under those from "better" suppliers, knowing that you base the buying decision on price alone.

Sealed-bid Buying

Sealed-bid buying is sometimes used by large hotels or chain operations where the head office does the purchasing for all units in the chain. It is basically a formalized method of competitive buying. Bid forms generally contain bid conditions, quantity of and specifications for products required, conditions concerning delivery, and the deadline date for bid submissions.

A bid may be written so that the purchaser pays for all products at the time of purchase, even though they may be delivered over a several-month period, or it may be written so that payment is made only as products are periodically received.

Sometimes bids are for a quantity of products to be delivered over a stipulated period at prices that can fluctuate with market prices. If this supplier flexibility were not part of the bid procedure, then potential suppliers are likely to protect themselves by quoting prices that are higher in total over the period than they would be if prices were allowed to fluctuate.

Sealed-bid buying is often used by hotels for quantity purchases of paper and cleaning supplies used in housekeeping areas. This method eliminates the problem of frequent pricing and purchasing. It may also have the advantages of reducing prices of products and eliminating supplier pressure on you to purchase from them.

A disadvantage of this purchasing method is that it requires a great deal of paperwork preparing and sending out bid forms to selected suppliers and scrutinizing bids received to ensure they meet requirements.

Another disadvantage of sealed-bid buying (particularly where long periods of time are involved) may be that, if you are the manager of an individual hotel that is part of a chain, you may not be able to benefit from subsequent local supplier price advantages as they occur, because sealed-bid buying generally requires that a contract be signed between the head office and the successful bidder for a stipulated quantity of product.

Cost-plus Buying

With cost-plus buying, you arrange with a supplier to purchase all of your requirements for a product or products at a specific percentage markup over the supplier's cost for a future fixed time period that can vary from 30 days to six months. The advantage to you is that this markup is generally smaller than would otherwise be the case. Time that would be spent dealing with a variety of suppliers is also reduced. An alternative to using cost-plus on a percentage basis might be to contract for cost plus a fixed fee per delivery.

The problem with this buying method is that it may be difficult, if not impossible, to verify the supplier's cost. What is "cost," and do you have the right to inspect or audit the supplier's records (or invoices from suppliers from which it purchases) to determine it? It is likely that a purchaser could impose a demand for an audit only if it were a major or chain operation. For example, a hotel chain that decided to purchase all its guest room furniture and/or linen requirements from a single supplier might be able to insist on an audit.

Cost-plus buying is not normally used by the typical individual hotel. Where it is used, however, the markup is usually 10 to 15 percent over cost compared to a normal 15 to 25 percent over cost. The actual percentage is usually negotiated. Suppliers are prepared to take a smaller markup because they consider it better to have a guaranteed small markup on volume sales rather than a higher markup on sales they are not guaranteed.

Cost-plus buying involves more risk than using long-term contracts because prices can rise sharply during the cost-plus term and you are commited to making those purchases rather than seeking alternatives. Obviously, a 30-day cost-plus contract is less risky than a six-month one.

One-stop Buying

One-stop buying is also sometimes referred to as prime-vendor purchasing. This involves the purchase of all items of a particular type (for example, paper and cleaning supplies) from one supplier.

The one-stop purchasing concept developed because suppliers were willing, because of guaranteed quantity sales, to reduce their markup from the normal 15 to 25 percent over cost to 10 to 12 percent, thus reducing your purchase costs by 3 to 15 percent.

This method eliminates or reduces the need to constantly compare suppliers' services and prices, eliminates constant negotiations, and builds up the selected supplier's trust. There are fewer orders required, fewer deliveries to be received, and fewer invoices to be processed and paid. Theoretically, this reduces your purchasing costs. However, because there is no competitive bidding, you must carefully review the financial advantages of one-stop buying before using this purchasing method.

One-stop buying may provide you with an overall cost advantage, even though the costs on some items may be higher than they would be if purchased elsewhere. Products with higher costs are theoretically compensated for by reduced costs on others and/or the supplier's willingness to offer a volume discount on the total purchase cost of all items.

Large suppliers offering one-stop buying may also have product specialists on their payroll who can give you detailed information on both existing and new product availability. The important ingredients in one-stop buying are careful selection of the supplier and periodic price comparisons to ensure that the supplier's prices are still in line.

The big risk with one-stop buying is that you become too dependent on the supplier and fail to stay alert to prices that are out of line or to newer products or additional services that have been introduced by the supplier's competitors. Another disadvantage is that the one-stop supplier will become a generalist rather than a specialist, thereby decreasing the availability of a variety of quality levels within any one product line.

For example, a generalist supplier might carry 3,000 to 4,000 different product lines, many of which are competitively priced quality products. However, along with those are other products that are priced higher than a specialist supplier might sell them for because the one-stop supplier will apply a higher than normal markup on these items.

Another risk with one-stop buying is that other suppliers will cut their prices, make them known to you, and try to convince you to revert to competitive bidding — at which point those suppliers will begin to raise their prices again. This is an example of "lowballing," where suppliers offer initial low prices then gradually raise them because they cannot maintain their profits over the long run at the offered low prices.

Cooperative Buying

Cooperative buying occurs when a group of hotel operators join together to purchase products. The operators benefit from quantity-discount prices as the result of bulk buying. For example, this could occur if a group of hotels joined together to contract for the purchase of the same quality of bed linen from a supplier.

An advantage of cooperative buying is that standardized quality as well as lower prices should result because of the group's volume purchasing. Also, as an individual group member you may have to spend less time with supplier sales representatives and thus will have more time to allocate to other day-to-day operations.

There are some disadvantages to cooperative buying. The purchasing decision is usually turned over to a committee. Committees are notorious for slowing down any process and sometimes find it difficult to arrive at a consensus. Further, individual members of the group may lose some control over supplier selection, loyalty, product variety, and quality because that task must be delegated to the committee.

Where cooperative purchasing is used, members have to agree on the quality standards and specifications for required products so that advantage can be taken of volume purchasing of identical products. This is a time-consuming task because, without agreement, the method cannot succeed. This often requires compromise by some participants in the cooperative.

Note that, when cooperative buying is used, it is not necessary that all products for all participants be purchased through the cooperative. You should still be free to independently purchase some products (particularly those unique to your operation), although this does decrease the ability of the cooperative to negotiate lower prices on all products.

If you do enter into a cooperative arrangement, make sure that the organization is set up and operates with proper legal advice so that you do not contravene antitrust laws. For example, the cooperative group could be liable for pressuring suppliers to offer discounts that are unfair to those purchasers who are not members of the group.

Volume Buying and Warehousing

Volume buying and warehousing is also known as *stockless purchasing*. In some situations, you may be able to buy in large quantity and obtain a major discount. In such cases, the supplier may agree to store or warehouse the product for an additional cost. Alternatively, you may be responsible for making storage arrangements off the premises (if there is not enough space on-site) and paying the storage costs.

Volume buying and warehousing usually requires you to pay in advance for products purchased and either pay in advance for storage or pay the storage fee monthly. In all these situations, you must balance the purchase cost savings against the costs incurred for storage and loss of interest on money tied up in inventory.

A variation of volume buying and warehousing is an agreement between you and a supplier by which the supplier agrees to deliver a contracted amount of a product over time and absorb all warehouse and storage costs until the goods are delivered to your establishment. This arrangement is sometimes used for items such as paper products, cleaning supplies, and linens. It can also be used where personalized items (such as guest room towels with your hotel's name and logo) need fairly large manufacturing runs to make their purchase cost-effective.

Volume buying and warehousing is often a good method to use if price increases are forecast. The added cost of warehousing may still make the products cheaper than if they were purchased later at higher prices. Obviously, there is a risk that the price will decrease rather than increase.

SELECTION OF SUPPLIERS

The supplier selection decision is important because selecting the right supplier can have significant impact on your profits. In other words, you need to use cooperative and reliable suppliers.

There are many types of suppliers, such as manufacturer, wholesaler, and local retailer. Depending on the product to be purchased, a different type of supplier may be contacted. For example, in the case of an item of capital equipment, it might be the manufacturer or his wholesaler representative. In the case of cleaning materials it might be a local supplier.

Factors Involved

You may need to go through the following steps before selecting suppliers:

- Find out who some of the supplier's present customers are to check with them about the supplier's competence, reputation, reliability, consistency of product quality, promptness and frequency of deliveries, and similar matters.
- Test the quality of the products offered. The "top" quality is not always the "best" in a particular situation. For example, in the case of a floor-cleaning compound you might find that the product available at the lowest price does the job just as well as the one with the highest price.
- Check product prices. Again, the highest price may not be the "best" price to pay, depending on the quality actually needed. Are a supplier's prices comparable to its competitors?
- Evaluate the degree to which the supplier provides information about new products as they appear on the market. Most hotel purchasers rely heavily on suppliers' sales representatives to provide product information. These representatives must therefore be knowledgeable and willing to provide this information. Large suppliers often provide monthly or weekly printed market information sheets that are automatically distributed to their purchasers and potential purchasers.
- Determine the "lead" time a supplier requires. Local suppliers of frequently required products normally accept orders a day ahead of delivery. Others may require two or more days lead time. For some products, some suppliers require even longer lead time.
- Check the supplier's delivery frequency and hours of delivery. Delivery costs are often a major expense to a supplier, and therefore an

area where price negotiation may be possible if you agree to have deliveries made at the convenience of the supplier. For example, instead of having daily deliveries from a regular supplier, can deliveries be reduced to two or three times a week with the supplier providing price concessions? Also, most suppliers have delivery schedules that peak in the morning. Can price concessions be negotiated for afternoon deliveries?

How Many Suppliers?

The typical medium-sized hotel may use as many as 50 separate suppliers. For any hotel, there is the question of how many suppliers to deal with. If your hotel is in a remote location there may be only a handful of suppliers to choose from for all products. But even in a large city, for some products there may be only one supplier. This could occur, for example, if the supplier has the sole distributorship or is the only one who carries a particular brand-name product.

Similarly, if you buy only in small volumes, you may find your choices among suppliers limited because large suppliers are not interested in accepting your business. For most products, however, you will have a choice among several competitive suppliers.

Note that fewer suppliers means larger orders. In turn, this means that the supplier's fixed delivery cost, as a percent of the total dollar value of the order, is less. This should lead to lower supplier prices because most suppliers have a pricing system that relates prices to the order size in dollars, weight, or cases.

Another advantage is that, by using as few suppliers as possible, you become a more important customer to each supplier and can use this as a form of price leverage to lower prices.

On the other hand, where there are many suppliers for a product, you have more ability to shop around and may be able to lower prices by playing one supplier against another. This would probably work when there is a large quality and price variance among suppliers for a particular product. It is in this situation that market quotations play an important role. Most suppliers operate in this very competitive situation.

Evaluating Suppliers and Sales Representatives

From time to time suppliers and/or sales persons must be evaluated. With some purchasers this is an ongoing process. Suppliers who continue to perform well are rewarded with repeat or additional business; those who are not performing are disciplined in some way.

A mild form of discipline might be to let the supplier know that it has competition by placing an order with another supplier for a week or two, then returning to the original supplier to see if a lesson has been learned. This approach often has to be used with suppliers for whom you have become a house account, with the supplier allowing product quality or service to slip, or prices to creep up higher than those of other suppliers. A house account is a hotel that purchases from a supplier (usually by telephone) without the supplier having a sales representative regularly calling at the hotel.

On the other hand, a bonus to a high-performing supplier may be for you to become a house account with that supplier, as long as it is made known that periodic evaluations will be part of the arrangement.

For new suppliers, a good idea is to allow them a trial period of a month or two to assess their level of performance, using measuring criteria such as number of occasions products were short-shipped, adherence to delivery schedules, consistency of product quality and services, and similar tools.

Rotating Suppliers

Astute purchasers will add new suppliers to approved-supplier lists, and discontinue those who are not performing. Some purchasers also regularly drop the bottom performers from the approved list and replace them with the top suppliers in the "also ran" list, leaving the dropped suppliers on that inactive list until they work their way to the top again.

The reason for doing this is to keep suppliers on their toes, retaining those who do a good job, and discontinuing business with those who do not. You should not have an unchangeable list of suppliers because they will become complacent. You should also be alert to new suppliers entering the market place who can be improved sources for purchasing.

ORDERING

Generally, the authority to request a needed item is vested in those responsible for running specific departments. For example, the housekeeper is in the best position to recognize the need to replenish housekeeping items such as linen and guest supplies. In many cases, in small properties, these same individuals may be responsible for actually ordering the items.

Purchase Orders

If your hotel is large enough, the ordering procedure should be formalized with the use of purchase orders. Three copies of the purchase order are required—one for the supplier, one for the person responsible for receiving, and one for the accounting office to be attached to the invoice when it is received for payment. A sample purchase order is illustrated in Figure 6.1.

To protect both you and the supplier from misunderstandings, the completed purchase order should contain the following information where appropriate:

- Quantity of product to be delivered.
- Product specifications. You must ensure on receipt that the products are those specified. This is an important step in receiving procedures in the event of contract dispute.
- Required delivery date. If the supplier agrees to ship by a certain date, this implies acceptance of the order. If the supplier fails to deliver on time, you have a basis for damages on condition that damages were suffered because the products were not delivered as agreed.
- Method and timing of payment.
- Responsibility for insurance.

Franklyn Hotel
1260 South St., Manchester
Telephone: (261) 434-5734

PURCHASE ORDER   #653

(The purchase order number must appear on all invoices,
bills of lading, or correspondence relating to this
purchase. Invoice must accompany shipment.)

Department_____   Purchase requisition #_____

Purchase order date _____   Delivery date _____

To supplier:

Description	Quantity	Price

Purchasing manager's signature_____

Figure 6.1 Purchase order.

- Responsibility for and method of delivery.
- Delivery location. If it is not stated it is generally assumed to be the supplier's business premises.
- When title to goods passes from the supplier to you. This is important because if the goods are lost or damaged during transportation, you need to know who the legal owner is at that time.

Note that, if receipt of a purchase order is acknowledged by a supplier, there is no contract until it is accepted. Therefore, purchase orders should be signed by the supplier under a statement such as, "We acknowledge and accept the above order and its conditions." Shipment of any part of an order implies that it has been accepted.

After a purchase order is placed, even though it is a valid legal contract, it may be necessary to change it. Most suppliers, particularly if they are local ones, will cooperate in such changes particularly if purchaser–seller relationships are on an amicable basis.

How Much to Order?

A question that arises in the ordering process is the quantity to order. This is often left to the discretion of the department head involved, either because he or she has authority to order directly what is needed, or is in the best position to advise the purchasing department of required quantities. In the case of items purchased only occasionally, the quantity required is not too difficult to determine from past experience. In some cases (for example, equipment purchases) a purchase might occur only once in ten years.

Even for products used regularly, however, daily purchasing should not be used. Generally it is preferable to buy more cases of an item and have them in stock for usage over several weeks than to buy one case every couple of days. One reason for this is that a better supplier price should be available for larger purchases.

If you do not maximize the quantity that you can accept on a delivery, you are requiring the supplier to charge higher prices because of your small order. Also, less frequent purchasing reduces ordering, receiving, and handling costs when purchase quantities are maximized each time.

SEVEN

Receiving, Storing, and Paying for Purchases

RECEIVING

In most hotels *invoice receiving* is practiced. This simply means that suppliers are asked to send a priced invoice with goods delivered so that the receiver can verify such matters as quantities received against those ordered and invoiced.

In all cases where purchase orders (see Figure 6.1) have been prepared, a copy of the purchase order should be on hand while receiving so that the receiver knows what is to be received. Prices on invoices should be checked against the purchase order.

Where specifications have been prepared, they should also be available so that delivered goods can be checked in detail against the specifications, and to ensure the supplier has not made substitutions. In some cases, a department head may be asked to verify the quality of an item if the receiver is in doubt.

Receiving Stamp

All invoices should be stamped, and the stamp initialed in the appropriate spots to indicate that the checking has been completed. A typical receiving stamp is illustrated in Figure 7.1. By insisting that employees responsible for checking deliveries stamp each invoice and initial the stamp where necessary, a form of psychological control is implemented.

Dummy or Memorandum Invoices

Sometimes suppliers fail to provide invoices, or copies of them, with a shipment. Without an invoice, it is difficult for a receiver to make all proper receiving checks. If an invoice is not received, then the receiver

```
┌─────────────────────────────────────────────────┐
│  Date  received _____           │
│  Quantity  checked  by _____        │
│  Quality  checked  by _____         │
│  Prices checked by _____            │
│  Listed on receiving report by _____         │
└─────────────────────────────────────────────────┘
```

Figure 7.1   Receiving stamp.

should prepare a dummy or memorandum invoice from other records (the purchase order or other type of order record), so that it can be later matched with the actual invoice sent in the mail by the supplier to the accounting office. The dummy or memorandum invoice is sometimes referred to as a "products received without invoice" form. A sample of such a form is illustrated in Figure 7.2.

Notice of Invoice Error

As the receiver carries out the receiving function, errors on invoices may be noticed. For example, invoice prices may be wrong. In such a case, the invoice should be corrected and the receiver should complete in duplicate a *notice of error correction form* such as that illustrated in Figure 7.3. A copy of this document should be sent to the supplier (either with the driver or by

Products Received Without Invoice Form			
Supplier _____ Date _____			
Products received without invoice:			
Quantity	Description	Unit Price	Total
Signature _____			

Figure 7.2   Products received without invoice form.

| | | | Your | Corrected | |
| | | Item | Invoice | Invoice | |
Item	Reason for correction	Price	Amount	Amount	Difference

Notice of Error Correction Form

Franklyn Hotel
1260 South St.
Manchester
Telephone: (261) 434-5734

Supplier _____ Date _____

Corrections have been made as follows on your invoice:

Invoice number _____ Date _____

Total corrections

Your invoice total

Correct invoice total

Figure 7.3   Notice of error correction form.

mail), and the other copy should be attached to the related invoice to alert the accounting office to the error and to ensure that proper adjustment is subsequently received from the supplier.

Credit Memorandum or Invoice

In some cases goods are invoiced but not received. In other words, they are short-shipped or "back ordered." On other occasions they are delivered and then returned to the supplier because they are not of acceptable quality or for some other reason. In these situations, a *credit memorandum* or credit invoice should be prepared in duplicate.

This memorandum will carry necessary details, including an explanation of why the credit memorandum has been prepared. It should be signed by the delivery driver, so that your hotel has proof that the goods were either not received or else returned. One copy should go to the supplier. The other copy remains with the hotel to ensure that proper credit is received from the supplier. Figure 7.4 is a sample credit memorandum.

In some situations suppliers' delivery drivers carry their own stock of

Supplier _____ Date _____			
Please issue a credit memorandum for the following:			
Quantity	Item description	Unit cost	Total
Reason for request for credit:			
Delivery driver's signature_____			

Figure 7.4 Credit memorandum.

credit forms, which are used instead of your hotel's having to provide them. Also, some operations use a request-for-credit form (see Figure 7.5) that the delivery driver signs and takes back to the supplier's accounting office so that a formal credit invoice can be issued by the supplier and sent to your accounting office.

Regardless of the system, a credit document should be initiated in the receiving area when products are delivered and the need for credit is apparent. Proper credit documentation should not be substituted by a written note on the invoice about the shortage or return of products, or by a driver's oral "promise" that the situation will be corrected with the next delivery. In all cases, the credit document should be cross-referenced to the invoice number, and vice versa if the credit document is numbered. Credit documents should be treated as if they were money.

Blind Receiving

Some hotels practice *blind receiving*. In this situation, the supplier is advised not to send an invoice with the goods but to send it through the mail to your accounting office. Instead of the invoice, a shipping, delivery, or packing slip accompanies the products. This slip shows no weights or counts but simply describes the products delivered. As a result, the receiver is forced to count each item and record the count on the slip, thus ensuring that this important aspect of receiving is carried out.

Blind receiving is used to prevent a dishonest receiver from removing part of a delivery for personal use, then altering the invoice to cover the

			Request for Credit Form			

Franklyn Hotel
1260 South St.
Manchester
Telephone: (261) 434-5734

Supplier _____   Date _____

Please credit our account as follows:

Invoice number _____   Date _____

Item	Reason for credit request	Item Price	Your Invoice Amount	Corrected Invoice Amount
		Total corrections		
		Your invoice total		
		Correct invoice total		

Figure 7.5 Request for credit form.

fraud. It also reduces the possibility of collusion between delivery driver and receiver. Blind receiving is not used today by most hotels because an accounting department verification of all purchasing and receiving documents and invoices will generally indicate dishonest practices.

COD Deliveries

If deliveries are made on a cash-on-delivery (COD) basis and the receiver is provided with a cash fund large enough to cover the invoice amount, that fund should be used to pay for the delivery. If there is no fund, or if it is not large enough, the receiver should accompany the delivery driver to the main cashier's office to authenticate delivery so that the invoice can be paid.

STORING

As soon after receiving as is practical, products received should be moved to their proper storage areas. Hand trucks must be made available to permit products to be easily moved.

Perpetual Inventory Cards

For items carried in storerooms that are under the control of an authorized person, a system of perpetual inventory cards is recommended. A separate set of individual perpetual inventory cards should be maintained for each storage location. For example, your housekeeper would have a set of cards for linens and other supplies required in the rooms department.

A card is required for each type and size of item carried in stock. A sample card is illustrated in Figure 7.6. The *In* column figures are taken from the invoices delivered with the goods. The figures in the *Out* column are recorded from the requisitions (to be discussed later) prepared and signed by persons in the department served by that particular storage location. Obviously, if all *In* and *Out* figures are properly recorded on the cards by the person in charge of the storeroom, the *Balance* column figure should agree with the actual count of the item on the shelf. Thus the cards aid in inventory control.

Other Uses of Cards

Perpetual inventory cards are also useful for cost control purposes because they carry the purchase prices of the items and allow requisitions to be costed; this ensures that each department is correctly charged with its share of costs. The cards are also useful for maintaining par stock for ordering purposes, and help ensure items are not overstocked or understocked because they can show the maximum stock for each individual item and

Item _____ Supplier _____ Tel. # _____				
Minimum _____ Supplier _____ Tel. # _____				
Maximum _____ Supplier _____ Tel. # _____				
Date	In	Out	Balance	Requisition cost information

Figure 7.6 Perpetual inventory card for a single item.

the minimum point to which that stock level can fall before the item needs to be reordered.

Without having to count quantities of items on the shelves, the person responsible only has to go through the cards in turn once a week, or however frequently it is practical to reorder. At that time, all items for which the balance figure is at or close to the minimum point are listed and the quantity required to bring the inventory up to par stock is ordered, keeping in mind possible delivery delays. Note that the cards can also be designed to carry the names and telephone numbers of suggested suppliers.

The advantages of perpetual inventory cards for inventory control and time saving in reordering are obvious. The major disadvantages are the time and cost to keep the cards up to date. Each establishment must weigh the costs against the benefits for its own operation in order to decide whether or not to use them.

Requisitions

Whether or not perpetual inventory cards are used to control items in stock and aid in ordering, requisitions should be used to allow authorized people to receive items from the storeroom and to ensure that the various departments are correctly charged with their share of costs. A sample requisition is illustrated in Figure 7.7.

Blank requisitions should only be made available, preferably in dupli-

#6329

Department ______________ Date ______________

Quantity	Item description	Item cost	Total

Authorized signature______________

***Figure** 7.7* Requisition.

cate, to those authorized to sign them. The original, listing items and quantities required, is delivered to the storekeeper. Duplicates are kept by the person ordering so quantities received from the storeroom can be checked.

If perpetual inventory cards are used, they should indicate the current price of the item in stock. Perpetual inventory card *Out* column figures can be recorded from the requisitions (and the *Balance* column figure adjusted) and the price of the item can be transferred from the card and recorded on the requisition in the *Item Cost* column. Frequently, the same item in stock may have been received with a different delivery date and price. In this case, a number of different methods are available for keeping track of the various prices on the perpetual inventory cards. These methods are discussed.

Most Recent Price.   The simplest method is to use the most recent price paid for an item in stock as the price for all of that item in stock. In other words, if there were 5 items in stock at $1.00 each and 12 new items were purchased at $1.10 each, then $1.10 would be recorded on requisitions as the cost for any of those 17 items subsequently requisitioned. If, before the 17 were issued, a new order of that item were received, the new order price would again prevail. For example, suppose stock on hand dropped to 2 and 18 were received at $1.05 each; it is now assumed that the 20 items in stock each have a price of $1.05. This is a simple method to use, but in times of wildly fluctuating purchase prices, it can be inaccurate. The other methods to be discussed take more time but are more accurate.

First-in/First-out Price.   With first-in/first-out (FIFO) pricing, it is assumed that proper stock rotation is in effect (this should be the case regardless of the requisition costing method) and that, as the items purchased earliest are issued first, they are issued at the price that was paid for them. Using the figures from the most recent price method already discussed, you will recall that we originally had 5 items on hand at $1.00 and 12 more were purchased at $1.10. If 6 items were then requisitioned, 5 would be costed on the requisition at $1.00, and 1 at $1.10 (for a total of $6.10). Because we have now used all the first group of items at $1.00, the $1.10 price will prevail on requisitions until that stock is used up, and so on.

It is obvious that the related perpetual inventory card must have recorded on it, in the Requisition Cost Information column, how many of that balance are on hand at each price. Alternatively, as items are received, the price can be handwritten or recorded in some other way on the case or carton or, if necessary, onto each separate item in the container.

Last-in/First-out Price.   Another method of requisition costing is last-in/first-out (LIFO). With LIFO the last items received are assumed to be the ones first issued, even if the items are actually issued on a first-in/first-out basis. In other words, with reference to the earlier figures used to illustrate FIFO, the six items issued would all be issued at the $1.10 price and total requisition cost would be $6.60.

Weighted Average Price.   The weighted average requires some simple calculations as each new delivery is received. Let us again use the quantities and prices we are familiar with:

$$
\begin{array}{ll}
\text{5 items on hand at \$1.00} = & \$\ 5.00 \\
\text{12 received at \$1.10} \quad = & \underline{\ 13.20} \\
\text{17 items total} \quad\quad\ = & \underline{\$18.20}
\end{array}
$$

The weighted average price is $18.20 divided by 17 = $1.07 (rounded to the nearest cent), and that is the cost recorded on all requisitions until another shipment is received. Assume that, just prior to the next shipment, we still have two items on hand at $1.07 and that 18 new items are received at $1.05:

$$
\begin{array}{ll}
\text{2 items on hand at \$1.07} = & \$\ 2.14 \\
\text{18 received at \$1.05} \quad = & \underline{\ 18.90} \\
\text{20 items total} & \$21.04
\end{array}
$$

The new weighted average price will drop from $1.07 to $1.05 ($21.04 divided by 20).

Dispensing with Perpetual Inventory Cards

If perpetual inventory cards are not used, the easiest method of recording item costs on the requisitions is to write the price of the item, taken from the invoice at the time of delivery, on the container or case, or even on each item in the container or case. Alternatively, pricing machines (such as those used in supermarkets) could be used. Recording the item price on the cases or items makes it easy to transfer this price to the requisition as the requisition is completed. This price recording method also has a psychological control advantage in that each person handling the items is made aware of their cost.

Costed requisitions can be later extended and totalled so that at the end of each accounting period each department can be charged with its proper share of expenses. Issuing blank requisitions of a different color to each department will aid in departmental identification. If necessary, for control purposes requisitions could also be numbered.

Of course, where establishments are large enough to support computerized inventory records, much of the paperwork that would otherwise be required with perpetual inventory cards and requisitions can be handled directly by the computer including, for example, a daily printout of all items whose level has dropped to the reorder point, and cost information for inventory on hand.

PAYMENTS

A valuable purchasing tool that you have is your operation's credit rating. When a hotel has a poor credit rating, it may find it difficult to deal or negotiate with suppliers, and may even find that deliveries will only be made on a COD basis.

In most cases where a hotel has an acceptable credit rating, suppliers expect invoices to be paid within 30 days of receipt or, alternatively, 30 days after the end of the month in which invoices are received. A hotel with an excellent credit rating may be able to negotiate an extension of credit terms beyond the normal 30-day limit, such as for a further 10, 20, or even 30 days.

When a hotel extends the credit period beyond what the supplier expects, it is the supplier who has to find other sources of cash to pay the businesses from which it purchases and receives credit. This added supplier cost must be included in the prices of the products sold to hotels, so the purchaser ends up paying for being delinquent in the first place!

Invoice Control

Most suppliers are paid once a month, with checks generally mailed to them so that they arrive on the last day for which credit has been agreed to. The first step in the invoice-paying process is to check invoice extensions (quantities of goods times purchase price) and then make sure invoice totals are correct. Depending on the situation, invoices may be paid from the invoice or by statement. Payment is made from the invoice(s) when there may be only one or two invoices for purchases from that supplier during a month.

When invoices are paid by statement, at the end of each month the supplier will send a summary form (statement) listing each invoice total for that month. This is the normal situation when an establishment makes frequent purchases from a supplier. With statements, you should ensure that the total of each invoice previously received and checked for extensions and total is properly recorded on the supplier's statement, and that the statement adds up correctly. In this situation, a single check is prepared to cover the statement total.

Opportunity Cost

The objective in making payments for purchases is to pay invoices when the most benefit will be received. To do this, you must consider the opportunity cost of money. An opportunity cost is the cost of doing something else with that money. For example, a hotel can invest its surplus cash in marketable securities at 10 percent, or leave it in the bank at 6 percent. If it invests in marketable securities, its opportunity cost is 6 percent. In other words, it is making 10 percent on the investment, less the opportunity cost of 6 percent, therefore the net gain is 4 percent. Applying this concept to purchasing, if a hotel pays its invoices ten days before it is necessary, the opportunity of earning interest on this money for a further ten days has been lost.

As far as paying for purchases is concerned, you must compare the opportunity cost of paying invoices on time with paying them after the end of the credit term, with the negative public relations that will generate along with a reputation as a slow payer, and the possibility that future deliveries will be on a COD basis.

Some argue that if an establishment is short of cash and must make a decision between paying off a bank loan or paying suppliers, it is preferable to pay the loan because suppliers will be more patient than the bank as they need to retain the establishment's business. There is likely some truth in this, except that such a situation cannot continue indefinitely.

Hotels that find themselves in a cash-short situation will likely receive more support from their suppliers if they advise them in advance that they need an extended credit period. Suppliers, of course, have to pay their own bills from businesses from which they buy products, and when they are under pressure to make their own payments they are less likely to want to extend lengthy credit to their hotel customers. This is why in many cases suppliers will only deliver on a COD basis, or offer only a short credit period such as seven to ten days.

Discounts

When a discount is offered, if you do not pay by the discount date and take the discount saving, you are in fact paying an extra cost for a product.

Some argue that a discount is not a saving on a product's cost, but that the discounted price is simply the lowest price available from a supplier for a product. However, it is rare today for suppliers to hotels to automatically offer a discount. Discounts are normally negotiated on an individual basis by the purchaser, and generally large establishments have more negotiating power than small ones. Where they are offered, discounts can also raise some problems:

- By deciding to stay with suppliers who offer a discount, you may ignore other suppliers who offer other services and, in effect, provide more product value. For example, a supplier offering a discount may gradually reduce the quality of products delivered to compensate for offering a discount.
- Separating invoices offering a discount from other invoices creates extra work and means establishing two or more separate payment schedules or systems.
- In order to make the payment on time to receive the discount, it may be necessary to borrow the cash. For example, suppose on a $1,000 purchase the terms are 2/10, net 60. This means that there is a 2 percent discount if you pay the invoice within ten days, otherwise it is payable within 60 days without a discount. On a $1,000 purchase paid within ten days, this would save $20. This may not seem a lot of money, but, multiplied many times over on all similar purchases made during a year, it could amount to a large sum. However, in the example cited, you may have to borrow the money ($980) in order to make the payment within ten days. Let us assume the money were borrowed for 50 days (60 days less 10 days) at an 8 percent interest rate. The interest expense on this borrowed money is:

$$(\$980 \times 50 \text{ days} \times 8\%)/365 \text{ days} = \$10.74$$

In this case, it would be advantageous to borrow the money, because the difference between the discount saving of $20.00 and the interest expense of $10.74 is $9.26.

Timing

Wherever possible, you should take advantage of a supplier's invoicing practices, particularly from suppliers you use frequently. Suppose that you buy a month's supply of products from a supplier at the beginning of each month, using the products as required during the month, and that the terms of the supplier's month-end statement are 2/10, net 30. In other words, there is a 2 percent discount off the total month's purchases if the statement is paid within ten days of the month-end; otherwise, the statement is payable within 30 days without discount. You thus have the use of the supplier's credit for 40 days if you take advantage of the discount, otherwise for 60 days. You can then use this "free" money to advantage, even if all you do is collect bank interest on it.

On the other hand, suppose you purchase from the same supplier but habitually buy at the end of each month sufficient items to carry you through until the end of the next month. In this case, you will have use of the "free" money for only ten days, if you take advantage of the discount, and otherwise only for 30 days.

These two cases are extreme, but they do point out that you can take advantage of a supplier's billing practices in order to increase profits.

Rebates

A rebate should be differentiated from a discount. With a rebate, you pay the full invoice amount but have some cash returned at a later date. The amount of the rebate may vary depending on the volume of purchases made during a period of time (for example, a month or a quarter), which is why the invoice is not discounted at the time of payment because the percentage rebate (discount) will not be known until the end of the period.

Rebates are really just a special form of discount that allow the supplier greater flexibility. They are quite legal (except in jurisdictions that do not allow them to be offered in connection with the purchase of alcoholic beverages), so long as the rebate is fully documented, and is not paid to an individual in your hotel for favoring that supplier. If rebates are given directly to an individual (for example, a purchaser) without any documentation, they are termed *kickbacks* and are illegal.

Kickbacks

Another form of kickback occurs when a supplier bills you a higher price than is equitable for a product, and the difference between that higher price and the real price is paid to the person approving the invoice. This can occur in small hotels where the purchaser, receiver, and invoice-approving employee are the same person, and in operations where there is no management supervision. It is unlikely to occur in large hotels where several people are involved in the purchasing, receiving, and invoice-approval system, because collusion (and sharing of the kickback "profits") would have to occur.

A more subtle form of kickback occurs when noncash payments are given by suppliers to those involved in purchasing. This type of kickback takes the form of free products or other gifts given to the employee, even to the extent of their being delivered directly to the employee's home. The line between what is an ethical token of gratitude and what may be a bribe from a supplier is thin, and for this reason many establishments maintain a policy disallowing any gifts, or any gifts above a nominal value, from suppliers.

EIGHT

Employee Policies

In your hotel, a major cost needing tight control is labor. Most hotels have legal requirements that they must conform to with regard to employees, including paying minimum wage levels, providing statutory holidays, using fair employment practices, allowing employees to unionize and bargain collectively, maintaining safety standards, and making pay withholdings such as for income tax and unemployment insurance.

INSTITUTING POLICIES

In addition, you need to institute some sort of employee practices (or personnel policies) as a minimum first step toward controlling your labor cost. The owner of even the smallest hotel usually has some personnel policies. For example, an owner who simply says "When I need a new employee, I'll hire the first person I can find who seems capable of doing the job, and I'll pay the minimum hourly rate" has established the following policies:

- When the decision to hire will be made.
- That no systematic advertising of job openings will be done.
- That the person hired must appear capable.
- What the rate of pay will be.

Job Descriptions

In formulating your hotel's personnel policies, you need to develop job descriptions for each type of job or employee position. A job description states

- What a job entails.
- What routines must be performed.
- When those routines must be performed.

In a small hotel, the job description may be as simple as specifying that an employee must welcome customers pleasantly and look after their needs.

In a large hotel, each job has more complexities, and it may be difficult—particularly if several different jobs need to be filled—to remember the many aspects of each. For that reason, job descriptions are best put into writing, and when employees are to be hired you can provide them with a written copy of the job description.

There are no standard job descriptions that fit every hotel. Although some common elements exist in job descriptions for any particular job type, the descriptions for each individual hotel must be prepared for that operation.

Job descriptions should not be too detailed, but they should include sufficient information to enable both employee and supervisor to be certain about what duties the job entails. Job descriptions must be kept simple, must be easily understood, and should include the skills (such as an ability to get along with the public) that are required if the employee is to perform well in the job.

Task Procedures

In many small hotels, positions or jobs require the employee to carry out a variety of different tasks during a shift or work period. Indeed, the smaller the hotel the wider the variety of tasks is likely to be, as several jobs might be assigned to a single worker. In such cases, exactly how a particular task is to be performed should be detailed step by step. Task procedures should also be in writing.

Task procedures could, of course, be demonstrated and taught without first being written down, but your new employees will probably feel more comfortable—particularly if they are being shown a number of different sets of procedures that their job entails—if the demonstrated steps can be supported in writing.

A sample set of task procedures concerning front office employees' handling of guest credit cards was listed in Chapter 4.

EMPLOYEE SELECTION

Once you have defined job skills through job descriptions and task procedures, the next step is to match appropriate employees with positions available.

Finding Applicants

In small hotels, advertising for employees can be done informally through family connections or friends of present employees. This is certainly a cost-free method. Some hotels offer current employees a cash bonus if they bring in successful applicants who stay with the hotel for a minimum period such as six months. Some hotels advertise available positions in local newspapers to encourage as many prospective applicants as possible to apply, although this does cost money.

Sometimes it is useful to use personnel agencies (whose offices are generally found only in large cities) to seek out needed employees. If you provide the personnel agency with job descriptions of the positions that need to be filled, it can use its professional skills to match suitable candidates to your vacancies. This can be an expensive method of hiring, but it does provide a screening service. If you do your own screening, it can be a time-consuming task that involves sifting through applications and then interviewing. You must weigh the time saved by using a personnel agency against the cost of this service.

Application Form

An application form should be used each time a person applies for a job. Even if a position is not open at the time someone asks about a job vacancy, it is a good idea to have the person complete an application form anyway. A few days or weeks from now, you may have a vacancy that the applicant's qualifications could fill.

An application form is useful for summarizing in an orderly way basic information about job applicants. The form permits initial screening without having to interview each applicant. A typical application form is illustrated in Figure 8.1.

Interviewing

Interviewing all candidates who have submitted an acceptable application form can take considerable time. You may need to spend an hour with each one (hence the advantage of using a personnel agency to carry out this work). The time spent in interviewing is necessary, however, to ensure that the person who is finally offered the job has the best combination of technical and human skills for your hotel.

Conduct all interviews in a private area or office. During the interview, you should have the individual's application form available and should be familiar with it so that relevant questions can be posed to the applicant about previous education or experience. You should have a prepared list of questions to ask all applicants, because consistency of evaluation is important.

You should ask questions about the applicant's present job (assuming that he or she has one) and why he or she wishes to leave that job. It may also be desirable to find out what the applicant's career expectations are. In

Position applied for _____ Date _____

How did you hear about this possible job opening? _____

_____

Are there any reasons you may be unable to carry out some of the

normal job duties in this position? _____

_____

If yes, explain _____

_____

Name _____

Address _____

Town _____ State _____ Code _____ Telephone _____

Social security # _____

What experience, training or education have you had that would

qualify you for this job? _____

_____

Why are you interested in this job? _____

_____

Are you available for work:

Saturdays _____ Nights 6 to 2 _____ Days 10 to 6 _____ Sundays _____

Are you now employed? _____ If yes, where? _____

_____

References (names of previous employers preferred):

    Name   Company Name/Address/Tel #   Dates employed

1. _____

2. _____

3. _____

Please sign below if you will consent to your present or previous
employer's release of information or discussion of previous performance with us.

Signature of applicant _____

Figure 8.1 Application for employment.

other words, is the applicant too ambitious for the job you have available
and for the offered wage or salary rate? If technical skills in specific areas
are required, you should ensure that the applicant possesses the necessary
competence in those areas.

Opportunity for Questions

The applicant should have an opportunity to ask questions. You should
provide a job description and be specific about working hours, rates of pay,
days off, and all other matters related to working conditions. If a prospec-

tive employee is to report to a supervisor, rather than to you, have the applicant and the supervisor meet. Let the supervisor have input into the final selection of the candidate. If the supervisor is to continue to do a good job, there must be compatibility between the supervisor and any new employee hired.

Taking Notes

During the interview, you should make notes about the applicant and his or her reactions. Written notes can be placed directly on the application form. Alternatively, you could use an interview evaluation form such as that illustrated in Figure 8.2. In summary:

	High 5	4	3	2	Low 1
Date _____ Position _____ Applicant name _____ Interviewer name _____					
1. General appearance and neatness					
2. Conduct during interview (poise, manners, tact, pleasantness)					
3. Communication skills, ability to explain, self-expression					
4. Apparent desire, motivation, and initiative					
5. Skills and apparent competence for job, previous experience, leadership potential					
6. Overall rating					

References contacted and comments:

1. _____

2. _____

3. _____

Summary of strengths and weaknesses:

_____

_____

_____

Interviewer's comments and recommendation for hiring or not:

_____

_____

Figure 8.2 Interview evaluation form.

- Have a plan or pattern for all interviews.
- Make sure the applicant is at ease.
- Be attentive and interested in what the applicant has to say, and do not interrupt.
- Give the applicant sufficient opportunity and time to respond to questions.
- Before closing the interview, invite the applicant to ask questions.
- If notes are not taken during the interview (because this can be distracting to the applicant), all resulting mental notes and impressions should be recorded immediately after the interview.

If an interview is well prepared and handled it can be an excellent screening device, can reinforce the information on the application form, and can reveal things that are not apparent on that form. Sometimes, a second interview is useful for obtaining an even clearer impression and understanding of an applicant.

Closing the Interview

A good way to end an interview is to advise the applicant how he or she will be informed if selected for the job and approximately when that decision will be communicated.

References

If references are provided on the application form, you should consult them by telephone. If you do not follow them up, there is no purpose in asking for them on the application form in the first place. Telephone reference comments are easy to record, and people giving information on the telephone are more likely to be candid than if they were required to provide the reference in the form of a letter.

Note that, if an applicant gives his or her present employer as a reference, you should not discuss with that employer the fact that the applicant has applied for a position with your hotel until you first receive the applicant's permission to do so.

Information that can be requested of the applicant's previous employers includes:

- Job title and tasks performed.
- Dates of employment.
- Reason for leaving.

- Quality of work performed.
- Absenteeism and punctuality record.
- Personal characteristics, strengths, weaknesses, and overall effectiveness.

It may also be worthwhile to ask if the previous employer would rehire the applicant, and determine the reason(s) if the employer would not.

With the information and knowledge gained from employment application forms, interviews, and reference checks, you are in a position to decide which applicant to choose.

Finally, once the selection has been made the application forms of the candidates not selected should be kept. A week or month later a position might be available for which one of the unsuccessful candidates would be very suitable.

EMPLOYEE ORIENTATION

Every person employed should be given an orientation. Many employees are uncomfortable in a new job, and the orientation program serves as an introduction to the job and to your business. In a small hotel, you should provide the orientation. In a large hotel, this orientation should be given by the supervisor with whom the employee is to work. The orientation could include information about any or all of the following:

- Your hotel's history, such as when it was started, who owns it, whether it is part of a chain or franchise, and its objectives.
- A copy of the organization chart (if your hotel is large enough to need one), showing where the employee fits in and to whom he or she reports.
- A copy of the job description and task procedures.
- When employee shifts are changed (frequency), how much advance notice of a change is given, and who produces these shift schedules.
- Employee vacation entitlement (how it is calculated and who produces vacation schedules) and statutory holidays.
- Employee dress and/or uniform requirements and (if uniforms are required) who maintains them and how frequently they are to be changed.
- Employee appearance and grooming requirements.
- Employee conduct expected (promptness, attendance, how and to whom absence or illness should be reported).

- Pay policies such as pay days, deductions made, overtime rates, pay advances, and how work hours are determined (time clocks, and so on).
- Employee benefit entitlements (sick leave, health and/or life insurance, dental plan, and educational assistance).
- Employee training: who does it and how long it lasts.
- Probationary period, if any. (It is a good idea to hire new employees on a probationary basis. The importance of the job or the skill level at which the person is hired will determine the appropriate length of the probationary period.)
- Employee evaluation process (how it is handled, who does it, when it is done, and what happens to its results).
- Grounds for dismissal and dismissal procedures.
- Any special rules (such as safety, sanitation, smoking, bonding, or special policies).
- Policy on customer complaints and how they are to be handled by the employee who receives them.
- An introduction to fellow employees.
- If you have a large hotel, you (or a delegated employee) should provide the new employee with a tour of the facilities to show restricted areas, staff entrance, location of time clocks, change rooms, parking areas, and so forth.
- Finally, you should provide an opportunity for the new employee to ask questions during the orientation.

This list is only a suggested one to be adapted for your operation. Many hotel operators compile orientation facts into a written manual or handbook that the employee is required to study at the start of employment.

EMPLOYEE TRAINING

The orientation is the beginning of an ongoing employee training process. This process includes such matters as employees' learning what your operation's standards are and how they can be met, what level of performance is expected of new employees, and how to adapt to day-to-day situations as they arise.

It should not be the employees' responsibility (even though in practice, unfortunately, that is often the case) to train themselves in these matters. The employee needs to be taught through discussion and demonstration, followed by practice.

In small hotels, training is usually done on the job by the owner or manager; in a larger operation, training is handled by the employee's supervisor. Proper training can

- Reduce employee stress and absenteeism.
- Lower employee turnover.
- Limit costs due to careless use of supplies and equipment.
- Improve sanitation and safety.
- Increase employees' morale, cooperation, interest in the job, job knowledge, productivity, and chances for promotion.

In short, training leads to more satisfied employees and fosters professionalism.

Job Rotation

Job rotation is another useful technique. Employees can be trained at different jobs so that they can be moved from one to another (where a union contract does not prohibit this) as the need arises. Besides giving the employee a variety of challenges, this ensures that employees can help out at different jobs in an emergency, reduces employee boredom, and (eventually) ensures that promoted employees make better supervisors because they have become familiar with all the jobs under their supervision.

EMPLOYEE EVALUATION

The final step in personnel planning is employee evaluation. If your hotel is very small, evaluation may be handled simply through observation. By personal observation, you should be able to determine quickly whether or not a new employee is able to do a good job following proper training. Incompetent employees may have to be released or, if open positions are available, moved to a job whose demands on their skills are not as great. On the other hand, competent employees should be encouraged to continue to do a good job and should be challenged (with more responsibility) or promoted when possible.

Formal Evaluation

If your hotel is a large one with many employees, evaluations will be more formal and may be carried out once or twice a year with each employee's supervisor instructed to fill out an evaluation form. In such situations, the employee should be allowed to read the completed evaluation and sign it to indicate acceptance of what it says. A sample evaluation form is illustrated in Figure 8.3.

In evaluating, your supervisors should judge employees with reference to the whole job. For example, an employee should be evaluated on his or her performance with customers, with other employees, and with the supervisor—not on just one of those three specific relationships.

The evaluation must be carried out objectively, despite the fact that the process itself is subjective. In other words, personal bias for or against an employee should not be allowed to affect the assessment. In some hotels, the responsibilities included in a job description are the basis for an employee evaluation. Indeed, some assessors believe that the points to be evaluated should match those on the job description.

Even if you do not formalize the evaluation on a document that the employee can see and read, the results of the evaluation—both the good and the bad—should be discussed with the employee. Communicating with employees concerning their performance should improve that performance.

Pay Raises

The evaluation process also necessitates your considering pay raises at least once a year (unless these are negotiated with a union). In the absence of a union contract, the factors that influence the size of an employee's wage increase are:

- Your hotel's ability to pay higher wages.
- The demands of each job.
- The pay rate for each job compared to the pay rate for a similar job in competitive hotels.
- The results of each employee's evaluation.
- The general inflation rate.
- The local supply of and demand for employees.

Promotions

Whenever job vacancies arise, it is usually a good idea to seek replacements from within the ranks of your present employees—particularly if this will create a promotion for a deserving employee. Employees who recognize that there are advancement opportunities within your hotel have an incentive to stay and they generally perform better.

Although seniority is sometimes the basis for promotion into a vacant

	Excellent	Good	Average	Below average	Poor
Employee name _____ Position _____ Date employed _____ Date of evaluation _____					
Knowledge of job: Clear understanding of duties related to job and ability to do the job					
Dependability: Conscientious, punctual, reliable					
Courtesy: To guests, fellow employees, and supervisor					
Cooperation: Ability and willingness to work with supervisors and fellow employees					
Work quality: Thoroughness, neatness, accuracy and completeness					
Work quantity: Ability to handle assigned volume under normal pressures and conditions					
Personal qualities: Personality, sociability, integrity, leadership potential					
Appearance: Hygiene and neatness					

Overall performance: Satisfactory ( )   Unsatisfactory ( )

Supervisor's signature _____

Employee's signature _____

Figure 8.3 Employee evaluation form.

position, that type of promotion should only occur if the person promoted has the necessary qualifications and capabilities for the new job, especially if it requires considerable responsibility and authority. Employee evaluation forms can be helpful in making promotion decisions.

Discipline

Your hotel will likely have employment rules and regulations that employees are to follow. Some of these rules and regulations will be restrictive; others will be for safety reasons; and others still may serve to protect employees' rights.

You should make sure that employees know and understand these rules during their orientation/training process. In some cases where rules are broken, employees should simply be reminded of the rule(s). In other cases, disciplinary action may be necessary.

Such action could take the form of a written memo to the employee explaining the measures being taken in response to breaking the rule, identifying the specific incident that prompted the action, detailing any further action that might be taken if the rule is broken again, specifying a time frame after which a review of the situation will occur, and providing a method for the employee to acknowledge receipt of the warning or disciplinary action.

A copy of the memo should remain with the employee, a copy should go to the employee's supervisor (if there is one), and a copy (preferably with the employee's signature on it acknowledging that he or she has been made aware of the situation) should be placed in the employee's file.

Termination

Sometimes, employees must be disciplined by termination of employment. This should only occur as a last resort, and should only be in response to the most critical of situations. Generally, you must show cause for dismissal. Cause can often be justified by the number of disciplinary action memos that have accumulated in the employee's file.

One of the values in having clearly written job descriptions is that they can indicate, at the time the employee is hired, the level of job performance required. If the employee has failed to meet that required level, and this fact can be supported by memos in the employee's file, then cause for termination can be documented.

If it is necessary to terminate an employee, the actual firing should be done in private on a one-to-one basis by the employee's supervisor or, in a small hotel, by you as owner or manager. The employee should be given the reason(s) for termination. A good way to terminate the process is to emphasize the employee's strong points and perhaps suggest alternative employment opportunities for that person's future.

EMPLOYEE RECORDS

Your hotel should maintain a record about each of its present (and former) employees. The record might be simply a file containing each employee's application form with a notation on it of the employee's current wage or salary, and attached to it any other information that needs to be recorded (such as disciplinary warnings).

Alternatively, a separate employee record card or file should be started as each new employee is hired. Such a card is shown in Figure 8.4. You can use this card to record the date on which the employee was hired, the position filled, and the initial rate of pay. Subsequent changes in the status of the employee can be recorded as they occur with the date of the change noted. Changes in status include such things as a move to another job within the operation, a change in wage or salary, and the date when employment was terminated. Each change recorded should be accompanied by the reason for the change summarized in the Comment column.

Employee record cards or files are useful for providing up-to-date information about current employees, and for preserving information about former employees who are being reemployed or reference-checked by other prospective employers. Also placed in each employee's file should be the evaluation form (Figure 8.3) if a formal evaluation process is used. Any other correspondence or notes about the employee should also be placed in the employee file. In this way all relevant information about each employee is maintained in a single centralized location.

It is a good idea to arrange employee files or cards in alphabetical order. The records for current employees should be kept together, and new files should be inserted as new employees are hired. As employees leave, their records should be removed from the current employee group and

Employee name _____ Date employed _____		
Initial position _____		
Starting wage/salary _____		
Date	Change status to	New wage/salary	Comments

Figure 8.4 Employee record card.

placed, again in alphabetical order, with the files of all other former employees.

As a general rule, you should keep the files of past employees for a minimum of two years and a maximum of five. When files are no longer needed, you should destroy all the information in them.

Because employee files contain confidential information, access to them should be restricted to yourself or (in a large hotel) a responsible person who is authorized to keep the employee records up to date.

EMPLOYEE TURNOVER

Because of the high cost of employee turnover you should try to reduce turnover in order to cut this cost. A turnover is the loss and replacement of an employee. One way to reduce turnover, particularly during a new employee's first few weeks on the job, is to observe the following four guidelines:

- Be honest about the job. Make sure that applicants understand both its good and bad aspects.
- Make sure that applicants are not overqualified for the job. Overqualified individuals are likely to become unhappy and leave because they are not challenged.
- Monitor new employees' performance from the first day and let each new employee have early feedback of preliminary assessment.
- Watch for signs of trouble such as absenteeism or drinking on the job. If problems are evident, get to the issue quickly to see if the problem can be resolved to everyone's satisfaction.

Turnover Cost

Turnovers occur for both voluntary and involuntary reasons. A voluntary turnover occurs when an employee leaves by choice. An involuntary turnover occurs when an employee has to be replaced because he or she is not suited for the job or for some other reason.

Both direct and indirect costs are associated with each turnover. Direct costs include such items as advertising, recruiting, selecting, orienting, and training new employees. Indirect costs are more difficult to measure but are nevertheless there.

For example, one cost is the low morale of other employees when good employees leave. This can also be translated into reduced customer satisfaction, compounded by the fact that new employees may not initially provide the same quality of service. Double staffing, or overtime, may also

Date __April 10__	Department __Coffee shop__
Employee name	Darlene Robertson
Date employed	April 6
Length of employment	4 days
Employee's reason for leaving __States she was not made aware__	
of shift hours	
Supervisor's comment __Was advised of shift hours when__	
employed but was unable to handle job pressure	
Action taken	None
Would supervisor reemploy? __No__	
Supervisor's signature	

Figure 8.5 Exit interview form.

be required while new employees are being trained. Also, an employee (knowing he or she is going to be leaving) might tend to reduce his or her level of service, adding to customer dissatisfaction and shifting the burden to other staff. Again, this affects staff morale.

Although turnover costs are difficult to calculate accurately, it is esti-

	VOLUNTARY					INVOLUNTARY				SERVICE				NUMBER OF SEPARATIONS		
	1.	2.	3.	4.		5.	6.	7.		a.	b.	c.				
DEPARTMENTS	Personal	Opportunity	Dissatisfied	Unknown	TOTAL	Performance	Conduct	Staff reduction	TOTAL	Less than 30 days	1-12 months	Over 1 year	TOTAL	Average number on payroll	This month	Year-to-date
Front Office																
Reservation																
Sales																
Service																
Housekeeping																
Telephone																

Figure 8.6 Labor turnover analysis form.

mated that they are as high as $500 per turnover. Because many hotels have turnover rates as high as 200 or 300 percent a year, total turnover cost can be extreme. In a hotel with 30 employees, a 200 percent turnover means that 60 job separations occurred during the year. If each turnover costs $500, total annual turnover cost is:

$$60 \times \$500 = \$30,000$$

Turnover Rate

One way to monitor turnover cost is to calculate the monthly turnover rate. The equation for this is:

$$\frac{\text{Number of separations during month}}{\text{Number of employees on payroll}} \times 100$$

Suppose your hotel has 30 employees and 6 separations occurred during a month. The turnover rate would be:

$$\frac{6}{30} \times 100 = 20\%$$

Annual turnover rates can be calculated in a similar way using annual figures.

Reducing Turnover Rates

Because of the high cost of employee turnover, your hotel can profit by trying to reduce the turnover rate. Some turnovers are uncontrollable (for example, death, disability, or retirement). The remaining turnovers are controllable to a greater or lesser degree.

One way to reduce the turnover rate is to determine the causes for turnovers and then attempt to correct the underlying problems. An exit interview form is useful for gathering information.

If an employee leaves without notice and with no opportunity for an exit interview, some relevant information may be obtainable from fellow employees. A word of caution: the reason employees give for leaving and the real reason may not be the same; you must try to determine the real reason. An exit interview form is illustrated in Figure 8.5, and a turnover analysis form in Figure 8.6.

NINE

Labor Cost Control

LABOR COST RATIOS

Because the hotel industry is so diverse, it is impossible to be specific in establishing guidelines within which the labor cost as a percentage of sales should fall for any particular operation. For example, the labor cost for most hotels will generally be between 25 percent and 35 percent of total sales. However, it could well be lower than 25 percent in some hotels, and higher than 35 percent in others.

Causes of Differences in Labor Cost

Many factors can cause these differences in labor cost from one hotel to another. Some of these are discussed.

Location.　A well-located hotel will usually enjoy a higher level of business (and thus a reduced labor cost percent) than a similar hotel less well located. For example, if you operate a hotel on a major highway it will, all other things being equal, enjoy a higher occupancy level on average than a competitive hotel located close by but not on a major highway.

Market Demands.　The particular clientele (market) that your hotel caters to can affect your labor cost ratio. For example, a hotel catering to the middle-income customer might find its sales dropping drastically and its labor cost percentage increasing as a proportion of revenue in recessionary times or when unseasonal weather continues for a long period of time during the peak summer vacation months.

Unions.　Hotels whose employees are covered by a union contract will generally have a higher labor cost relative to sales than establishments whose employees are not covered by union contract. Unions generally obtain higher levels of pay and more fringe benefits (which are a part of total labor cost) for their members than those received by nonunion employees.

115

Use of Equipment. If you can use and afford certain items of hotel equipment, you may be able to reduce the number of employees and thus their labor cost. More sophisticated front office and housekeeping equipment may mean that fewer employees are required.

PROBLEM OF PRODUCTIVITY

One of the key words in measuring employee performance and in labor cost control is productivity. Traditionally, it is thought that for many reasons the productivity of employees in the hotel industry, which is measured in different ways, has been low compared with productivity in many other industries. Whether comparisons with other industries (such as manufacturing) are fair is open to question. Some of the reasons why productivity may be low and some possible ways of improving it are discussed.

Fluctuating Sales Volume

The peaks and valleys of demand for the products and services offered by the typical hotel, combined with an insensitivity of much of the labor cost to fluctuating and frequently unpredictable demand, can mean that at certain times you can do nothing about the productivity (or lack of it) of some employees.

In other words, the industry generally has a high fixed labor cost, so that minor changes in volume of sales can have a major effect on labor cost ratios and net income. Figure 9.1 illustrates this. On a normal day, labor cost is 40 percent of revenue. On a good day, it drops to 37 percent; and on a poor day, it jumps to 45 percent. The reason for these swings is that, even if you could adjust the variable portion of labor (for example, housekeeping employees) to revenue, the fixed portion (for example, front office employees) cannot be changed.

	Normal Day		Poor Day		Good Day	
Sales	$1,000	100%	$800	100%	$1,200	100%
Labor cost:						
Fixed	$ 200	20%	$200	25%	$ 200	17%
Variable (20% × sales)	200	20	160	20	240	20
Total	$ 400	40%	$360	45%	$ 440	37%
Income before other expenses	$ 600	60%	$440	55%	$ 760	63%

Figure 9.1   Effect of volume on labor cost.

Limited Ability to Produce for Inventory

Manufacturing industries that are subject to cyclical demand can continue to produce during low-demand periods and hold the goods in inventory until demand again increases. Productivity is stabilized and the labor cost per unit of production can be held constant. This is not true of a hotel. Since the industry is a service one selling space (guest rooms), it is impossible to store the labor cost.

An additional problem is that, if a room's space is not sold on a particular night that revenue is lost forever. It cannot be regained by selling the room twice on the following night.

Lack of Labor-Saving Equipment

Since the industry is highly labor intensive because of its service nature, it is difficult for you to replace employees with machines. Customers expect personal service. Where equipment can be introduced to reduce labor cost, then you should seriously consider this.

Poor Facilities Layout

Poor facilities layout is probably more of a problem for older properties. For example, many older hotels were designed when less concern was placed on labor cost. However, many new hotels are still designed without enough consideration given to employee movement (and thus employee productivity).

Poor Management and Supervision

One of your most important tasks in the improvement of productivity and the reduction of labor cost is to hire and train the right kind of supervisors (department heads or managers). These managers must in turn be competent at training their employees to be efficient.

Such managers should be hired on the basis of their administrative skills combined with technical skills — not just on the basis of their technical skills. A good technical employee may not be a good administrator. A superior room maid may make a poor head housekeeper.

The manager's or supervisor's skills should include such abilities as selecting good employees, training them to be more productive, enforcing standards, motivating employees, preparing staffing schedules, maintaining employee morale (to reduce employee turnover), and implementing procedures to control both labor and other costs. A poor manager or supervisor will fail to extract the full potential from employees and thus will add to overall labor costs.

Part-time Employees

Part-time employees are often viewed as a solution to reducing a high labor cost. However, these employees can create problems if their use is not carefully planned and implemented. Properly determining what is known as the "employee mix" between full- and part-time employees requires experience and judgment.

One of the problems is the hidden cost of a part-time employee. Although the total cost per day for a part-time person is obviously less than that for a full-time employee, you will need more individual employees than if only full-time ones were used. This entails a higher training cost for the extra people. There is also likely to be a higher turnover cost, which in turn increases the training cost for replacement employees.

Other hidden costs relate to the potential unreliability of part-time employees. For example, because they may not have the same commitment to your hotel that full-time employees have, and because they may have full-time jobs elsewhere, absenteeism can occur because the full-time job takes precedence. That full-time job may even be a commitment as a homemaker. If the part-timers are students, their school work (or even school vacations) can take precedence.

Overtime

Overtime pay is sometimes inevitable — for example, in an emergency when service must be continued beyond normal hours because of an unanticipated demand, or when there is no time for you to call in part-time people to cope with an unexpected demand. Overtime work is often seen as a cause of a higher labor cost, but it can be used strategically as a tool to reduce labor cost.

For example, if you need an extra employee for two hours of work but that employee if called in must legally or by union agreement be paid for a minimum of four hours, it is more profitable (less costly) to pay a full-time employee who has already worked a full shift to perform the extra two hours at time-and-a-half pay — which in this case amounts to the equivalent of three hours. The net saving is thus one hour of labor cost.

It is also likely that the full-time employee is more skilled and better trained than the part-time employee who is called in only when the perceived need to avoid overtime arises. Overtime becomes an unnecessary cost when it is the result of poor planning.

You may want all overtime to be supported by an overtime authorization form documenting the reason for the overtime. Such a form is illustrated in Figure 9.2.

Date___April 5___   Department_____Banquet_____

Employee name_____Jones_____

Position_____Houseman_____

Hours of overtime___2___   Rate of pay_____$6.00/hour_____

Total overtime cost___$12.00___

Reason: To set up meeting room for early breakfast on April 6

Authorized by_____J. L. Hinton_____
                      Department head

Figure 9.2   Overtime authorization form.

Incentive Schemes

Some hotels have successfully introduced incentive schemes to increase productivity. These include such practices as paying bonuses for low absenteeism and/or a good record of punctuality, and extra pay for high productivity (for example, cleaning more guest rooms than your hotel's standard — although, in such cases, you must consider the possible reduction in quality of cleanliness provided in guest rooms).

Increasing Demand

Mention was made earlier in this chapter about the high fixed labor cost of most hotels. Rather than concentrate solely on a reduction of labor cost to conform to anticipated demand, an alternative might be to increase the demand during the slack periods. This is a matter of analyzing your market and establishing sales strategies that will increase demand.

An optimum situation, though it may be difficult to achieve in practice, would be to have your hotel always operating at peak occupancy. In this way, productivity of all employees can be maximized. For example, many hotels catering to the business traveller have high mid-week occupancies, but low weekend occupancies. For this reason they often offer lower weekend rates to the family trade to encourage business and build up total weekly occupancy.

PAYROLL PROCEDURES

Labor cost control begins by ensuring that payroll hours paid for are correct. Each employee's net pay is calculated from hours worked during the pay period at regular and overtime rates, less any amounts deducted for government withholdings such as income tax and unemployment insurance and other withholdings such as union dues.

Regular hourly rates of pay are decided at the time each employee is hired. In many cases the starting rate is either a legally required or union mandated minimum rate. Any subsequent pay rate increases should be authorized and approved on a change in rate pay form such as that illustrated in Figure 9.3.

Computerized Process

Because of the repetitive nature of payroll preparation, many hotels today computerize this process, either using an in-house computer or an external service bureau that specializes in payroll preparation. Payroll control, however, involves more than just computerizing the process of calculating and verifying the mathematical accuracy of each employee's paycheck.

For example, a computerized payroll system cannot verify that employees

- Were physically on duty when they were supposed to be.
- Worked a specified number of hours.
- Were paid at the correct rate.
- Were needed for all the time they were on duty.
- Were justified in receiving overtime pay.

It is generally a department manager's responsibility to control most of these steps prior to the actual preparation of each employee's pay.

AUTHORIZATION FOR CHANGE IN RATE OF PAY

Employee _____
Position _____
Present pay rate _____
New pay rate _____
Effective date _____
Supervisor's signature _____
Manager's approval _____

Figure 9.3 Authorization for change in rate of pay form.

Time Clocks

Most hotel employees are required to use a time clock that records on each employee's individual time card the hours during which he or she was on duty. Unfortunately, time cards reflect only the time when the employee entered and left your hotel's premises and not the number of hours actually worked nor the hours they were supposed to work. Therefore, to control this situation it is generally each department head's responsibility to review and approve time cards before they are submitted for payroll preparation.

Alternatively, department heads can record on a separate form (without reference to the time cards) the hours when each employee started and finished work each day of the pay period. In this situation, it is then the responsibility of a payroll department employee to verify that each employee's time card record of hours worked compares correctly with the supervisor's record. Any differences between time card and time sheet can then be questioned with the department head and, if necessary, with the employee involved so that only the correct number of hours are paid for.

In many small hotels overtime is not permitted without the prior approval of the general manager. In larger hotels, department heads are usually given the authority to approve overtime. Overtime approval forms (see Figure 9.2) are generally attached to employee time cards at the end of each pay period.

Vacation Periods

Employee vacation time is also a payroll expense. A minimum vacation period is established by law, but many union contracts allow employees to extend their legal vacation time by one or more weeks based on length of service. You or an authorized department head, however, have the right to stipulate when vacations can be taken. Obviously, since most hotels operate on a seasonal basis, the best time to schedule employee vacations is usually during slow periods.

Department heads can also try to schedule vacation periods to minimize employee replacement costs. You or your department heads must decide whether you should cover each employee's vacation period with a temporary or part-time replacement employee or by paying other employees overtime.

If an employee requests time off without pay beyond the normal vacation allowance, and if a replacement employee's wage cost is less or if a replacement is not required, then extended vacations should be encouraged because this will reduce total labor cost.

Cash Wages

You should also discourage cash wages because cash wage forms can be forged by a dishonest department head, or a department head may use cash wage payments to circumvent staffing restrictions that you have established.

However, in some situations cash wage payments are inevitable. In such cases, each employee's cash wage should be justified on a cash wage form that the employee must sign acknowledging receipt of the cash.

Cash Advances

You should also discourage cash advances and authorize them only if a hardship need is determined. Employees who receive cash advances often find it difficult to catch up, and most requests for advances are made by employees with a history of previous loans.

Distribution of Checks

A common procedure for payroll check distribution is for department heads to receive, sign for, and distribute the payroll checks to employees in their departments. A control procedure used by some hotels in issuing these checks is to ensure that there is actually an employee for each check prepared.

The procedure requires an employee of the accounting department each payday to randomly select a department and distribute the checks without the department head's involvement. Because in a large hotel it is usually not possible for the accounting department employee to recognize and identify each person who receives a check, each employee must sign for his or her check on a form listing all employees who, according to payroll department records, are working in that department. In some hotels, the procedure is carried one further step by comparing each employee's signature with the signature on that employee's initial job application form or other personnel department record.

LABOR COST PERCENT

A traditional measure of labor cost is the labor cost percentage, that is, labor cost from payroll records divided by sales and multiplied by 100. However, there may be difficulties in relying solely on the percentage as a basis for evaluating your actual operating results.

There may also be risks in relying on payroll labor cost percent as a measure of labor cost control because labor cost percentage depends on five variables, some of which cannot be controlled:

1. The number of rooms occupied. This number is predictable where reservations have been made, but unpredictable where a hotel has a great deal of "walk-in" trade—that is people who arrive without having made prior reservations.
2. The average room rate. This is relatively predictable, based on past performance.
3. The number of employees called in on duty. This can usually be predicted and controlled based on occupancy forecasts.
4. The hours worked by employees who are not on a fixed salary. This is a known factor (other than when unforeseen emergencies such as those requiring overtime hours arise).
5. The hourly wage rate. This is normally a known and predictable figure.

Changing Variables

All of these variables are continually shifting. Some of them (such as the number of rooms occupied) shift randomly from day to day, others (such as wage rates) are relatively constant, but shift over time. Therefore, you should use labor cost as a percent of sales only as a planning and operating guideline. It should not be used as a real measure of payroll cost and employee productivity.

For example, labor cost percent can decrease if your room rates are increased, while productivity goes down (for example, as customers resist the higher rates and fewer rooms are occupied). This problem is not even apparent when you use labor cost percent as a measure of labor cost control.

Additional Problem

An analysis of labor cost that relies entirely on labor cost percent has an additional pitfall. This problem, which was illustrated in Figure 9.1, relates to the fixed nature of a certain proportion of labor cost. The effect of this fixed element may be hidden over time, when labor cost percentage peaks and valleys offset each other and tend to smooth out what might otherwise be a volatile cost percent.

If you exclude fixed salaries from labor cost before it is calculated as a percentage of sales, however, the measure may have some validity— particularly if fixed salaries are low in comparison to variable wages.

On the other hand, labor cost based on a standard of employee productivity predetermined on the basis of forecast volume of business overcomes the cost percent problems. The remainder of this chapter discusses how to establish employee productivity standards and use them in labor cost planning and control.

LABOR PRODUCTIVITY STANDARDS

A preliminary step to the preparation of labor productivity standards is to ensure that your hotel's quality standards are well understood. For example, the productivity of a housekeeping employee measured in number of rooms cleaned per day can be increased easily by reducing the time spent on each room. This would not be a good idea if it reduces your quality standards and results in customer complaints.

Jobs in the hotel industry can generally be categorized into three broad types: fixed cost employees, semifixed cost employees, and variable cost employees.

Fixed Cost Employees

Fixed cost employees, sometimes referred to as nonproductive employees, are those employees whose positions are not dependent on volume of sales unless there is a major change in this volume. These employees are generally on a monthly or annual salary, regardless of number of hours actually worked. So long as analysis of each position in this category shows that the employee is needed, no productivity standard would normally be established.

Although fixed cost employee positions, as mentioned, are not generally affected by sales, employees in these positions can sometimes be used in slack times to assume jobs, either part- or full-time, that would otherwise be carried out by employees in the semifixed or variable categories. While this does not affect the labor cost of fixed employees, it does reduce overall labor cost.

Semifixed Cost Employees

The semifixed cost production-related group of employees are those whose positions are dependent to some extent on the volume of sales. This dependence could be on a daily basis, or, alternatively, the employee might work each day with the hours of work (subject to a minimum guaranteed number of hours) fluctuating daily according to volume. In order to have cost flexibility, semifixed cost positions normally have an hourly pay rate attached to them.

This category includes employees such as housekeeping supervisory personnel and certain front desk employees. For each of these positions, productivity standards should be established.

Variable Cost Employees

The employees in the variable cost group are entirely dependent on guest rooms occupancy, both as to number of employees required each day and number of hours worked by each employee. Note that, if your employees are covered by a union contract, they might still have to be paid for a minimum number of hours (for example, four) if called in any particular day. This category includes housekeeping employees and bell desk personnel. The establishment of productivity standards is most critical for this group of employees, particularly if your hotel's volume fluctuates widely on a daily basis.

Establishing Productivity Standards

Although you could establish productivity standards based on past performance, there is no guarantee that past results were appropriate. For example, based on historical records, the number of rooms cleaned in a standard eight-hour shift might be established at 16 per maid. How can you be sure 16 is the most productive number?

Observation of employees on the job is helpful in determining the optimum number of guest rooms that the average, reasonably good housekeeping employee can cope with, keeping your quality standards in mind. The number will vary from one hotel to another because of such matters as the layout of the property, size and layout of guest rooms, and location of equipment and linen storage areas relative to guest rooms.

After each type of position has been appropriately studied and all necessary factors considered, final standards should be established in discussion with the appropriate supervisor, such as the head housekeeper.

Once standards have been established, you should review them from time to time and revise them if necessary. For example, the introduction of a new piece of housekeeping equipment could change the affected employees' productivity.

Note that, in some hotels the standards may be written into the union contract and thus not subject to unilateral change by either party.

Staffing Guides

After standards are established, you must develop staffing guides to indicate the number of employees required on duty for various levels of guest-room occupancy. These staffing guides should be prepared on a daily volume basis because for complete labor cost control you must be able to adjust your staffing daily in accordance with anticipated volume.

In developing the guides, you must consider both minimum and maximum occupancy levels. The minimum level identifies the minimum number of employees necessary to maintain a smooth operation. The maximum level is the point beyond which no additional staffing is allowed. For example, it would be useless to staff beyond the level required to handle 100 percent occupancy. Figure 9.4 shows a partial weekly staffing guide. Just as productivity standards must be revised as conditions warrant, so, too, should your staffing guides.

Forecasting

The next step in labor cost control is forecasting guest room occupancies. These forecasts are developed from records of past performance adjusted for current factors. Although for budgeting purposes many hotels forecast in months, for staffing purposes these budgeted figures must be broken down on a weekly basis prior to each week of actual operations and then on a daily basis for each day of the week. In this way, the figures can be adjusted to reflect current conditions and recent trends that can affect your volume of business.

Staff Scheduling

There are two basic types of staff schedules: stacked or shift schedules and staggered schedules. Stacked (or shift) schedules are used for fixed and/or semifixed cost employees who would normally work a full shift regardless of volume of business. For all other employees, staggered schedules must be used.

Daily Number of Occupied Rooms	Head Housekeeper	Room Inspectors	Maids
15	1	0	1
30	1	0	2
45	1	1	3
60	1	1	4
75	1	1	5
90	1	2	6
105	1	2	7
120	1	2	8
135	1	3	9
150	1	3	10

Figure 9.4 Staffing guide.

Empl.	A.M.	P.M.
	6 7 8 9 10 11 12	1 2 3 4 5 6 7 8 9 10 11 12
A		
B		
C		
D		
E		
F		
G		

Figure 9.5   Staggered schedule.

Even though your staffing guides indicate the number of employees or person-hours that are to be used for each level of occupancy, they do not indicate when those employees are to work. Generally, an analysis of the time of day that departing guest room occupants leave and new occupants arrive must be made. This analysis will indicate the low, the medium, and the high room turnover periods. You should schedule employees so that the maximum number are on duty during high-turnover periods and the minimum number during low-turnover periods, thus staggering the hours when employees are working.

A staggered schedule might appear as shown in Figure 9.5. This type of schedule reduces idle time, provides for overlap of employees, recognizes variations during the day in usage of rooms, and can lead to reduction or elimination of overtime costs. In most cases, you would prepare schedules in advance of each weekly period. The schedule would show each day for each employee the scheduled times of arrival and departure. The times would be subject to daily review prior to each work day for adjustment (where necessary) to a changed forecast. Days off also appear on the schedule. A completed individual employee schedule is illustrated in Figure 9.6.

Once staff schedules have been completed, it may be useful to cost them, calculating the cost percent to see whether it meets your hotel's overall labor cost percent goal (if it has one). If the cost percent does not meet this goal, rescheduling must be done where feasible within the established standards. Sometimes rescheduling is not feasible because of the way the peaks and valleys of occupancy occur.

Labor Cost Analysis

Since you can prepare occupancy forecasts and labor schedules daily, an analysis of actual labor cost with forecast or budgeted cost can also be made daily.

Week Commencing					April 8		
Employee	Sunday	Monday	Tuesday	Wednesday	Thursday	Friday	Saturday
C. Jones	9–5	9–5	9–5	9–5	9–5	off	off
J. Hathaway	off	off	8–4	8–4	8–4	8–4	8–4
S. Heil	7–3	7–3	7–3	7–3	7–3	off	off
P. Mintz	12–8	12–8	12–8	off	off	12–8	12–8
A. Smith	7–3	7–3	off	off	7–3	7–3	7–3
C. Cody	10–5	10–5	10–5	10–5	off	off	8–4

Figure 9.6   Employee schedule.

The analysis compares the actual person-hours or person-days used and to be paid for with the forecast person-hours or person-days for that day. In a small hotel, it might well be that overstaffing and understaffing on individual days will even out and only minor variances will occur overall.

However, because the objective of labor cost analysis is to discover all variances, analysis should preferably be done daily. In this way, you can determine the causes of all variances and the entire process of forecasting and thus controlling labor cost can be made more effective. Generally, variances can result from one or more of the following:

- Inappropriate staffing guidelines.
- Inaccurate forecasts.
- Poor scheduling and excessive overtime.
- Unpredictable volume fluctuations.

When making comparisons between forecast and actual hours, and when this comparison is made on a person-days basis, the hours of part-time employees must be converted to equivalent person-days. If the standard person-day for a full-time employee were eight hours, then equivalent person-days would be calculated by dividing total part-time hours for all such employees by eight. The actual hours figures would be taken from payroll records (time cards or sign-in/sign-out sheets).

Comparisons between forecast and actual figures can also be made on a dollar basis. This requires converting hours forecast and hours actually worked to dollars. In the case of hourly paid employees, hours are simply multiplied by the related hourly rate of pay. In the case of salaried employees, the daily rate will vary depending on the number of days in a month. For example, a department head paid $1,500 a month is assumed

Date ___April 11___

Department	Number of employees today		Labor cost today		Labor cost to date		Labor cost variance	
	Budget	Actual	Budget	Actual	Budget	Actual	Today	To date
Rooms								
Front office	10	10	$ 440	$ 440	$1,320	$1,320		
Housekeeping	42	43	1,280	1,310	3,840	3,900	$ + 30	$ + 60
Service	8	8	320	320	960	930		– 30
Switchboard	6	6	274	274	822	822		

Figure 9.7 Labor cost summary and analysis.

to be responsible for that department even on days off, and will have a daily rate of $50 during a 30-day month and $48.39 during a 31-day month.

If desired, the labor cost analysis could include labor cost percentage figures. This simply involves dividing labor cost dollars by sales and multiplying by 100. But again, do not rely too much on the percentage figures for analysis purposes. A sample daily labor cost analysis form is illustrated in Figure 9.7.

TEN

Income Statement Analysis

COMPARATIVE STATEMENTS

A periodic income statement is useful for presenting information about your hotel's operations and for monitoring the progress of the business, particularly if monthly financial statements are produced.

The income statement is more meaningful, however, if it is compared with the income statement for the previous period. When the current period's income statement is placed alongside the previous period's income statement, changes that have occurred between the two periods can be seen. A straight side-by-side comparison of the two sets of figures, however, is not easy because the extent of changes is not always obvious. Therefore, to aid in making the comparison it is useful to use *comparative analysis* (also known as horizontal analysis) so that you have additional information calculated and added to the two statements.

Additional Information

For example, refer to the two income statements illustrated in Table 10.1, showing Martha's Motel's operating results for each of the years 0001 and 0002. Alongside the income statements are two additional columns — one showing the difference in dollars for each item, and the other expressing this dollar difference as a percentage increase or decrease over the previous year.

The two extra columns help Martha to pinpoint large changes that have occurred, either in dollars or in percentages, from one year to the next. The percentage change figures are calculated by dividing the dollar change figure by the base figure in year 0001 and multiplying by 100. For example, sales have gone down 2.5 percent, calculated as follows:

$$\frac{\$1,300}{\$529,200} \times 100 = 2.5\%$$

131

TABLE 10.1

Comparative Income Statement Analysis

	Year Ending Dec. 31, 0001	Year Ending Dec. 31, 0002	Change from year 0001 to year 0002	
			Dollars	Percent
Sales	$529,200	$527,900	− $ 1,300	− 2.5%
Expenses				
Salaries and wages	$277,400	$304,500	+ $27,100	+ 9.8%
Employee benefits	34,500	37,800	+ 3,300	+ 9.6
Operating supplies	37,200	38,000	+ 800	+ 0.2
Marketing	7,500	8,400	+ 900	+ 12.0
Utilities	10,200	12,100	+ 1,900	+ 18.6
Administration	6,500	7,200	+ 700	+ 10.8
Maintenance	2,900	4,000	+ 1,100	+ 37.9
	376,200	412,000	+ 35,800	+ 9.5
Profit	$153,000	$115,900	−$37,100	− 24.2%
(before fixed charges)				

The other percentage change figures are calculated in the same way.

Even though the total sales decrease was relatively small, however, profit before fixed charges has declined $37,100, or 24.2 percent. This is a drastic change. With sales relatively constant and all other things being equal, profit should not have declined so much. All other things, obviously, are not equal, because analysis of costs shows that the majority of them have increased considerably.

To select only one as an example, the salaries and wages expense has increased by $27,100 over the year, or 9.8 percent. Why is this? Was there a wage increase? Has Martha's operation become less efficient in staffing? Was a one-time bonus paid to employees?

Martha needs to analyze each expense so that large changes such as that for the salaries and wage expense can be accounted for. In this particular illustration, assuming the increased costs were inevitable, perhaps they have not yet been adjusted for by Martha in room rates.

Absolute versus Relative Changes

In carrying out comparative analysis you should distinguish between absolute and relative changes. Absolute changes show the dollar change from one period to the next. The relative change is the absolute change expressed as a percentage. For example, the wage cost in Table 10.1 shows an absolute change of $27,100 which in relative terms is a change of 9.8 percent.

An absolute change may sometimes appear large (for example, $10,000) but when compared to its base figure (for example, $1,000,000) it represents a relative change of only 1 percent.

By the same token, a relative change may seem high (for example 50 percent) but when compared to its base figure is quite small in absolute terms (for example, $50 base figure increasing to $75). In terms of the total income statement this $25 change (even though it shows a relative increase of 50 percent) is insignificant.

Therefore, when analyzing comparative income statements, both the absolute and relative change should be looked at, and only those that exceed both acceptable norms would be of concern.

For example, a particular hotel might establish absolute changes of concern at $10,000 and relative changes at 5 percent, and only those changes that exceeded both $10,000 and 5 percent will be investigated. The following changes would not be investigated:

- Above $10,000 but below 5 percent.
- Above 5 percent but below $10,000.
- Below $10,000 and below 5 percent.

COMMON-SIZE STATEMENTS

Another type of income statement analysis is known as vertical or *common-size analysis*. Common size simply means that all income statement dollars are converted to a percentage basis. Total sales are given the value of 100 percent, and all other items are expressed in ratio to that 100 percent. Table 10.2 illustrates Martha's two income statements from Table 10.1 converted to a common-size basis.

Note how labor cost for year 0001 is converted to a percentage of sales by dividing it by sales and multiplying by 100 as follows:

$$\frac{\$277,400}{\$529,200} \times 100 = 52.4\%$$

Other expenses and profit are converted to common size in the same way. For example, profit before fixed costs in year 0001 is

$$\frac{\$153,000}{\$529,200} \times 100 = 28.9\%$$

Figures for year 0002 are calculated in a similar way, using sales for that year as the denominator.

Comparative, Common-size Income Statements

Even though an individual periodic common-size income statement can be of some value, it is of more value if two or more successive income statements are compared to each other on a common-size basis, as illustrated in Table 10.2. In this way, changes from one period to the next are more apparent.

The reason for converting dollar amounts to percentages for purposes of comparison is that it makes comparison a lot easier. For example, refer to Table 10.2 and note that Martha's profit (before fixed costs) was $153,000 in year 0001 and $115,900 in year 0002. These figures tell us that, in absolute terms, the profit has declined—but how much is the profit relative to sales in each of the two years? This is not easy to tell by looking only at the dollar figures.

By converting the net profit to a percentage of sales, however, Martha can see that it has declined from 28.9 percent of sales in year 0001 to 22.0 percent of sales in year 0002. That is to say, out of each dollar of sales in year 0001 there were almost 29 cents profit, while in year 0002 this had declined to 22 cents. In other words, in year 0001 Martha had a larger proportion of sales represented by profit, and a declining ratio of profit to sales is not normally a desirable trend.

TABLE 10.2

Common-size Income Statement Analysis

	Year Ending Dec. 31, 0001	Year Ending Dec. 31, 0002	Year Ending Dec. 31, 0001	Year Ending Dec. 31, 0002
Sales	$529,200	$527,900	100.0%	100.0%
Expenses				
Salaries and wages	$277,400	$304,500	52.4%	57.7%
Employee benefits	34,500	37,800	6.5	7.2
Operating supplies	37,200	38,000	7.0	7.2
Marketing	7,500	8,400	1.4	1.6
Utilities	10,200	12,100	1.9	2.3
Administration	6,500	7,200	1.2	1.4
Maintenance	2,900	4,000	0.6	0.6
	376,200	412,000	71.1	78.0
Profit	$153,000	$115,900	28.9%	22.0%
(before fixed charges)				

135

Causes of Changes.   What is the reason for this trend? One cause that is obvious is that salaries and wages have increased from 52.4 to 57.7 percent of sales. This 5.3 percent increase translates into almost $28,000 (5.3 percent of sales of $527,900). In other words, if salaries and wages had remained at 52.4 percent of sales in year 0002 (rather than increasing to 57.7 percent), profit would have been almost $28,000 higher.

What is the reason? Have increased labor costs not been passed on in higher room rates? Was Martha in year 0002 less effective in controlling this cost, that is, is there a problem in the labor cost control system?

Although there are minor increases relative to sales in other expenses, none is very serious compared to labor cost.

SALES AND COSTS PER ROOM

Another analysis method that Martha could use is to convert the income statements to a per room basis: using either cost per room available or cost per room occupied.

Sales and Costs per Room Available

Table 10.3 shows Martha's annual sales and costs per room available. Assuming Martha's Motel has 36 rooms, rooms available for the year are:

$$36 \text{ rooms} \times 365 = 13{,}140$$

Each sale and cost figure for each of the two years is divided by 13,140. The results show again that the major problem is in labor, where the cost per room has increased from $21.11 to $23.17, or an increase of $2.06, while the average revenue per room declined by $0.09 (from $40.27 to $40.18). These changes, combined with increases in other costs, resulted in a decline in profit before fixed charges of $2.82 ($11.64 less $8.82).

Sales and Costs per Room Occupied

Perhaps a better way to analyze sales and cost figures is on a rooms occupied (rather than rooms available) basis. Assuming Martha's occupancy in 0001 was 65 percent, then

$$13{,}140 \text{ available rooms} \times 65\% = 8{,}541$$

rooms were occupied in that year, and each of the sale and cost figures for 0001 is divided by 8,541. If Martha's occupancy in 0002 was 60 percent, then

TABLE 10.3

Sales and Costs per Room Available

	Year Ending Dec. 31, 0001	Year Ending Dec. 31, 0002	Year Ending Dec. 31, 0001	Year Ending Dec. 31, 0002
Sales	$529,200	$527,900	$40.27	$40.18
Expenses				
Salaries and wages	$277,400	$304,500	$21.11	$23.17
Employee benefits	34,500	37,800	2.63	2.88
Operating supplies	37,200	38,000	2.83	2.89
Marketing	7,500	8,400	0.57	0.64
Utilities	10,200	12,100	0.77	0.92
Administration	6,500	7,200	0.49	0.55
Maintenance	2,900	4,000	0.22	0.30
	376,200	412,000	28.63	31.36
Profit	$153,000	$115,900	$11.64	$8.82
(before fixed charges)				

$$13{,}140 \text{ available rooms} \times 60\% = 7{,}884$$

rooms were occupied in that year, and each of the sale and cost figures for 0002 is divided by 7,884.

The results have been tabulated in Table 10.4 and indicate that the changes are now larger than on a per room available basis because they are compounded by the declining occupancy percent.

SELECTION OF ANALYSIS METHOD

Note that, even though several different methods of income statement analysis have been demonstrated in this chapter, you would not in practice use all of them. Each is useful, and each shows basically where problem areas are. Therefore, you must select whichever one you think is most appropriate in your operation and illustrates the situation most clearly to you.

Monthly Analysis Preferable

Tables 10.1, 10.2, 10.3, and 10.4 show methods of analyzing annual income statements. However, in your hotel it would be preferable to make monthly calculations because you need to be alerted to worsening trends more frequently than once a year.

Comparison with Budget

One other way in which to make income statement comparisons is to compare actual results with budgeted figures. This subject will be covered in more depth in Chapter 16.

OPERATING RATIOS

A number of operating ratios are also useful in analyzing your hotel's sales.

Occupancy Percentage

Occupancy is calculated by dividing the rooms used during a period (a night or a week) by the rooms available (rooms in the establishment times days in the period) during that period and multiplying by 100. For example, if Sonny's Snoozery had 100 rooms of which 80 were occupied overnight, Sonny's occupancy for that night is

TABLE 10.4

Sales and Costs per Room Occupied

	Year Ending Dec. 31, 0001		Year Ending Dec. 31, 0002		Year Ending Dec. 31, 0001		Year Ending Dec. 31, 0002
Sales		$529,200		$527,900		$61.96	$66.96
Expenses							
Salaries and wages	$277,400		$304,500		$32.48		$38.62
Employee benefits	34,500		37,800		4.04		4.79
Operating supplies	37,200		38,000		4.36		4.82
Marketing	7,500		8,400		0.88		1.07
Utilities	10,200		12,100		1.19		1.53
Administration	6,500		7,200		0.76		0.91
Maintenance	2,900	376,200	4,000	412,000	0.34	44.05	0.51 52.26
Profit		$153,000		$115,900		$17.91	$14.70
(before fixed charges)							

$$\frac{80}{100} \times 100 = 80\%$$

Double Occupancy Percentage

Double occupancy percentage is the percentage of rooms occupied that are occupied by more than one person. For example, if 20 of Sonny's 80 occupied rooms on that night were occupied by more than one person, the double occupancy is

$$\frac{20}{80} \times 100 = 25\%$$

Double occupancy is sometimes expressed by calculating the average number of people per room occupied (total number of guests for a period divided by total rooms occupied during that period). For example, if Sonny's 80 occupied rooms were occupied by 100 guests, the double occupancy is

$$\frac{100}{80} = 1.25$$

Double occupancy is usually higher for resort hotels catering to the family trade than for transient hotels catering primarily to the business person traveling alone.

Obviously, a high occupancy and a high double occupancy are both desirable because this indicates greater use of the rooms facilities, and also potentially greater usage of other hotel facilities by guest-room occupants. Therefore, the trend of this information is important.

Note that, when an occupancy percent is calculated for a period of time (such as a week), this does not mean that was the occupancy every night of the week. For example, a hotel could have an average occupancy of 70 percent for a week, with an occupancy of over 90 percent per night from Monday to Friday and a very low occupancy percent at the weekend.

Average Rate per Room Occupied

The average rate per room occupied can be calculated daily by dividing rooms occupied into revenue from rooms. For example, if Sonny had total revenue for a night of $7,200 from 80 occupied rooms, average rate per occupied room is

$$\frac{\$7,200}{80} = \$90$$

If the average rate per occupied room is calculated on a monthly basis, this is done by dividing total rooms occupied during the month into total revenue for the month. The method is similar for an annual average rate, except that annual figures are used.

The trend of this figure is important. It can be influenced upward by directing sales efforts into selling higher priced rooms rather than lower priced ones or by increasing the rate of double occupancy.

Average Rate per Guest

Another useful measure of performance is the average daily rate per guest. This is calculated by dividing total room revenue for a period by the total number of guests accommodated during that period. For example, if Sonny had 80 rooms occupied overnight by 110 guests (that is, 30 rooms were double occupied) average rate per guest is

$$\frac{\$7,200}{110} = \$65.45$$

Average rate per guest can be calculated monthly by using monthly figures and annually by using annual figures.

Average Length of Stay

The average length of stay is calculated by dividing the rooms occupied for a period of time by the number of guests registered during that period.

For example, if rooms occupied during a month were 2,400 and 1,500 registrations occurred, average length of stay is

$$\frac{2,400}{1,500} = 1.6 \text{ days}$$

To increase rooms occupancy and maximize sales, you should try to increase the guests' length of stay through advertising and other marketing methods. If guests can be encouraged to stay an extra night or two, that means more revenue for your hotel and thus more profit.

Manager's Daily Report

Many of the operating statistics that are useful for analyzing the ongoing operations of your hotel can be calculated on a daily basis so that you can monitor the success of your operation continually. A sample of such a report was illustrated in Figure 4.1.

TREND RESULTS

Earlier in this chapter we limited our analysis of the income statement to only two periods. However, limiting an analysis to only two periods (weeks, months, or years) can be misleading if anything unusual distorted the results for either of the two periods. Looking at results over a greater number of periods can often be more useful. For example, consider trend figures for Monty's Motor Inn for six successive months:

Month	Sales	Change in Sales	Percentage Change
1	$25,000		
2	30,000	+$5,000	+20%
3	33,000	+ 3,000	+10
4	35,000	+ 2,000	+ 6
5	36,000	+ 1,000	+ 3
6	36,000	0	0

In the above figures the change in sales dollar amounts for each period is calculated by subtracting from each period's sales the sales of the preceding period. For example, in period 3:

$$\$33,000 - \$30,000 = \$3,000 \text{ change in sales}$$

The percentage change figures are calculated by dividing each period's change in sales amount by the sales of the previous period and multiplying by 100. For example, in period 3:

$$\frac{\$3,000}{\$30,000} \times 100 = 10\%$$

Over a long enough period of time, trend results show the direction in which your hotel is going. In Monty's case, the trend results indicate that, although business has been increasing over the past few months, it now seems to have levelled off. Has Monty reached his maximum potential in sales? Trend information such as this is useful in forecasting or budgeting (as we shall see in Chapter 16).

Index Trends

An *index trend* is a method of looking at trends by first converting the dollar amounts to an index. For example the following sales and wages cost dollars have each been converted to an index trend:

Period	Sales	Wage Cost	Sales Index	Wage Cost Index
1	$25,000	$ 7,500	100	100
2	30,000	9,200	120	123
3	33,000	10,300	132	137
4	35,000	10,800	140	144
5	36,000	11,100	144	148
6	36,000	11,200	144	149

An index is calculated by assigning a value of 100 (or 100 percent) in period 1 (the base period) for each item tabulated. The index figure for each succeeding period is calculated by dividing the dollar amount for that period by the base period dollar amount and multiplying by 100. For example, in period 2 (with reference to the above) the sales index is:

$$\frac{\$30,000}{\$25,000} \times 100 = 120$$

In period 4 the wage cost index is:

$$\frac{\$10,800}{\$ 7,500} \times 100 = 144$$

The completed index trend results in this particular case show that the wage cost has been increasing faster than sales. Expressed another way, sales are up 44 percent (144 − 100) and wage cost is up 49 percent (149 − 100). This is normally an undesirable trend needing investigation and possible correction.

Adjusting for Inflation

When comparing operating results, and in particular when you analyze trend figures, you must be aware of the effect changing dollar values have on the results. One hundred gallons of cleaning compound a few years ago provided the same quantity as one hundred gallons today; but the amount of money required to buy one hundred gallons today is probably considerably higher than the amount of money needed a few years ago. This is true of all expenses because prices change over time. Therefore, when you compare income and expense items over a period of time, you must consider the implications of inflation.

Consider a small hotel with the following sales in two successive years:

Year 1 $200,000
Year 2 $210,000

This is a $10,000, or a 5 percent ($10,000 divided by $200,000), increase in sales from year 1 to year 2. But if the hotel's room rates have been increased in year 2 by 10 percent over year 1 because of inflation, then the year 2 sales should have been at least $220,000 just to stay even with year 1 sales.

In other words, when comparing sales for successive periods in inflationary times you are comparing unequal values. Last year's dollar does not have the same value as this year's. What a dollar would buy last year may now require $1.15, or even more. Is there a method that will allow you to convert previous period's dollars into current period dollars so trends can be analyzed more meaningfully? The answer is: Yes, with the use of index numbers.

Selecting an Appropriate Index

The Consumer Price Index is probably one of the most commonly used and widely understood indexes available. But many other indexes are produced by the government and other organizations. By selecting an appropriate index, conversion of previous period's dollars into current year dollar values is simple. Consider the following, showing trend results for sales of Ivy's Inn for the past five years.

Year	Sales	Change in Sales	Percentage Change
1	$420,000	0	0
2	450,000	$30,000	7.1%
3	465,000	15,000	3.3
4	485,000	20,000	4.3
5	510,000	25,000	5.2

The trend shows increasing sales each year—generally a favorable trend. But, is it reasonable for Ivy to compare $420,000 of sales in year 1 with $510,000 of sales in year 5? By selecting an appropriate index (such as the Consumer Price Index) and adjusting all sales to comparable year 5 dollar values, a more realistic picture of Ivy's sales may emerge.

To do this, Ivy must use an index that is based on the same period of time for which she wishes to adjust her sales (or expenses). Assume the index numbers were as follows:

Year	Index Number
1	100
2	107

3	113
4	122
5	135

The equation for converting past period's (historic) dollars to current (real) dollars is:

$$\text{Historic dollars} \times \frac{\text{Index number for current period}}{\text{Index number for historic period}} = \text{Current dollars}$$

The following shows Ivy's sales dollars converted by the index numbers to express the five-year sales in terms of today's current dollars:

Year	Index	Historic Sales	Conversion Equation	Current Dollars
1.	100	$420,000 ×	135/100	= $567,000
2	107	450,000 ×	135/107	= 568,000
3	113	465,000 ×	135/113	= 556,000
4	122	485,000 ×	135/122	= 537,000
5	135	510,000 ×	135/135	= 510,000

As you can see, the resulting picture is quite different from the unadjusted historic figures. In fact, Ivy's annual sales have generally declined from year 1 to year 5, and this would not normally be a desirable trend.

ELEVEN

Ratio Analysis

In the previous chapter you saw some of the ways in which income statement information can be presented and analyzed. In this chapter you will see how a balance sheet, in conjunction with some income statement information, can be used in ratio analysis. For this we will use the information from Figure 11.1 (balance sheet) and Figure 11.2 (income statement) for Rusty's Resort—a resort hotel that owns its own land and building.

RATIOS

In its simplest terms, a *ratio* is a comparison of two figures. A comparison can be expressed in several ways. For example, you have already seen one type of ratio comparison in the previous chapter where common-size income statements were compared using percentages. A percentage is a ratio. You will see other types of ratios in this chapter.

Current Ratio

The *current ratio* is one of the most commonly used ratios to measure a hotel's liquidity or its ability to meet its short-term debts (current liabilities) without difficulty. The equation for this ratio is:

$$\frac{\text{Current assets}}{\text{Current liabilities}}$$

or, using figures from Rusty's balance sheet

$$\frac{\$92,200}{\$68,400} = 1.35$$

The ratio shows that for every $1.00 of short-term debt (current liabilities) Rusty has $1.35 of current assets. In general business, a rule of thumb is

RUSTY'S RESORT BALANCE SHEET AS OF DECEMBER 31, 19X1		
ASSETS		
Current Assets		
Cash	$ 25,400	
Accounts receivable	15,200	
Marketable securities	32,000	
Inventory	4,700	
Prepaid expense	14,900	$ 92,200
Fixed Assets		
Land	$ 60,500	
Building	882,400	
Furniture and equipment	227,900	
Linen and uniforms	18,300	
	$1,189,100	
Less: Accumulated depreciation	(422,000)	767,100
Total Assets		$859,300
LIABILITIES AND OWNERS' EQUITY		
Current Liabilities		
Accounts payable	$ 16,500	
Accrued expenses	4,200	
Income taxes payable	20,900	
Credit balances	800	
Current portion of mortgage	26,000	$ 68,400
Long-term Liability		
Mortgage payable		486,800
Total Liabilities		$555,200
OWNERS' EQUITY		
Common shares	$ 200,000	
Retained earnings	104,100	304,100
Total Liabilities and **Owners' Equity**		$859,300

Figure 11.1   Balance sheet.

that there should be $2.00 or more of current assets for each $1.00 of current liabilities.

However, most hotels can operate without difficulty with a current ratio considerably lower than 2 to 1. A reason for this is that a current ratio of 2 to 1 is typical of manufacturing businesses that must normally carry

RUSTY'S RESORT INCOME STATEMENT FOR YEAR ENDING DECEMBER 31, 19X1		
Sales		$755,800
Expenses		
Payroll and related expense	$319,200	
Operating supplies	101,400	
Administration and general	57,900	
Marketing	20,700	
Maintenance and repairs	15,400	
Energy	25,100	
Property taxes	28,800	
Insurance	13,100	
Depreciation	41,900	623,500
Profit before interest and tax		$132,300
Interest		51,900
Profit before tax		$ 80,400
Income tax		40,200
Net profit		$ 40,200

Figure 11.2 Income statement.

large inventories as part of their current assets because it takes weeks, and sometimes months, to have inventory delivered once it is ordered.

In comparison, most hotels carry relatively small inventories because they can purchase daily most of what they need. Indeed, for most hotels a current ratio of 2 to 1 would show an inefficient use of its current assets if that high ratio were due to carrying too much inventory. Money tied up in inventory is money that is not earning interest it could earn if it were left in the bank.

For your hotel, you must determine what the most effective current ratio is in order to have a current ratio position that neither creates short-term liquidity problems (too low a ratio), nor sacrifices profitability for safety (too high a ratio). If the ratio is too high, you have too much money tied up in *working capital* (current assets less current liabilities) that is not earning a profit.

With the current ratio, as with most ratios, its trend is important. Conditions of short-term loans from banks often require that this ratio be at or above a certain level at each balance sheet date. If it drops below the required level, the bank may have the right to call in (terminate) the loan. In such circumstances, the ratio should be assessed immediately prior to your balance sheet date to ensure that it is at a "safe" level so far as your bank is concerned.

Quick Ratio

Because total current assets include some assets that are not very liquid, bankers and other lenders frequently like to calculate the *quick* (or acid test) *ratio*. The quick ratio has as its numerator only cash, accounts receivable, and marketable securities:

$$\frac{\text{Cash} + \text{Receivables} + \text{Marketable securities}}{\text{Current liabilities}}$$

In Rusty's case this is

$$\frac{\$25,400 + \$15,200 + \$32,000}{\$68,400}$$

$$= \frac{\$72,600}{\$68,400} = 1.06$$

Under normal circumstances, lenders like to see this ratio at 1 to 1 or higher. In Rusty's case it is 1.06 to 1, or about what is normally considered an acceptable level. However, note again that this is a hotel, and the "normal" ratio of 1 to 1 is more applicable to manufacturing and similar companies, and hotels can often effectively operate with a quick ratio of less than 1 to 1.

Accounts Receivable Ratios

Many hotels that have extensive credit sales run into financial and cash flow difficulties because they lose control over their accounts receivable. There are several useful ratios for assessing your receivables.

Accounts Receivable to Charge Sales.   The ratio of accounts receivable to charge sales is usually expressed as a percentage. This percentage indicates the accounts receivable that are uncollected and is calculated as follows:

$$\frac{\text{Accounts receivable}}{\text{Charge sales for year}}$$

For Rusty, assuming that out of total annual sales of $755,800, $320,000 was for charge sales, the figures are

$$\frac{\$\ 15,200}{\$320,000} = 0.0475 \text{ or } 4.75\%$$

This is a very small percent of sales. In this ratio charge sales should be separated from cash sales so that only the charge sales figure is used in the denominator as was demonstrated for Rusty. However, for many hotels it is not practical to keep a separate record of these two types of sale.

Although the trend of this ratio is of some value, some other accounts receivable ratios are often more useful because they provide additional information.

Accounts Receivable Turnover.   The accounts receivable turnover is calculated as followed:

$$\frac{\text{Charge sales for year}}{\text{Accounts receivable}}$$

For Rusty, this is

$$\frac{\$320,000}{\$\ 15,200} = 21 \text{ times}$$

In a typical hotel that allows a 30-day limit for payment of accounts, and that is successful in collecting its accounts close to this time limit, an annual turnover of 12 would be acceptable. If the turnover is higher than 12, this is good. If lower, this is normally not considered good. In Rusty's case, he is considerably higher than 12.

Days Sales in Receivables.   Another way of assessing the receivables situation is to calculate the days sales outstanding in receivables. This requires two steps. First you must calculate the average daily charge sales:

$$\frac{\text{Charge sales for year}}{365}$$

In Rusty's case, the figures are

$$\frac{\$320,000}{365} = \$877 \text{ average daily charge sales}$$

The next step is to calculate the average number of days that the accounts receivable figure represents. The equation for this is:

$$\frac{\text{Accounts receivable}}{\text{Average daily charge sales}}$$

For Rusty, this is

$$\frac{\$15,200}{\$877} = 17.3 \text{ days}$$

Again, this figure for Rusty shows that his average accounts receivable are being collected in about 17 days. This is very acceptable if 30 days is the normal credit limit in Rusty's operation.

When your accounts receivable results indicate that the turnover rate or number of days outstanding is over the desirable limit of, let us say, 30 calendar days, you need to ask and answer the following questions:

- Can you continue to carry these overdue accounts without impairing your cash position?
- Is a 30-day limit normal for your type of hotel?
- Have you been unwise in extending more than 30 days credit to some customers?
- Can anything be done to encourage more prompt payment of outstanding accounts?
- Would an interest charge on overdue accounts speed up collections?
- Has the bad debt loss amount increased because some customers do not pay within the normal 30-day limit?

Aging of Accounts.   One other method of evaluating accounts receivable is to age the accounts. This technique will be demonstrated in Chapter 17.

Inventory Turnover

Another useful balance sheet ratio is inventory turnover. A discussion of this ratio is also deferred until Chapter 17.

Total Liabilities to Total Equity Ratio

Total assets in a hotel can be financed either by liabilities (debt) or equity (shares and retained earnings in an incorporated company, and total capital in a proprietorship or partnership). The total liabilities to total equity ratio (commonly called the debt to equity ratio) illustrates the relationship between these two forms of financing. It is calculated as follows:

$$\frac{\text{Total liabilities}}{\text{Total owners' equity}}$$

In Rusty's case, the figures are

$$\frac{\$555,200}{\$304,100} = 1.83$$

This ratio tells us that for each $1.00 that Rusty has invested, the creditors (or lenders) have invested $1.83. The higher the creditors' ratio, or debt to equity ratio, the higher is the risk to the creditor or lender. In such circumstances, if a hotel needed additional money to expand its operations it might find it difficult to borrow the funds.

The contradiction is that, while your creditors prefer not to have the debt to equity ratio too high, you will often find it more profitable to have it as high as possible. A high debt to equity ratio is known as having high leverage. Using leverage, or trading on the equity, will be discussed later in the chapter.

Number of Times Interest Earned

Another measure that creditors sometimes use to measure the safety of their investment is the number of times interest is earned during a year. The equation for this is:

$$\frac{\text{Profit before interest and income tax}}{\text{Interest expense}}$$

or, for Rusty's

$$\frac{\$132,300}{\$ 51,900} = 2.55 \text{ times}$$

Generally an investor or creditor considers the investment safe if interest is earned two or more times a year because profit before interest could decline significantly without reducing the risk to creditors.

Net Profit to Sales Ratio

The *net profit to sales ratio* (also known as the *profit margin*) is one of the more common measures of the profitability of a hotel. The equation is:

$$\frac{\text{Net profit}}{\text{Sales}} \times 100$$

For Rusty, the figures are

$$\frac{\$40,200}{\$755,800} \times 100 = 5.3\%$$

This means that, out of each $1.00 of sales Rusty has only 5.3 cents net profit. In percentage terms, the profit margin may not be too meaningful because it does not necessarily fully represent the profitability of the business. Consider the following two cases:

	Hotel A	Hotel B
Sales	$100,000	$100,000
Net profit	5,000	10,000
Net profit to sales ratio	5%	10%

With the same sales it seems that Hotel B is better. It is making twice as much net profit in absolute terms as is Hotel A ($10,000 to $5,000). This doubling of net profit is supported by the net profit to sales ratio (10% to 5%).

If these were two similar hotels, or two units of the same hotel chain, the figures would indicate the relative effectiveness of the management of each in controlling costs and generating a satisfactory level of profit. However, in order to determine the true profitability of a hotel you need to relate the net profit to the owners' investment by calculating the return on the owners' equity.

Return on Owners' Equity

The equation for return on owners' equity is:

$$\frac{\text{Net profit}}{\text{Owners' equity}} \times 100$$

In Rusty's case this is

$$\frac{\$40,200}{\$304,100} \times 100 = 13.2\%$$

This ratio shows the effectiveness of the use of owners' funds (or equity). How high should the ratio be? This is a matter of individual opinion. If you could put money either into the bank at a 10 percent interest rate or into a hotel investment at only 8 percent (with more risk involved), the bank might look like the better of the two choices. Many people feel that 15 percent (after tax) is a reasonable return for the owner of a hotel operation (with all its risks) to expect.

If we return now to the Hotel A and Hotel B situation discussed earlier, assume that the investment in A were $40,000 and in B $80,000. The return on investment of each would be:

$$\text{Hotel A } \frac{\$5,000}{\$40,000} \times 100 = 12.5\%$$

$$\text{Hotel B } \frac{\$10,000}{\$80,000} \times 100 = 12.5\%$$

As you can see, despite the wide difference in net profit, and net profit to sales ratio (calculated earlier), there is no difference between the two hotels as far as profitability is concerned. They are both equally as good, yielding a 12.5 percent return on owner's equity. You could therefore conclude that it makes sense to first determine the return on owner equity that is desired, then establish what profit to sales ratio (profit margin) is required to achieve this.

For example, suppose that the amount of money desired next year to provide an adequate return on owner equity in your hotel is $20,000, and that estimated sales next year are $400,000. The required profit as a percentage of sales is

$$\frac{\$20,000}{\$400,000} \times 100 = 5\%$$

By taking this approach you will know what level of sales you have to achieve to have an adequate return on owner equity. Obviously, if anticipated sales do not reach $400,000, then the profit to sales ratio will be less than 5 percent and the profit less than $20,000.

It is unfortunate that most hotel operators do not know what their sales level has to be or relate their required profit to their owner equity in advance. They just wait until the results are out without any advance profit planning.

RATIO COMPARISONS

A ratio by itself has little value. For example, a hotel's profit margin of 4 percent may appear good, but it can be fully judged only after you compare it with some standard, such as what is normal in the hotel industry for that type of hotel. It is only when compared with some base figure or standard that ratios have any meaning.

Use of Standards

One of the standards you could use is an industry average for your type of hotel. That standard of comparison, however, is generally the least valuable of all, because it generally includes all hotels of the same type, and those hotels might be spread over a very broad territory where different operating conditions prevail in different locations. As a result, there may not be a single hotel that is just like the "average" hotel.

Another basis of comparison might be a comparable figure from a direct competitor. However, how do you find out your competitor's ratios? Also, if your figure differs from your competitor's, which one is better?

There may be many reasons to explain why particular ratios differ among competitors.

A better standard is to compare a ratio with previous periods' ratios. How does it compare with the same ratio last month, or the same month last year? What is the trend of the ratio? Is that trend good or bad and how do you know if it is good or bad? One of the problems with comparing ratios with prior periods is that hotels operate in a dynamic environment, and comparing current ratios with previous ratios might be like comparing apples and oranges.

The best comparison of all is to judge any ratio against a standard determined for your own hotel. This standard can consider both internal and external factors about your operation. Internal factors might include such matters as your fixed and variable costs, operating policies, changes in operating methods, and similar matters. External factors can include such matters as the general economic environment and what the competition is doing.

Often these standards can be determined for your hotel by establishing operating plans (including ratio standards) in an annual budget. Budgets can consider not only the past and the present, but also expectations about the future. Because of the importance of budgeting for any hotel, this topic is covered in some depth in Chapter 16.

Ratio Limitations

You should be aware of some of the limitations of ratios.

- Many of the ratio guidelines or rules of thumb given in this (and in previous) chapters have assumed ownership of all assets. If assets (particularly land, building, and furniture and equipment) are leased rather than owned, then comparison with industry guidelines or with competitors' figures can be quite meaningless.
- Even though there are many ratios available, it is not a good idea to try to use all of them all the time. Selectivity is important. You should use only those that are of benefit in evaluating the results of your hotel in relation to its objectives (that is, its plan or budget).
- Ratios should not be an end in themselves. For example, a hotel's objective might be to have the lowest labor cost percent in town. But to achieve this, room rates might have to be raised so high that customers stay away and the hotel does not survive.
- Financial ratios are generally produced from historical accounting information. As a result, some accounting numbers reflect historic costs rather than present values. An example is a building's cost

recorded on the balance sheet at its original purchase price and offset by accumulated depreciation to produce net book value. A ratio based on total assets may show a result that is more than acceptable, but if based on the current replacement cost of those assets would produce a much more realistic ratio that can then be compared with alternative investments.

- Ratios are of value only when two related numbers are compared. For example, the current ratio compares current assets with current liabilities. This is a meaningful comparison. On the other hand, if current assets are compared to owner equity this has little value because there is no direct relationship between the two numbers.
- Finally, ratios cure no problems. Analysis of ratios shows only that problems may exist. Only your analysis of problems and subsequent action can solve them. For example, the trend of the accounts receivable ratio may show that the time it is taking to collect the average account receivable is becoming longer. That is all the ratio shows. Only management analysis of this problem to discover the causes can correct this deteriorating situation.

INCREASING PROFIT LEVELS

There are, of course, limits to the amount of profit that a hotel can achieve without expanding its premises or starting another hotel. For example

- The number of guest rooms limits the number of guests who can be accommodated at any one time.
- Competition controls your room rates to a great extent.
- Quality of service cannot be reduced (to save on labor cost) without losing business from customers who will not accept this reduced quality.

Nevertheless, you can increase profit in two basic ways: increasing sales and/or decreasing expenses, given your hotel's limitations or constraints. Generally, to increase profit it is easier to decrease expenses than to increase sales. The reason is that, to increase sales part of each extra sales dollar has to be spent on certain costs (variable costs) that increase with sales.

For example, to sell more rooms, part of the additional room revenue has to be spent to pay for more housekeeping labor and guest room supplies (such as laundry and soap). This is true even though many of your hotel's costs may be fixed (do not change with a change in sales). Examples of fixed costs are management salary, rent, and interest on borrowed money.

On the other hand, if expenses can be reduced by more effective operating procedures, each dollar of expense saved adds directly to profit. Consider the following situation for Vicky's Vacation Villas—a property whose average monthly sales are $30,000:

Sales		$30,000
Expenses:		
Variable (60% of sales)	$18,000	
Fixed	9,000	27,000
Profit		$ 3,000

Suppose that Vicky could increase sales by 10 percent or $3,000 per month. The new income statement will be

Sales		$33,000
Expenses:		
Variable (60% of sales)	$19,800	
Fixed	9,000	28,800
Profit		$ 4,200

In this case, the sales increase of $3,000 contributed an additional $1,200 to profit because 60 percent of the sales increase (or $1,800) had to be paid out for additional variable costs. The fixed costs, of course, did not change.

As an alternative to increasing profit by $1,200, Vicky may be able to reduce a fixed expense by the same amount with a lot less effort than is required to increase sales by $3,000. If this occurred, the following would result:

Sales		$30,000
Expenses:		
Variable (60% of sales)	$18,000	
Fixed	7,800	25,800
Profit		$ 4,200

In other words, profit has been increased by the full amount of the expense saving. Obviously, if Vicky's sales can be increased and combined with an expense saving, an even better situation would result.

FINANCIAL LEVERAGE

Earlier in this chapter the concept of *financial leverage*, or trading on the equity, was introduced. To illustrate this, consider the case of a new resort that two partners (Stew and Brew) are considering leasing and operating. Their investment would be $250,000.

Stew and Brew have the cash available, but they are considering not using all their own money. Instead, they wish to compare their relative return on equity based on using either all their own money (100 percent equity financing) or using 50 percent equity and borrowing the other 50 percent (debt financing) at a 10 percent interest rate.

Regardless of which financing method they use, sales will be the same, as will all operating costs. With either choice, they will have $50,000 profit before interest and taxes.

There is no interest expense under 100 percent equity financing. With debt financing, interest will have to be paid. However, interest expense is tax deductible.

Assuming a tax rate of 50 percent on taxable profit, Table 11.1 shows the comparative operating results and the return on the partners' equity (ROE) for each of the two options.

In this situation, not only do Stew and Brew make a better ROE under a 50/50 debt/equity ratio (15 percent ROE versus 10 percent), but they still have $125,000 cash that they can invest in a second venture.

Therefore, you could ask, if a 50/50 debt to equity ratio is more profitable than 100 percent equity financing, would not an 80/20 debt to equity ratio be even more profitable? In other words, what would be the

TABLE 11.1

Effect of Leverage on ROE

	Option A	Option B
Investment required	$250,000	$250,000
Equity financing	$250,000	$125,000
Debt financing	0	$125,000 @ 10%
Income before interest and income tax	$ 50,000	$ 50,000
Interest expense	0	(12,500)
Income before income tax	$ 50,000	$ 37,500
Income tax (50%)	(25,000)	(18,750)
Net income	$ 25,000	$ 18,750
Return on equity	$\dfrac{\$ 25,000}{\$250,000} \times 100$	$\dfrac{\$ 18,750}{\$125,000} \times 100$
	=10%	=15%

TABLE 11.2

Effect of High Leverage on ROE

	Option C
Investment required	$250,000
Equity financing	$ 50,000
Debt financing	$200,000 @ 10%
Income before interest and income tax	$ 50,000
Interest expense	(20,000)
Income before income tax	$ 30,000
Income tax (50%)	(15,000)
Net income	$ 15,000
Return on equity	$\dfrac{\$15,000}{\$50,000} \times 100 = 30\%$

ROE if Stew and Brew used only $50,000 of their own money, and borrowed the remaining $200,000 at 10 percent? Table 11.2 shows the result of this more highly levered situation.

Under this third option, the return on initial investment has now increased to 30 percent, and Stew and Brew still have $200,000 cash—enough for four more similar business ventures.

Advantages of Leverage

The advantages of leverage are obvious: the higher the debt to equity ratio, the higher will be the ROE. However, this only holds true if profit (before interest) as a percent of debt is greater than the interest rate to be paid on the debt. For example, if the debt interest rate is 10 percent, the profit before interest must be more than 10 percent of the money borrowed (the debt) for leverage to be profitable.

With high debt (high leverage) there is a risk. If profit declines, the more highly levered the business is the sooner it will be in financial difficulty. In 50/50 financing in Table 11.1 (relatively low leverage), profit before interest and income tax could decline from $50,000 to $12,500 before net profit would be zero. In Table 11.2 (relatively high leverage) profit before interest and income tax could decline from $50,000 to only $20,000.

TWELVE

Cost Management

TYPES OF COST

Most of the cash from hotel sales goes towards expenses — as much as 95 cents or more of each sales dollar may be used to pay for them. Therefore, expense or cost management is important. In order to manage costs, you must understand that there are many different types. If you can recognize the type of cost you are dealing with, then you can make better decisions about it. Some of the more common types of costs are defined in the following sections.

Discretionary Cost

A *discretionary cost* is one that may, or may not, be incurred at the discretion of a particular person — usually the hotel owner or manager. Nonemergency maintenance is an example. Your hotel's exterior could be painted this year, or the painting could be postponed until next year. In either case, sales should not be affected. As the owner, you can use your own discretion — thus it is a discretionary cost.

Relevant Cost

A *relevant cost* is one that makes a difference to a decision. For example, a hotel is considering replacing its front office guest accounting equipment with a computerized system. The relevant costs are the cost of the new equipment (less any trade-in on the old one), the cost of training employees on the new equipment, and maintenance and stationery supply costs for the new machine.

Sunk Cost

A *sunk cost* is a cost already incurred and about which nothing can be done because it cannot affect any future decisions. For example, if the hotel in the preceding paragraph had spent $250 for a consultant to study the relative merits of available front office computer systems, the $250 is a sunk cost. It cannot make any difference to the decision.

Standard Cost

A *standard cost* is what the cost should be for a given volume or level of sales. For example, if it takes half an hour to clean a guest room, and your maids are paid $6 an hour, the standard cost per room occupied is $3.

Fixed Cost

Fixed costs are those that, over the short run (a year or less), do not change or vary with volume. Examples of these are a hotel manager's salary, insurance expense, and interest on a bank loan. Over the long run all these costs can change. But, in the short run they are normally fixed.

Variable Cost

A *variable cost* is one that varies with sales. Very few costs are truly variable, except for cost of sales in your gift shop if you operate one.

Mixed Costs

Many costs do not fit into either the fixed or variable category. Most have an element of fixed expense and an element of variable — and the variable element is not always variable directly to sales. Examples of these *mixed costs* include labor, maintenance, and energy costs. In order to make useful decisions, you must break down these mixed costs into their fixed and variable elements.

BREAKING DOWN MIXED COSTS

A number of different methods can be used to break down mixed costs into their fixed and variable elements. Two will be illustrated:

1. Maximum/minimum method
2. Multipoint graph method

Maximum/minimum Method

To demonstrate the two methods of breakdown of a mixed cost, consider Charlene's Chalets — a resort hotel that has an annual salary and wage (labor) cost of $120,000. Since the cost of labor is closely related to the number of rooms sold, Charlene needs a month-by-month breakdown of the sales for each month and the related wage cost for each month. (This information could be broken down by week, but there should be sufficient accuracy for all practical purposes with a monthly analysis). The sales and labor cost monthly breakdown is:

	Sales	Labor
January (minimum)	$ 5,000	$ 7,200
February	9,000	8,000
March	14,000	9,000
April	13,000	10,700
May	13,000	12,300
June	15,000	12,000
July	21,000	13,000
August (maximum)	21,000	13,200
September	15,000	11,900
October	10,000	7,600
November	10,000	7,600
December	7,000	7,500
Totals	$153,000	$120,000

Note that the month of January has the word "minimum" alongside it. In January, sales and wage cost were at their lowest for the year. In contrast, August was the "maximum" month.

Three Steps.   There are three steps in the *maximum/minimum* method:
   Step 1: Deduct the minimum from the maximum figures for both wages and sales:

	Sales	Labor
August (maximum)	$21,000	$13,200
January (minimum)	5,000	7,200
	$16,000	$ 6,000

   Step 2: Divide the wage difference by the sales difference to get the variable cost per dollar of sales:

$$\frac{\$\ 6,000}{\$16,000} = \$0.375 \text{ variable cost per dollar of sales}$$

Step 3: Use the answer to Step 2 to calculate the fixed cost element:

August total wages	$13,200
Less variable costs $21,000 × $0.375	7,875
Fixed wage cost	$ 5,325

Note that in Step 3 we used the maximum month (August) to calculate Charlene's fixed cost. We could equally well have used January (the minimum month) with no change in the result:

Step 3:

January total wages	$7,200
Less variable costs $5,000 × $0.375	1,875
Fixed wage cost	$5,325

Charlene's fixed labor cost is $5,325 a month or:

$$12 \times \$5,325 = \$63,900 \text{ a year}$$

(or $64,000 to the nearest thousand)

We can now break down Charlene's total annual labor cost into its fixed and variable elements:

Total annual wages	$120,000
Fixed cost	64,000
Variable cost	$56,000

Using a Two-point Graph. The calculation of the monthly fixed cost figure has been illustrated arithmetically. The maximum/minimum figures could equally as well have been plotted on a graph, as illustrated in Figure 12.1.

In this illustration, the maximum figure is first plotted (the upper right-hand point) and then the minimum figure is plotted (the lower left-hand point) and the two points are joined by a solid line. The solid line is then continued by a dotted line down and to the left and the fixed cost is where the dotted line intersects the vertical axis. If the graph is accurately drawn, the same monthly fixed wage cost figure of approximately $5,300 is arrived at as calculated arithmetically earlier.

The maximum/minimum method is quick and simple. It uses only two sets of figures. Unfortunately, either one or both of these sets of figures may not be typical of the relationship between sales and labor costs for the

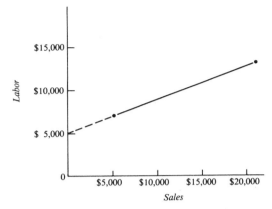

Figure 12.1 Maximum/minimum graph.

year (for example, a one-time wage bonus may have been paid during one of the months selected), thus distorting the figures. As long as you are aware of them, these distortions can be eliminated by adjusting the raw figures.

Another way to improve the maximum/minimum method and remove possible distortions in individual monthly figures is to plot the cost and sales figures for each of the twelve months (or however many periods there are involved) on a multipoint graph.

Multipoint Graph Method

Figure 12.2 illustrates a *multipoint graph* for Charlene's sales and labor cost for each of the twelve months. Sales and costs were taken from the figures listed earlier. The graph illustrated is for two variables (sales and labor). In this case labor is given the name *dependent variable* and is plotted on the vertical axis. Labor is dependent on sales—it varies with sales. Sales, therefore, are the *independent variable*. The independent variable is plotted on the horizontal axis.

Note that, in drawing this graph the point where the vertical and horizontal axes meet should be given a reading of zero. The figures along each axis should then be plotted to scale from zero.

After plotting each of the twelve points, Charlene has what is known as a scatter graph—a series of points scattered around a line that has been drawn through them. A straight line must be drawn.

There is no limit to how many straight lines could be drawn through the points. The line Charlene wants is the one that, to her eye, seems to fit

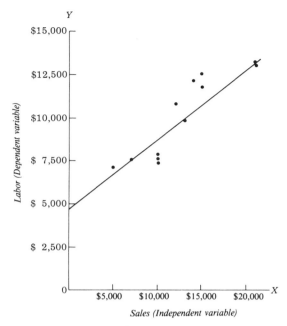

Figure 12.2   Multipoint graph.

best. Each hotel operator doing this exercise would probably view the line in a slightly different position, but most people with a reasonably good eye would come up with a line that is close enough for all practical purposes.

The line should be drawn so that it is continued to the left until it intersects the vertical axis (the dependent variable). The intersect point reading is the fixed cost (wages in this case). Note that, in Figure 12.2, the fixed cost reading is $5,000 (approximately). This is Charlene's monthly cost. Converted to an annual cost it is:

$$\$5,000 \times 12 = \$60,000$$

The total annual wage cost is then broken down as follows:

Total wages	$120,000
Less fixed	60,000
Variable	$60,000

Difference in Methods

With the maximum/minimum method, Charlene's total annual fixed cost was $64,000. With the multipoint graph method it is $60,000—a difference of $4,000. This difference is due primarily to the fact that with the maximum/minimum method there is a higher risk of inaccuracy because only two of the twelve months were used and, as was mentioned earlier, these two months may not be typical of the entire year. For this reason, the multipoint graph is generally more accurate.

Other Mixed Costs

This chapter has attempted to show how one type of mixed cost can be broken down into its fixed and variable elements using two different methods. Once a method has been selected, you should apply it to each of the mixed costs that you have so that each one can be broken down into its two elements.

Alternatively, a simpler method is to add all mixed costs together before separating them in total into their fixed and variable elements. This method has the advantage of considerably reducing the number of calculations that you have to make. As a result, it may give a less accurate breakdown of the fixed and variable costs. Nevertheless, the figures arrived at can probably still be used for most decisions.

Let us look at some of the ways in which a breakdown of costs into their fixed and variable elements helps in decision making.

CAN WE SELL BELOW COST?

The obvious answer to the question "Can we sell below cost?" is "Not unless you want to go broke." But before you can intelligently answer that question, you should first ask: "Which cost?". If the answer is: "Below total cost but above variable cost" then, yes, indeed, you can sell below total cost under certain circumstances.

Consider the situation of Charlene's Chalets. She rents the land on which the chalets sit for $80,000 a year and has other fixed costs (including management salaries, insurance, and furniture and equipment depreciation) of $66,000 a year. This is a total fixed cost of $146,000 or:

$$\frac{\$146,000}{365} = \$400 \text{ a day}$$

Since there are 20 chalets, the daily fixed costs per chalet are $20. During the summer season each chalet rents for $50 a day, and variable costs per unit rented out are $15. During the winter season Charlene is approached by a conference group that wishes to rent all 20 chalets for a week during which she has no other reservations. The conference group is prepared to pay only $30 per night per chalet. Normally, Charlene would not cut her rates so low. If she accepts the business, the income statement would look like this per night for those 20 units:

Sales 20 × $30.00	$600
Variable costs 20 × $15	(300)
Fixed costs	(400)
Net loss	($100)

For the week, Charlene's "loss" will be $700. The loss does not look good, but what is the loss if Charlene does not accept this group? It will be $2,800 ($400 × 7), because the fixed costs for that week for those chalets will still have to be met. But, by selling below total cost per day of $700 ($400 fixed and $300 variable), Charlene's loss is less than it would otherwise be.

In the short run, as long as sales are greater than variable costs, it pays to accept business because the excess of sales over variable costs will contribute to (help pay for) the fixed costs which are there in any case. We can arrange Charlene's daily income statement to illustrate this concept of contribution margin as follows:

Sales	$600
Variable costs	(300)
Contribution margin	$300
Fixed costs	(400)
Net loss	($100)

SHOULD WE CLOSE IN THE OFF SEASON?

One of the uses of a breakdown of fixed and variable costs is to decide whether or not to close in the off season. Consider the case of Rosa's Resort that has the following annual income statement:

Sales	$150,000
Expenses	130,000
Net profit	$ 20,000

Rosa decided to do an analysis of her sales and costs by month, and found that for ten months she was making money and for two months had a loss. The following summarizes her findings:

	10 months	2 months	Total
Revenue	$135,000	$15,000	$150,000
Variable costs	$ 25,000	$ 1,000	$ 26,000
Fixed costs	80,000	24,000	104,000
Total costs	$105,000	$25,000	$130,000
Net income	$ 30,000	($10,000)	$ 20,000

Rosa's analysis seems to indicate that she should close to eliminate the $10,000 loss during the two-month loss period. But if she does, the fixed costs for the two months ($24,000) will have to be paid out of the ten months' profits, and $30,000 (10 months' net profit) less the two months' fixed costs of $24,000 will reduce her annual net profit to $6,000 from its present $20,000. If she does not want a reduction in annual net profit, she should not close.

There might be other factors in such a situation that Rosa needs ɩo consider and that would reinforce the decision to stay open. For example, there could be sizeable additional close-down and start-up costs that would have to be included in the calculation of the cost of closing.

Also, would key employees return after an extended vacation? Is there a large enough pool of skilled labor available and willing to work on a seasonal basis only? Would there be recurring training time (and costs) at the start of each new season? These are some of the questions that would have to be answered before any final decision to close was made.

WHICH BUSINESS TO BUY?

Just as a business owner/manager has to make choices between alternatives on a day-to-day basis, so too does an entrepreneur going into the hotel business or expanding an existing hotel frequently have to choose between alternatives. Let us look at one such situation, again involving fixed and variable costs.

Ernie Entrepreneur has an opportunity to take over one of two similar existing hotels: Dan's or Claudia's. The two hotels are close to each other in location, have the same type of clientele and size of operation, and the asking price is the same for each. Each is presently doing $1,000,000 a year in sales, and each has a net profit of $100,000 a year. With only this information, it is difficult for Ernie to make a decision as to which would be the more profitable investment. But a cost analysis as shown in Table 12.1 illustrates there are differences between the two hotels.

TABLE 12.1

Statements Showing Differences in Cost Structure

	Dan's		Claudia's	
Revenue	$1,000,000	100.0%	$1,000,000	100.0%
Variable costs	$ 500,000	50.0%	$ 300,000	30.0%
Fixed costs	400,000	40.0%	600,000	60.0%
Total costs	$ 900,000	90.0%	$ 900,000	90.0%
Net income	$ 100,000	10.0%	$ 100,000	10.0%

Structure of Costs

Although the sales and net profit are the same for each hotel, the structure of their costs is different, and this will affect the decision about which one could be more profitable.

Ernie is optimistic about the future. He feels that without any change in fixed costs he can increase annual sales in either business by 10 percent. What effect will this have on the net profit of Dan's versus Claudia's? The net profit for each of the two hotels will not increase by the same amount. Dan's variable cost is 50 percent. This means that, out of each dollar of additional sales, it will have variable expenses of $0.50 and a net profit of $0.50 (fixed costs do not change). Claudia's has variable costs of 30 percent (or $0.30 out of each sales dollar) leaving a net profit of $0.70 from each additional sales dollar (again, fixed costs do not change).

Assuming a 10 percent increase in sales and no new fixed costs, the income statements of the two hotels have been recalculated in Table 12.2. Note that Dan's net profit has gone up by $50,000 (to $150,000), but Claudia's has gone up by $70,000 (to $170,000). In this situation, Claudia's would be the better investment.

TABLE 12.2

Effect of Increased Revenue on Costs and Net Income

	Dan's		Claudia's	
Revenue	$1,100,000	100.0%	$1,100,000	100.0%
Variable costs	$ 550,000	50.0%	$ 330,000	30.0%
Fixed costs	400,000	36.4%	600,000	54.5%
Total costs	$ 950,000	86.4%	$ 930,000	84.5%
Net income	$ 150,000	13.6%	$ 170,000	15.5%

High Operating Leverage

A business that has high fixed costs relative to variable costs is said to have *high operating leverage*. Compared to Dan, Claudia has high operating leverage. From a profit point of view, Claudia will do better in times of rising sales than will Dan with *low operating leverage* (low fixed costs relative to variable costs). A business with low fixed costs, however, will be better off when sales start to decline. Table 12.3 illustrates the new situation for Dan's and Claudia's given the assumption that each is going to have a decline in sales of 10 percent from the present $1,000,000 level and that there will be no change in fixed costs.

Table 12.3 shows that with declining sales, Dan's net profit will be higher than Claudia's. In fact, if sales decline far enough, Claudia will be in financial difficulty long before Dan. If the *break-even point* were calculated (the break-even point is that level of sales at which there will be neither a profit nor a loss), Dan's sales could go down to $800,000, while Claudia would be in difficulty at $857,000. This is illustrated in Table 12.4.

TABLE 12.3

Effect of Decreased Revenue on Costs and Net Income

	Dan's		Claudia's	
Revenue	$ 900,000	100.0%	$ 900,000	100.0%
Variable costs	$ 450,000	50.0%	$ 270,000	30.0%
Fixed costs	400,000	44.4%	600,000	66.7%
Total costs	$ 850,000	94.4%	$ 870,000	96.7%
Net income	$ 50,000	5.6%	$ 30,000	3.3%

TABLE 12.4

Break-even Revenue Level Depends on Cost Structure

	Dan's		Claudia's	
Revenue	$ 800,000	100.0%	$ 857,000	100.0%
Variable costs	$ 400,000	50.0%	$ 257,000	30.0%
Fixed costs	400,000	50.0%	600,000	70.0%
Total costs	$ 800,000	100.0%	$ 857,000	100.0%
Net income	0	0	0	0

You could determine the break-even level of sales by trial and error (although this would be rather tedious). However, there is a formula available for quick calculation of this level. The formula, and a more in-depth discussion of fixed and variable costs and how an awareness of them can be of great value in many types of decision, will be covered in Chapter 13.

PAYING A FIXED OR A VARIABLE LEASE

Another situation where fixed and variable cost knowledge can be useful is in comparing the alternative of a fixed lease cost versus a lease based on a variable percent of sales. For example, consider the case of Stella's—a hotel that has an opportunity to pay a fixed rent for its premises of $5,000 a month ($60,000 a year) or a variable rent of 6 percent of its revenue. What Stella needs to first determine is the break-even point of sales at which the fixed rental payment for a year would be identical to the variable rent. The equation for calculating this is:

$$\text{Annual break-even revenue} = \frac{\text{Fixed annual lease cost}}{\text{Variable lease percent}}$$

and inserting the figures we can determine Stella's sales level as follows:

$$\frac{\$60,000}{6\%} = \$1,000,000$$

In other words, at $1,000,000 of sales it would make no difference whether Stella paid a fixed rent of $60,000 or a variable rent of 6 percent of sales. At this level of sales she would be indifferent. For this reason, the break-even revenue point is sometimes referred to as the indifference point.

If Stella expected sales to exceed $1,000,000, she would select a fixed rental arrangement. If sales were expected to be below $1,000,000, then she would be better off selecting the percent of sales arrangement.

THIRTEEN

Using Break-Even Analysis

QUESTIONS BREAK-EVEN ANALYSIS CAN ANSWER

A great many questions can be asked by the owner of a hotel, such as:

- At what level of sales will I start losing money—that is, what is my break-even sales level?
- What will my net profit be at a certain level of sales?
- What is the extra sales revenue I need to cover the cost of additional advertising and still give me the profit I want?
- By how much must sales be increased to cover the cost of a wage increase and still give the profit to sales ratio I want?

These and many other questions cannot be easily answered from the traditional income statement. However, if you break down your operating costs into their fixed and variable elements as demonstrated in Chapter 12, you can then use this information in a technique known as *break-even analysis*. However, before you use break-even analysis, you must clearly understand its assumptions and limitations.

Assumptions and Limitations

The following are the assumptions and limitations of break-even analysis:

- It assumes that the costs associated with the present level of sales can be fairly accurately broken down into their fixed and variable elements (see Chapter 12).
- It assumes that fixed costs will remain fixed during the period affected by the decision being made.
- It assumes that variable costs vary directly with sales during the period affected by the decision being made.

- It is limited to situations where economic and other conditions are assumed to be relatively stable. In highly inflationary times, for example, when it is difficult to predict sale and/or cost prices more than a few weeks ahead, it would be risky to use break-even analysis for decisions that affect the distant future.
- Finally, break-even analysis is only a guide to decision making. The break-even approach might indicate a certain decision, but other factors (such as employee or customer relations) may dictate a decision that contradicts the break-even analysis.

Contribution Margin Concept

In this chapter we shall use the following annual income statement information for Heidi's Hideaway, a 30-room hotel:

Income Statement

Sales		$306,000
Variable costs	$113,000	
Fixed costs	181,000	294,000
Profit		$12,000

In break-even analysis, the income statement is sometimes presented in the form of a contribution statement. Heidi's contribution statement is:

Contribution Statement

Sales	$306,000
Variable costs	113,000
Contribution to fixed costs	$193,000
Fixed costs	181,000
Profit	$ 12,000

The contribution to the fixed cost figure (in Heidi's case $193,000) is commonly referred to as the *contribution margin* and is simply sales less variable expenses. Note that presenting the fixed and variable costs in the form of a contribution statement does not change the profit figure.

From the above information we can calculate Heidi's variable cost as a percent of sales:

$$\frac{\$113,000}{\$306,000} \times 100 = 37\%$$

Therefore, because total sales are given the value of 100 percent, the contribution margin percent is

$$100\% - 37\% = 63\% \text{ or } 0.63$$

Alternatively, contribution margin percent can be calculated directly by dividing the contribution margin by the sales:

$$\frac{\$193,000}{\$306,000} \times 100 = 63\% \text{ or } 0.63$$

Break-Even Equation

The easiest way to use break-even analysis is to use the following equation:

$$\text{Sales level} = \frac{\text{Fixed costs} + \text{Profit desired}}{\text{Contribution margin}}$$

USING THE BREAK-EVEN EQUATION

Let us use the equation to answer some questions for Heidi.

At What Sales Level Will I Break Even?

Suppose Heidi wants to know the level of sales at which she will make neither a profit or a loss, that is, the break-even point. The solution is:

$$\text{Sales level} = \frac{\$181,000 + 0}{0.63}$$

$$= \$287,302, \text{ rounded to } \$287,000$$

(It makes sense to round figures when using the equation because the breakdown of fixed and variable costs may not be accurate in the first place and, in the situation just illustrated, an answer to the closest $1,000 would normally be quite acceptable.)

At What Sales Level Will I Make a Desired Profit?

Suppose Heidi wanted to know the sales level required to provide her with a profit of $39,000 (rather than the present profit of $12,000). She can use the same equation for the answer, substituting $39,000 for the profit desired:

$$\text{Sales level} = \frac{\$181{,}000 + \$39{,}000}{0.63}$$

$$= \frac{\$220{,}000}{0.63}$$

$$= \$349{,}206, \text{ rounded to } \$349{,}000$$

How Much Must Sales Increase to Cover a New Fixed Cost?

Normally, if fixed costs increase and no change is made in room rates, Heidi would expect profits to decline by the amount of the additional fixed cost. She could then ask, by how much must sales be increased to compensate for a fixed cost increase and not have a reduction in profit?

A simple answer would be that sales have to go up by the same amount as the fixed cost increase. But this is not correct, because to increase sales (with no increase in room rates) you have to sell more rooms, and if you sell more your variable costs (housekeeping and related costs) are going to increase.

By trial and error you could arrive at a solution, but the break-even equation will quickly solve this kind of question. You simply add the new fixed cost to the old fixed cost and add the profit desired to the numerator of the equation and divide—as before—by the contribution margin.

For example, suppose Heidi wished to spend $5,000 more on advertising a year. How much more in sales must she have (assuming no room rate changes) to maintain her present profit level of $12,000?

$$\text{Sales level} = \frac{\$181{,}000 + \$5{,}000 + \$12{,}000}{0.63}$$

$$= \frac{\$198{,}000}{0.63}$$

$$= \$314{,}286, \text{ rounded to } \$314{,}000$$

Heidi can easily prove the correctness of the result (as she can with any solution to a problem using the break-even equation) as follows:

Sales		$314,000
Variable costs		
37% × $314,000 = $116,000		
Fixed costs	186,000	302,000
Profit		$ 12,000

The solution tells Heidi that sales must be $314,000—an increase of $8,000 over the present sales level of $306,000—to pay for the $5,000 advertising cost.

What Additional Sales Do I Need to Cover a Change in Variable Expenses?

You saw in the preceding section how a change in fixed costs can be easily handled in the equation. How do we handle a change in variable costs? A change in the variable costs will change the contribution margin percent. Therefore, the contribution margin must be recalculated by first calculating the new variable cost percent.

You will recall that Heidi's present variable cost of 37 percent was calculated by dividing total variable costs by total sales and multiplying by 100. Let us assume an increase in wages is to be put into effect that will increase Heidi's variable costs as a percentage of sales from 37 percent to 39 percent. The new contribution margin percent will therefore be:

$$100\% - 39\% = 61\% \text{ or } 0.61$$

and Heidi can now use 0.61 as the denominator in the equation.

What About Multiple Changes in the Variables?

So far, we have considered making only one change at a time. Multiple changes can be handled without difficulty. For example, assume the $5,000 is to be spent on advertising, that the employees will be given the wage increase (changing the contribution margin to 0.61), and that the profit is to be increased from $12,000 to $20,000. What will Heidi's new sales level have to be? The answer is

$$\frac{\$181,000 + \$5,000 + \$20,000}{0.61}$$

$$= \frac{\$206,000}{0.61}$$

$$= \$337,705 \text{ or } \$338,000$$

and to prove this:

Sales		$338,000
Variable costs		
39% × $338,000	$132,000	
Fixed costs	186,000	318,000
Profit		$ 20,000

How Can I Convert the Sales Level Directly into Units?

In the equation used so far the denominator has been

$$100\% - \text{Variable costs as a percent of sales}$$

If we use the break-even equation and express the contribution margin in percentages (which we have been doing), then our sales level will be expressed in sales dollars. If we use the equation and express the contribution margin in dollars, we shall have a sales level expressed in units (rooms to be sold). Let us test this.

If Heidi's average room rate is $40 and the variable costs total $15.60 (39% × $40) per room sold, the contribution margin is $24.40 per room sold. Assuming fixed costs are $186,000 (including the $5,000 additional for advertising) and that $20,000 profit is desired, the number of rooms to be sold will have to be:

$$\text{Sales level} = \frac{\$186,000 + \$20,000}{\$40.00 - \$15.60}$$

$$= \frac{\$206,000}{\$24.40}$$

$$= 8,443 \text{ rooms}$$

This can again be proved as follows:

Sales 8,443 × $40,000 =		$337,700
Variable costs 8,443 × $15.60 =	$131,700	
Fixed costs	186,000	317,700
Profit		$ 20,000

The reason Heidi might want the solution in rooms to be sold is that it might be useful to have the sales level converted to an occupancy percent, and this can be calculated quickly from the sales level in rooms to be sold.

For example, from information given earlier about Heidi's present level of business ($306,000 annual sales), and knowing that the average rate is $40, we know that Heidi is presently selling 7,650 ($306,000 divided by $40) rooms per year in her 30-room hotel. In terms of an annual occupancy this is

$$\frac{7,650}{30 \times 365} \times 100 = \frac{7,650}{10,950} \times 100 = 69.9\% \text{ (rounded to 70\%)}$$

To cover the proposed changes in costs, we know that Heidi must now sell 8,443 rooms. Converted to an occupancy percentage this is

$$\frac{8,443}{10,950} \times 100 = 77\%$$

This represents 7 percent more rooms per night on average or approximately two more rooms per night (7% × 30 rooms).

If We Change Room Rates, How Will This Affect Rooms Sold?

The contribution margin expressed in dollars is also useful in answering questions concerning a change in room rates. For example, assuming Heidi's fixed costs are $186,000, profit required is $20,000, and variable costs are $15.60 per room sold, what will her occupancy have to be to offset a 10-percent reduction in room rates? In other words, the new average rate will be $36 instead of $40.

$$\text{Sales level (in rooms)} = \frac{\$186,000 + \$20,000}{\$36,000 - \$15.60}$$

$$= \frac{\$206,000}{\$20.40} = 10,098 \text{ rooms}$$

In terms of an occupancy percent this is:

$$\frac{10,098}{10,950} \times 100 = 92\%$$

Thus, to compensate for the 10-percent reduction in room rates, Heidi's occupancy will have to increase from 77 percent to 92 percent — an increase of 15 percentage points. On average, Heidi will have to sell 4.5 more rooms per night (15% × 30 rooms).

What About a New Investment?

The break-even equation has been used in this chapter to illustrate how historical information from accounting records can be used to make decisions about the future. But break-even analysis is equally useful when there is no past accounting information to help you. For example, in a proposed new hotel, or expansion of an existing one, you simply make intelligent estimates of what the fixed and variable costs are likely to be and then project potential profits from those figures.

INCOME TAX AND BREAK EVEN

To this point in the discussion of break-even analysis the effect of income taxes has been ignored. Obviously, at the break-even level of sales there are no tax implications because there is no profit. Also, with a proprietorship or partnership the organization pays no income taxes. Any profits are deemed to be paid out to the owner(s), who then pay income tax at personal tax rates.

An incorporated company that has a taxable net income must, however, consider the tax implications when using break-even analysis for decisions. Unfortunately, income tax is neither a fixed cost nor a variable cost dependent on sales. Taxes vary with income before tax and thus require special treatment in break-even analysis. This necessitates adjusting the break-even equation, substituting the term *profit desired* with *profit before tax*.

Consider the figures used earlier in this chapter where Heidi's profit desired was $39,000 and the sales required to achieve this were calculated to be $349,000. Assume now that Heidi's Hideaway is in a 45-percent tax bracket. What sales are required to achieve a $39,000 *after-tax* profit? The $39,000 can be converted to a before-tax figure as follows:

$$\text{Profit before tax} = \frac{\text{After-tax profit}}{1 - \text{Tax rate}}$$

and substituting our figures:

$$= \frac{\$39,000}{1 - 0.45}$$

$$= \frac{\$39,000}{0.55}$$

$$= \$70,909 \text{ (rounded to } \$71,000)$$

This can be proved:

Before-tax profit	$71,000
Income tax 45%	32,000
After-tax profit	$39,000

Thus, if Heidi, with fixed costs of $181,000 and a contribution margin of 0.63, wanted a before-tax profit of $71,000, the sales would have to be

$$\frac{\$181,000 + \$71,000}{0.63} = \frac{\$252,000}{0.63} = \$400,000$$

rather than the $349,000 calculated earlier when income tax was ignored. This can be proved as follows:

Sales		$400,000
Variable costs 37% $\times$ $400,000 = $148,000		
Fixed costs	181,000	329,000
Before-tax profit		$ 71,000
Tax 45%		32,000
After-tax profit		$ 39,000

FOURTEEN

Establishing Room Rates

The way in which you establish room rates in your hotel is going to dictate, to a degree, whether you will achieve your financial goals. If your rates are too high you might drive away customers who do not believe they are obtaining value for money. If your rates are too low, you will not be maximizing your sales potential. In either event, your profits will be lower than they should be.

PRICING METHODS

A number of different methods, each with its pros and cons, are used by hotel operators to establish rates.

Intuitive Method

The intuitive method requires no real knowledge of the business (costs, profits, room rates, competition, the market). The operator just assumes that the rates established are the right ones. This method has no advantages. Its main disadvantage is that the rates charged are unrelated to profits.

Trial-and-error Method

With the trial-and-error method, rates are changed up and down to see what effect they have on sales and profits. When profit is apparently maximized, rates are established at that level. However, this method ignores the fact that there are many other factors (such as general economic conditions and the competition) in addition to room rates that affect sales and profits, and what appears to be the optimum pricing level may later be affected by these other factors. This method can also be confusing to customers during the rate-testing period.

Rate-cutting Method

Rate-cutting occurs when prices are reduced below those of the competition. This can be a risky method if it ignores costs, because if variable costs are higher than rates then profits will be eroded. To use this method, the reduction in rates must be more than compensated for by selling additional rooms. If the extra business gained is simply taken away from your competitors, then the competitors will be forced to reduce their rates also and a rate war may result.

High Rate Method

Another method is to deliberately charge more than competitors, then emphasize in advertising such factors as quality that many customers equate with price. If this strategy is not used carefully, however, it can encourage customers to move elsewhere when they realize that a high room rate and high quality are not synonymous.

Competitive Method

Competitive pricing means matching rates to those of the competition and then differentiating in such areas as location, atmosphere, and other non-price factors. When there is one dominant hotel in the market that generally takes the lead in establishing rates, with its close competitors matching increases and decreases, this method is then referred to as the follow-the-leader method.

Competitive pricing tends to ensure there is no rate cutting and resulting reduction in profits. In other words, there is market price stability. This may be a useful method in the short run. However, if competitive pricing is used without knowledge of the differences in such matters as product and costs that exist between one hotel and another, then this method can be risky.

Rule-of-thumb Method

One of the methods developed many years ago for setting an appropriate room rate is the so-called $1 per $1,000 approach. Since the greatest cost in hotel construction is the investment in building (from 60–70 percent of total investment), it was argued that there should be a direct relationship between the cost of the building and the room rate to be charged. From this developed the rule of thumb that for each $1,000 in building cost $1 of room rate should be charged in order for the investment to be profitable. In other words, if a 100-room hotel had a building cost of $4,000,000, its average cost of construction is

$$\frac{\$4,000,000}{100} = \$40,000 \text{ per room}$$

Then, for each $1,000 of construction cost per room, there should be $1 of room rate. The average room rate would then be

$$\frac{\$40,000}{\$ 1,000} = 40 \times \$1 = \$40.00$$

This rule of thumb worked under certain circumstances and assumptions. Some of these assumptions were that the hotel was a relatively large one (several hundred rooms), that there was sufficient rent from shops and stores in the building to pay for interest and real estate taxes, that other departments (food, beverages, and so on) were contributing a profit to the overall hotel operation, and that the average year-round occupancy was at least 70 percent.

Consider, however, the following two small hotel operations: Hotel A, which has no public facilities, and Hotel B, with more spacious lobbies and a dining-room/coffee shop and banquet rooms.

	Hotel A	Hotel B
Building cost	$2,000,000	$2,600,000
Number of rooms	50	50
Cost per room	$40,000	$52,000
Room rate at $1 per $1,000	$40	$52

If the $1 per $1,000 rule of thumb were used, Hotel B would find itself at a distinct disadvantage to Hotel A, assuming the two properties were in the same competitive market.

The $1 per $1,000 rule also leaves room rates tied to historical construction costs and ignores current costs, including current financing costs.

USING THE RIGHT METHOD

Many of the pricing methods briefly reviewed above are commonly used because hotel operators understand them and find them easy to implement. Unfortunately, if your hotel is not operating as efficiently as it should, the use of one of these methods simply tends to perpetuate the situation, and sales and profit will not be maximized.

Hotel owners or managers who use these methods are not fully in control of their operations and are probably failing to use their income statements and other financial accounting information to guide them in improving their operating results.

Pricing your rooms properly is a marketing tool that you can effectively use to improve profitability. The dilemma is often a matter of finding the balance between rates and profits. In other words, rates should only be established after considering the effect they have on profits. For example, you can lower your rates to attract more customers, but if those rates are reduced to the point that they do not cover the costs of serving those extra guests, profits will decline rather than increase.

Long-run or Strategic Pricing

Over the long run, price is determined in the marketplace as a result of supply and demand. When rates are established to compete in that marketplace, they must be set with your hotel's overall long-term financial objectives in mind. A typical objective could be any one of the following: to maximize sales revenue, to maximize return on owners' investment, to maximize profitability, to maximize business growth (in a new hotel), or to maintain or increase share of market (for an established hotel).

A clearly thought-out pricing strategy will stem from the objective or objectives of your business, as well as recognize that these objectives may change over the long run.

TACTICAL PRICING

As well as a long-run pricing strategy, you also need short-run or tactical pricing policies to take advantage of situations that arise from day to day. Some of these situations might be

- Reacting to short-run changes in rates made by competitors.
- Adjusting rates because of a new competitor.
- Knowing what discount to offer to accommodate group business while still making a profit.
- Knowing how much to increase rates to compensate for an increase in costs.
- Knowing how much rate increases can be justified to compensate for renovations made to your premises.
- Adjusting rates to reach a new market segment.
- Knowing how to discount rates in the off-season to attract business.
- Offering special promotional rates.

In order to use tactical pricing effectively, you must keep four factors in mind. These factors are *elasticity of demand, cost structure*, the *competition*, and *product differentiation.*

Elasticity of Demand

Elasticity of demand has to do with the responsiveness of demand for a product when rates are changed. When there is a large change in demand resulting from a small change in rates, this is referred to as elastic demand. When there is a small change in demand following a large change in rates, this is referred to as inelastic demand.

Perhaps the easiest way to test whether demand is elastic or inelastic in your hotel is to note what happens to total sales when rates are changed. If demand is elastic, a decline in rate will result in an increase in total sales because, even though a lower rate is received per room sold, enough additional rooms are now being sold to more than compensate for the lower rate.

Elastic Demand.   For example, assume that your hotel's average room rate is $50.00 and that an average of 1,000 rooms per week are sold. Total revenue per week is $50,000. If the average rate is reduced by 5 percent to $47.50, and average weekly occupancy goes up 10 percent to 1,100, total revenue will now be 1,100 × $47.50 or $52,250, which is $2,250 more than before. Demand is elastic. A generalization is that, if demand is elastic, a change in rate will cause total revenue to change in the opposite direction.

Inelastic Demand.   If demand is inelastic, a rate decline will cause total revenue to fall. The small increase in sales that occurs will not be sufficient to offset the decline in average rate. Again, you can generalize and say that, if demand is inelastic, a change in rate will cause total sales to change in the same direction.

In other words, when demand is inelastic, a rate change will have little or no effect on the number of rooms sold, but it will affect total revenue. If your room rates are increased, total revenue will increase, and if rates are decreased, total revenue will decrease. Therefore, when demand is inelastic, there is little value in cutting room rates because your revenue and net profit will decline.

Availability of Substitutes.   One of the factors that influences elasticity of demand is the availability of substitutes. Generally, hotels that charge the highest rates are able to do so because there is little substitution possible by customers. An elite hotel with little competition can charge higher rates

its customers expect to pay higher rates, can afford to do so, and
.ily would not move to a lower-priced, less luxurious hotel if room
were increased. Demand is inelastic.

On the other hand, a hotel that is one of many in a resort catering to
.e family tourist trade that wants budget-priced rooms would probably
lose considerable business if it raised its room rates out of line with its
competitors. Its trade is very elastic. Its rate-conscious customers will
simply take their business to another hotel. That is to say, one hotel can
easily be substituted for another by customers.

In general, you can therefore say that, the lower the income of a hotel's
customers, the more elastic is their demand and vice versa.

Customers' Habits.   Closely related to income levels are the habits of a
hotel's customers. The more habitual the customers are, the less likely they
are to resist some upward change in rates, because customers tend to have
"brand" loyalties to hotels just as they have with other products they buy.

Nevertheless, if your hotel counts on repeat business you must be very
conscious of the effect that room rate changes may have on that loyalty.
For example, loyalty and demand for a product (or a particular hotel) tend
to be more elastic the longer the time period under consideration. Even
though customers are creatures of habit and do develop loyalties, those
habits and loyalties can change over time.

You must therefore be aware of the elasticity of demand of the market
in which you operate and how loyal your customers are. In other words,
you must have a market-oriented approach to pricing. This market orientation is particularly important in short-run decision making such as in
promoting special room rates during slow periods. These reduced rates are
particularly appropriate where demand is highly elastic.

Cost Structure

The specific cost structure of your hotel is also a major factor influencing
pricing decisions. Cost structure in this context means the break-down of
costs into fixed and variable ones. Fixed costs are those that normally do
not change in the short run, such as a manager's salary or insurance
expense. Variable costs (such as housekeeping costs) are those that increase
or decrease depending on occupancies.

If your hotel has high fixed costs relative to variable costs, the less
stable your profits are likely to be as occupancy increases or decreases. In
such a situation, having the right rates for the market becomes increasingly
important. In the short run, any rate in excess of the variable costs will
produce a contribution to fixed costs and profit, and the lower the variable
costs the wider is the range of possible rates.

For example, if a hotel's variable costs to sell an extra room are $10, and that room normally sells for $50, any price between $10 and $50 will contribute to fixed costs and net profit.

Note that this concept of variable or marginal costing is only valid in the short run. Over the long run rates must be established so that all fixed and variable costs are covered in order to produce a long-run net profit.

The Competition

Your hotel's competitive situation is critical in pricing. Very few hotels are in a monopolistic situation, although some may be, such as a hotel with an exclusive access to a beach area.

Where there is a monopolistic or near-monopolistic situation, you have greater flexibility in determining rates and may, indeed, tend to charge more than is reasonably fair. In these situations, nevertheless, the customer still has the freedom to stay or not stay at that hotel. Also, in most monopolistic free-enterprise situations where high rates prevail, other new hotel entrepreneurs are soon attracted to offer competition.

Most hotels, however, are in a purely competitive situation where the demand for the rooms of any one is highly sensitive to the rates charged. In such situations, there is little to choose, from a rate point of view, from one hotel to the next. Rates, therefore, tend to be highly competitive.

Where there is close competition, competitive pricing will often prevail without thought to other considerations. Unfortunately, an operator practicing competitive pricing may fail to recognize that his particular hotel is superior in some ways to his competitors' and could command higher rates without reducing demand.

Product Differentiation

In a highly competitive situation, an astute hotel operator will not copy competitors' rates but rather look at the strengths and weaknesses of his own situation as well as those of his competitors. In analyzing strengths and weaknesses, you should try to differentiate yourself and your products from your competitors and emphasize your uniquenesses.

The hotels that are most successful in differentiating have more freedom in establishing their rates. This differentiation can be in such matters as ambiance and atmosphere, decor, location, view, and similar things. Indeed, with differentiation psychological pricing may be practiced.

With psychological pricing, the rates are established according to what the customer expects to pay for the unique products offered. The greater the differentiation, the higher your rates can be. For example, this situation prevails in fashionable hotels where a particular market niche has been created, and a monopolistic or near-monopolistic situation may prevail.

Summary

umary then, there is no one method of establishing rates for all s. Each hotel will have somewhat different long-run pricing strategies ied to its overall objectives, and will adopt appropriate short-run pric-ʒ tactics depending on its market situation.

A LOGICAL APPROACH TO PRICING

In the discussion so far, the role of profit in establishing room rates has been generally ignored. Because there is a relationship between prices charged and total sales, prices must affect your hotel's ability to cover all costs and provide a profit that yields an acceptable return on investment.

A useful approach in pricing, therefore, might be to start with the profit that is required, calculate fixed and variable costs, and determine what sales are required and what prices are to be charged in order to achieve the desired profit.

Profit as a Cost

This approach assumes that profit is a cost of doing business, which indeed it is. If a bank lends money at a particular interest rate to your hotel, the interest cost is considered to be an expense for your business. The bank is an investor. You, as owner, are also an investor. You too expect interest on your investment of money and/or time, except that your "interest" is called profit. Therefore, profit is just another type of cost. This concept can be useful in calculating what your room rates should be to yield the desired profit.

Let us consider the following about the 50-room Motorway Motel. The Motorway wishes to determine what its average room rate should be next year. The Motorway's fixed costs, including the profit desired, are $411,000 and its variable costs are 25 percent of sales. If variable costs are 25 percent of sales, then fixed costs must be 75 percent (because total sales are given the value of 100 percent). Therefore, total sales next year to give the desired profit are calculated as follows:

$$\text{If } 75\% \text{ of sales} = \$411,000$$

$$\text{Then } 100\% \qquad = \$411,000/75\% = \$548,000$$

Assuming the motel is going to continue to operate at a 70-percent occupancy, it will sell the following number of rooms per year:

$$50 \times 70\% \times 365 = 12,775$$

Its average room rate will therefore have to be:

$$\frac{\text{Revenue required}}{\text{Rooms to be sold}} = \frac{\$548,000}{12,775} = \$42.90, \text{ rounded to } \$43.00$$

Note that this figure, $43.00, is only an average room rate and is not necessarily the rate for any specific room. Most hotels have a variety of sizes and types of rooms, each type having a rate for single occupancy and a higher rate for double occupancy.

Where there are multiple types of rooms and multiple rates, the calculated average rate can only be a guide to what the actual rate for each specific type of room will be. Size of room, decor, and view will be some of the factors to consider in arriving at a balance of rates that will be fair to customers and allow the actual average rate to work out to the required figure.

Double Occupancy

Another factor to consider is the rate of double occupancy of rooms. Because a room that is occupied by two persons normally has a higher rate than the same room occupied by one person, the higher the proportion of double occupancies, the higher the resulting average rates.

In our example, a safe way to assure that the Motorway Motel achieved at least a $43.00 average would be to make that the minimum single rate for any room. Any rooms then sold that have a higher single rate, or any rooms sold at the double occupancy rate, would guarantee that the average rate will end up higher than $43.00. Unfortunately, competition and customer resistance may preclude this approach.

Calculating Single and Double Rates

In a simple situation, with only one standard type of room and all rooms having the same single or double rate, is there a method of calculating what these rates should be? The answer is yes—as long as you decide what the spread will be between the single rate and the double, and as long as you have a good idea of the double occupancy percent.

To illustrate this we will use the information about our 50-room Motorway Motel. We know that $43.00 is the average rate required to cover all costs and provide the return on investment desired. Present average occupancy is 70 percent. Assume we know from past experience that the double occupancy rate is 40 percent (that is, 40 percent of all rooms occupied are occupied by two persons), and that we want a $10.00 difference between the single and the double rates. The double occupancy rate is calculated as follows:

Total number of guests during year	17,885
Less number of rooms occupied	12,775
Equals number of rooms double occupied	5,110

$$\text{Double occupancy rate} = \frac{5,110}{12,775} \times 100 = 40\%$$

On a typical night in the 50-room motel with a 70-percent occupancy and a 40-percent double occupancy, there will be

$$70\% \times 50 = 35 \text{ rooms occupied}$$

of which

$$40\% \times 35 = 14 \text{ will be double occupied}$$

and

$$35 - 14 = 21 \text{ will be single occupied}$$

Also, in this operation on a typical night, total revenue will be

$$35 \text{ rooms} \times \$43.00 \text{ average rate} = \$1,505$$

The question now is, at what room rates can we sell 21 single rooms and 14 double rooms (at a price $10.00 higher than the singles) so that total revenue is $1,505? Expressed arithmetically this becomes (with $ x the unknown single rate):

$$21\$\,x + 14(\$\,x + \$10) = \$1,505$$
$$21\$\,x + 14\$\,x + \$140 = \$1,505$$
$$35\$\,x \qquad\qquad = \$1,505 - \$140$$
$$35\$\,x \qquad\qquad = \$1,365$$
$$\$x \qquad\qquad = \$1,365/35$$
$$\$x \qquad\qquad = \$39.00$$

Therefore, the single rate is $39.00 and the double rate is $39.00 + $10.00 = $49.00. Let us prove the correctness of these rates.

21 singles × $39.00 =	$ 819.00
14 doubles × $49.00 =	686.00
35 rooms × $43.00 =	$1,505.00

These, then, are the rates under the given circumstances. They are the rates that the Motorway Motel should be charging, given the correctness of assumptions about next year. They may not be the rates actually charged since the factors discussed earlier in this chapter may oblige the Motorway Motel to reduce them—in which case there will be a smaller return on investment than desired.

On the other hand, newer establishments in the area with higher construction and operating costs and higher rates with a customer willingness to pay them, may allow the Motorway Motel to increase its rates above the calculated ones. In this case there will be a higher return on investment than required.

In trying to determine appropriate room rates, other influencing factors tending to decrease the average rate include

- Reduced rates for families
- Commercial traveler discounts
- Travel agent commissions (unless accounted for separately)
- Convention or group rates
- Special government employee rates
- Weekly or monthly rates

On the other hand, extra charges for three or more persons in a room would influence the average in an upward direction.

Average Occupancy

An analysis of occupancy by day of the week can also be revealing. Refer to the following:

	Harry's Hotel	Hilary's Hotel
Saturday	40%	60%
Sunday	40	60
Monday	70	70
Tuesday	90	70
Wednesday	90	80
Thursday	90	80
Friday	70	70
	490%	490%
Average	$\frac{490}{7} = 70\%$	$\frac{490}{7} = 70\%$

Both hotels have the same average occupancies, but the analysis by day shows a different picture for each. Harry's has very low occupancy at weekends and very high occupancy during the week. An advertising campaign directed toward bringing in weekend guests would benefit the property. On the other hand, Hilary's has a relatively high weekend business, and good but not high occupancy during the week. Her advertising should be geared not just toward weekend promotions but also toward improving mid-week occupancy.

FIFTEEN

Room Rate Discounting and Yield Management

ROOM RATE DISCOUNTING

Room rate discounting is the practice of reducing prices below the rack rate. The *rack rate* is defined as the maximum rate that will be quoted for a room. When rates are discounted for some rooms on any night, this prevents your hotel from achieving its maximum potential total revenue for that night.

Room rates are typically discounted for groups such as convention delegates and corporate and government travellers who are regular customers of your hotel. The discounts given are a normal cost of business to maintain occupancy levels. The reduced room revenue is often compensated by extra profits achieved from those room guests' patronizing your hotel's other facilities.

Discount Grid

In reviewing room rates and deciding on the discounts to be offered, it is useful to prepare a discount grid. This grid shows the impact of various room rate discounts on total room revenue.

To prepare the grid, you must know the variable costs of selling each additional room. Normally, variable costs occur only in the housekeeping department, because no extra costs are incurred in the reservations or front office departments to sell an extra room.

Housekeeping costs include such items as employee time to clean the room, cost of linen and laundering, cost of guest supplies (soap, shampoo, and similar items), and additional utility costs for lighting and heating or air conditioning. For most hotels, variable costs are easy to determine.

Let us assume that Rusty's Resort, a 100-room hotel, had variable costs for renting each additional room of $10. The following equation can be used by Rusty to calculate the equivalent occupancy needed to hold total revenue less variable costs constant if the rack rate is discounted:

$$\text{Current occupancy} \times \frac{\text{Rack rate} - \text{Variable cost}}{[\text{Rack rate} \times (1 - \text{discount percent})] - \text{Variable cost}}$$

Assume that all of Rusty's rooms have the same rack rate of $80 and that the hotel currently operates at a 70-percent occupancy. If Rusty's rates are discounted by 10 percent, the equivalent occupancy required (using the above equation) would be:

$$70\% \times \frac{\$80 - \$10}{[\$80 \times (1 - .10)] - \$10}$$

$$= 70\% \times \frac{\$70}{(\$80 \times .9) - \$10}$$

$$= 70\% \times \frac{\$70}{\$72 - \$10}$$

$$= 70\% \times \frac{\$70}{\$62}$$

$$= 70\% \times 1.13 = 79.1\%$$

This can be proved. Nightly room revenue before discounting is:

$$70\% \text{ occupancy} \times 100 \text{ rooms} \times \$80 \text{ rack rate} = \$5,600$$

and total variable costs are:

$$70\% \text{ occupancy} \times 100 \text{ rooms} \times \$10 = \$700$$

Net revenue (total revenue less variable costs) is therefore $5,600 − $700 = $4,900.

After discounting, nightly revenue at 79-percent occupancy will be:

$$79\% \text{ occupancy} \times 100 \text{ rooms} \times \$72 \text{ rate} = \$5,688$$

and total variable costs will be:

$$79\% \text{ occupancy} \times 100 \text{ rooms} \times \$10 = \$790$$

Net revenue is therefore $5,688 − $790 = $4,898. In other words, net revenue is the same as before. (The small difference is due to rounding out the required occupancy level to 79 percent from 79.1 percent.)

Similar calculations can be made for various occupancy levels and discount percentages, and the results tabulated in a grid such as that in Figure 15.1. Once this has been done, the grid shows the equivalent occupancy that must be achieved to maintain room revenue (less variable

Current Occupancy	New Occupancy Level Necessary to Maintain the Same Profitability if an $80 Rack Rate Is Discounted by			
	5%	10%	15%	20%
70%	74.2%	79.1%	84.7%	91.0%
65	68.9	73.5	78.7	84.5
60	63.6	67.8	72.6	78.0
55	58.3	62.2	66.6	71.5
50	53.0	56.5	60.5	65.0

Figure 15.1 Discount grid.

costs) at a stipulated level as discounts are increased or decreased. Thus the grid allows Rusty to make sensible pricing decisions.

For example, the grid shows that if the hotel discounted room rates by 15 percent and its current occupancy is 70 percent, the equivalent occupancy after discounting would have to be 84.7 percent. In Rusty's 100-room hotel, this means an additional 15 rooms would have to be sold per night. If there is an advertising cost to sell 15 extra rooms this must be considered, as would additional revenue that the additional guests might provide in other departments. In other words, Rusty should use the grid only as an aid in decision making and not as the only factor to consider.

Potential Average Room Rate

The potential average room rate is defined as the average rate that would result if all rooms occupied overnight were sold at the rack rate without a discount. You can use this potential average rate to monitor the actual average room rate.

To this point, we have stated that the rack rate is the maximum rate that will be charged for a room. But in fact, most hotels have two or more rack rates for each room. There may be a rack rate for single occupancy, a rack rate for double occupancy, and even a rack rate for three or more occupants. How can a potential average room rate be determined in such a situation?

If your hotel sold all its rooms at single occupancy, your potential average rack rate would be the average rate if all rooms were single occupied. If your hotel sold all its rooms at double occupancy, your potential average rate would be the average rate if all rooms were double occupied. For most hotels, neither of these extremes is likely.

For most properties on a typical night, some rooms will be single occupied and others will be double occupied. A further complication is that there may be different types of rooms whose single or double rack rates are different. Thus the potential average rate must be calculated by taking your hotel's normal sales mix into consideration.

To illustrate, assume that all of a 100-room hotel's various rooms were each occupied by one person (single occupancy) at the maximum single-occupancy rack rate, and that in this situation total revenue would be $7,500. Potential minimum average rate is therefore

$$\frac{\$7,500}{100} = \$75$$

On the other hand, if all 100 rooms were double occupied at the maximum double-occupancy rack rate, total revenue would be $8,500. Potential maximum average rate is therefore

$$\frac{\$8,500}{100} = \$85$$

(Note that if the hotel had suites or special rooms at higher rates, these can be included in the maximum potential double rate calculation).

The difference between $85 and $75 is known as the rate spread. If this hotel's percentage of double occupancy were 40 percent (that is, 40 percent of all rooms occupied are occupied by two people), the potential average room rate can be calculated as follows:

Potential average single rate + (Percent of double occupancy × Rate spread)

In our case, this results in a potential average room rate of

$$\$75 + (40\% \times \$10.00)$$
$$= \$75 + \$4 = \$79$$

Comparing Actual Average to Potential Average

Once you calculate the potential average room rate, you can compare each day or each period your actual rate to this potential. There may be occasions when the actual rate will be higher than the potential. This could occur when the double occupancy rate exceeded the normal 40 percent and/or if additional charges were made for a third person in a room and/or if front desk employees were doing a good job of selling the most expensive rooms first.

In other cases, the actual average rate will be below the potential rate and can be measured by dividing it by the potential rate and converting to a percentage to arrive at the average rate ratio. For example, if your actual rate achieved during a particular week were $72, the average rate ratio is

$$\frac{\$72}{\$79} \times 100 = 91\%$$

This means your hotel achieved only 91 percent of its potential average rate. This could occur because the double-occupancy ratio declined below normal and/or because the front desk employees did a poor job and sold the lower-priced rooms first. Alternatively, all other things being equal, it could mean that rack rates had been discounted 9 percent on average.

Room Rates for Each Market Segment

With reference to the $79.00 potential average room rate calculated earlier, it is possible to calculate the room rate for each type of market (market segment) that your hotel deals with. Suppose you have the following information for each of three segments:

Market Segment	Annual Room Nights	Percent	Rack Rate
Business travelers	5,110	40%	100%
Conference groups	4,471	35%	90%
Tour groups	3,194	25%	80%
	12,775	100%	

The Percent column figures show how much each segment produces out of total business. For example, business travelers constitute 5,110/12,775 × 100 = 40 percent of total room nights.

The rack rate column tells you the percent of the rack rate that you are going to charge customers in that market segment. For example, business travelers are going to pay 100 percent of the rack rate (and receive no discount), conference groups will be charged 90 percent of the rack rate (or receive a 10 percent discount), and tour groups 80 percent of the rack rate (or receive a 20 percent discount). What must those rates be for each market segment to ensure that you continue to achieve a $79 average room rate?

You must first calculate what the new potential average rack rate is going to be for the business travelers who receive no discount. You know that it will be higher than before because some segments are going to receive a discounted rate, and thus the new rack rate must increase to compensate for these discounts.

You make the calculation by weighting the discount percent for each market segment and, at the same time, taking into account the percent of business that each market segment generates as follows:

$$\frac{\$79.00}{(40\% \times 100\%) + (35\% \times 90\%) + (25\% \times 80\%)}$$

Note that, in each set of parentheses in the denominator the first figure represents the portion of the business provided by that segment and the second represents the rack rate percentage for that segment. For example, in the first set of figures the business travelers provide 40 percent of the business at the full rack rate. Following through on the calculations you have

$$\frac{\$79.00}{40\% + 31.5\% + 20\%} = \frac{\$79.00}{91.5\%} = \$86.34$$

as the rack rate for the business travelers. The discounted rates for the other segments are:

Conference groups $\$86.34 \times 90\% = \$77.70$

Tour groups $\$86.34 \times 80\% = \$69.07$

You can prove that these rates will generate the sales required to yield your desired potential average room rate:

Market Segment	Room Nights	Average Rate	Total Sales
Business travelers	5,110 ×	$86.34	= $ 441,197
Conference			
groups	4,471 ×	$77.70	= 347,397
Tour groups	3,194 ×	$69.07	= 220,610
Totals	12,775		$1,009,204

and

$$\frac{\$1,009,204}{12,775} = \$79.00$$

YIELD MANAGEMENT

The main goal of the rooms department in many hotels is to sell hotel rooms to increase the occupancy percent. Management's objective is to maximize the revenue (or yield) from the rooms available. Unfortunately, many of the methods presently used to measure a hotel's marketing effort do not generate sales decisions that maximize revenue. Marketing effort has been traditionally judged on either the occupancy percent or the average room rate achieved.

Measurement Problems

The problem with occupancy percent is that it does not show if revenue is being maximized. For example, your hotel may be 100 percent occupied, but many of those guest room occupants may be paying less than the maximum (rack) rate for the room. In other words, managers measured by rooms occupancy are tempted to increase occupancy at the expense of room rate.

Other managers are judged by the average room rate. Again, the average room rate can be increased by refusing to sell any rooms at less than the rack rate, thus turning away potential customers who are unwilling to pay this rate. Average room rate will be maximized at the expense of occupancy. Average room rate can be slightly more meaningful if it is expressed as a ratio of the maximum potential average rate, as discussed in an earlier section of this chapter.

Yield Statistic

Instead of focusing on a high occupancy or a high average rate, however, a better measure of a manager's performance is the yield statistic. Yield is defined as

$$\frac{\text{Actual revenue}}{\text{Potential revenue}} \times 100$$

Potential revenue is defined as the room sales that you would generate if 100 percent occupancy were achieved and each room were sold at its maximum rack rate. For example, if your hotel had 150 rooms, each of which had a maximum rack rate of $100, potential revenue is

$$150 \times \$100 = \$15,000$$

and if actual revenue on a particular night were $10,000, then yield is

$$\frac{\$10,000}{\$15,000} \times 100 = 66.7\%$$

Yield thus combines two factors: the number of rooms available (rooms inventory) and rooms pricing. Rooms inventory management is concerned with how many rooms are made available to each market segment and that segment's demand for rooms. Pricing management is concerned with the room rate you quote to each of these market segments.

Various Combinations

Note that there can be different combinations of room rates and occupancies that achieve the same yield percentage. For example, consider the following three situations that each show various combinations that generate the same actual revenue, and thus the same yield percentage:

> Case A 100 rooms occupied × $100.00 average rate = $10,000
>
> Case B 120 rooms occupied × $ 83.33 average rate = $10,000
>
> Case C 140 rooms occupied × $ 71.43 average rate = $10,000

In each of these three situations, if potential revenue were $15,000 the yield will be the same: 66.7 percent. However, even though each of these situations is equal insofar as total room revenue and yield percent are concerned, they may not be equal in terms of other factors.

For example, in Cases B and C there are more rooms occupied than in Case A, thus there will be additional housekeeping and energy costs. On the other hand, Cases B and C also mean more guests in the hotel, who are likely to patronize and increase revenue in other departments. Further, if those additional customers were first-time guests of your hotel and leave with a favorable impression, they are likely to be repeat customers and will provide positive word-of-mouth advertising, thus increasing future revenue.

Finally, note that because the yield statistic is a combination of occupancy percent and average room rate, you can also calculate it by multiplying the actual occupancy percent by the average rate ratio. The average rate ratio in this case is the actual average rate expressed as a percentage of the average maximum potential rate.

In our 150-room hotel, the maximum average potential rate is $100 ($15,000 potential maximum revenue divided by 150 rooms). In Case A above, with 100 rooms occupied (66.7 percent occupancy), and an average rate ratio of 1.0 or 100 percent (because the actual average rate is the same as the maximum potential rate), the yield statistic can be calculated as

$$66.7\% \times 1.0 = 66.7\%$$

In Case B it would be

$$\frac{120}{150} \times \frac{\$83.33}{\$100}$$

= 80% occupancy $\times$ 0.8333 average rate ratio = 66.7% yield

and in Case C it would be

$$\frac{140}{150} \times \frac{\$71.43}{\$100}$$

= 93.33% occupancy $\times$ 0.7143 average rate ratio = 66.7% yield.

Even though the occupancy percent and the average rate ratio by themselves do not provide complete information, by multiplying them together to provide the yield percent, you have a single integrated statistic that is much more meaningful and a more consistent measure of your hotel's performance. In an attempt to maximize this statistic, a practice known as *yield management* has recently been adopted by some hotels.

The objective of yield management is to maximize hotel room revenue by using basic economic principles to allocate the right type of room to the right type of guest at a price the guest is prepared to pay.

The concept of maximizing revenue is not new. Indeed, hotel managers have always known that during slow periods they can increase the demand for rooms by looking at the number of reservations they already have for future periods and then reducing the prices of still-available rooms to stimulate further demand.

Conversely, during high demand periods when occupancy will be at or near 100 percent, they can increase room rates knowing that customers are prepared to pay higher rates to guarantee having a reservation. Most hotel operators have traditionally used this concept of supply and demand in their pricing.

Airline Practices

Other branches of the tourism industry also use the discounted price approach to stimulate demand. For example, airlines have many different fares for the same aircraft seat and either directly—or through a travel agency—quote a price for that seat depending on who the customer is and what he or she is prepared to pay to fly.

Over the years, airlines have developed sophisticated yield management computer programs to help them determine how many seats on each aircraft can be allocated in advance for each type of discounted fare in order to fill all seats and maximize their revenue on each flight.

What makes airline yield management different from traditional hospitality industry discount pricing is that the airlines constantly update the price decision-making process. The computer systems allow discounted prices to change daily to match each day's demand from the various market segments the airlines deal with. In other words, airlines constantly adjust the number of seats available at any one price to maximize their revenue or yield.

Similarity of Hotels and Airlines

In many ways, hotel guest rooms are similar to aircraft seats. For example

- There is a fixed supply in the short run. The objective is to use this fixed availability in the most profitable way to maximize revenue.
- In many cases, a known proportion of aircraft seats and hotel rooms are reserved some time ahead of their actual usage.
- A guest room not sold (just like an aircraft seat unsold) is lost revenue that can never be recovered. In other words, the inventory is extremely perishable.
- Demand for both airline seats and hotel rooms can fluctuate a great deal, particularly on a seasonal basis. However, it can also vary monthly, and even daily by day of the week.
- Variable costs (the cost to sell an extra aircraft seat or hotel room) are relatively low compared to marginal revenue. For example, to sell an extra hotel room does not require any more labor in the reservations or front office areas. The only additional costs are for housekeeping labor, guest room laundry and supplies expense, and energy.
- Customer characteristics (that is, the market segments that airlines and hotels deal with) are similar. These segments can be easily identified from past demand.
- There is a certain amount of price and time sensitivity for some market segments for both airline seats and hotel rooms. For example, vacation travelers usually reserve both airline seats and hotel rooms well ahead of travel time. These customers reserve primarily based on price. Thus, to reach this market, prices must be reduced and made known to potential customers well in advance. Last-minute price reductions to fill airline seats or hotel rooms are unlikely to generate additional volume from the vacation market.

In order to use yield management in a hotel, you must know how and when each market segment makes reservations (by time of year and day of week), must have an overbooking policy for each market segment, and must know the elasticity of demand for each market segment. Computers can easily provide this information by analyzing past experience so that it can be used in forecasting. Indeed, demand forecasting is the basis of effective yield management.

Complications for Hotels

Note, however, that the yield management practices of the airline industry become somewhat more complicated when applied to the hotel industry. For example, when a customer makes a hotel reservation, that reservation can be for one night, for one night that the guest after arriving extends for two or more nights, or for more than one night with the guest subsequently staying for a shorter period than originally reserved. This creates questions such as

- Will a guest making a low-demand day reservation at a discounted price be allowed to extend that stay subsequently at the same price through one or more high-demand days that follow?
- In a situation where a guest enquires about a rate for a stay starting on a low-demand day but extending into high-demand days, should a high-demand price be quoted for the entire period? If so, will the potential customer decide to shop around for a better price at a competitive hotel? The yield management system must consider this type of trade-off possibility.

In addition, when guests make reservations the derived demand they provide other departments must be considered, along with the market segment that the guest is in. Guests of one market segment might be more likely to use your hotel's food and beverage areas (if your hotel has them) and increase revenue in those areas than guests of another market segment. Thus, your yield management system must be programmed to consider revenue and profitability from more than the rooms department.

Note also that airlines have many different prices for the same seat on an aircraft, and customers know that the earlier they make a reservation for a flight the lower the price is likely to be. This has not traditionally been the way hotels operate, and a hotel converting to a yield management pricing system must consider the effect this will have on its potential customers.

Further, in North America the major airlines presently operate in an oligopolistic environment, and the airline customer often has little choice about using a particular airline to fly from point A to point B. Hotels, on the other hand, generally operate in a highly competitive environment, and the potential customer (other than in extremely high-demand periods) can shop around for a room rate appropriate to his or her budget.

Note also that on a national basis and in the general market area where a hotel is located, total demand for hotel rooms is relatively inelastic. At the local level, however, demand for any particular hotel's rooms (and thus the elasticity of demand for its rooms) can be affected by its pricing decisions. It is thus important that you know what your market segments are and to determine how elastic the demand is for each market segment so that you can adjust your prices to obtain a larger share of each segment.

Implementing Yield Management

Many hotels have adopted yield management and abandoned the practice of pricing rooms according to traditional methods such as room type and season of the year. By using computers to forecast rooms demand, they have eliminated a great deal of guesswork from the room rate decision-making process. This process involves the number of rooms that should be sold at various room rates.

Currently, hotels do not generally have as wide a variety of rates as airlines. If you decide to implement yield management you might find it appropriate to parallel the airlines by having a much wider variety of rates in order to maximize the benefits that yield management can offer. By having more room rates, a yield management system is better able to influence demand and even length of stay to improve profits. In other words, yield management controls rooms inventory availability.

Potential hotel customers may initially consider it unfair (because they are not used to this) to be quoted a different room rate depending on how far in advance they make a reservation. What you therefore require when you implement yield management is a customer-education program and flexibility in the system to allow reservation department employees to use their judgment when they feel that potential customers are resisting quoted high prices.

Need for Compromises

Clearly, yield management involves compromises. For example, the preferred situation would be to have 100 percent rooms occupancy with all rooms sold at the rack rate. For most hotels, however, this is unrealistic on a year-round basis and would likely lead to empty rooms and lost revenue because there is insufficient demand for rooms at the maximum rate.

An alternative might be to lower all rates to ensure that there is 100 percent occupancy year round. Again, however, this will lead to lost revenue because some of the customers paying low rates would have been prepared to pay higher rates.

Thus, in both of these situations yield (revenue) is not maximized. The objective of yield management is to decide what the trade-off will be between maximizing room rates and maximizing occupancy and how many rooms at rack rates and how many at discounted rates will be offered during each time period to each different market segment.

Group Sales

Yield management can be a problem in group bookings. Employees responsible for booking group sales often have their job performance measured by the volume of sales (number of room nights) that they make. The group booking department's objective is to sell rooms, and to make those sales they usually have the authority to reduce room rates to obtain the business.

Yield management, however, may show that some low-rate group sales do not maximize revenue at certain times of the year when those rooms could be sold to transient (business) travelers at a higher rate. Thus, yield management may prevent a sales employee from making a group sale. This obviously reduces that person's incentive to sell.

Another consideration is that a group booking often creates a situation where transient travelers who would otherwise stay at your hotel at higher rates are displaced. Those displaced transients will then reserve rooms at a competitor hotel. They may also be encouraged to stay at that competitor hotel on future visits. Obviously, this reduces future revenue of your hotel.

It is also argued that group rooms sales should be separated from other room sales under yield management and that the group sales department's effectiveness should not be measured on number of room nights booked over a period (such as a month) but on a combination of room nights times average rate to arrive at total revenue.

Summary

In summary, yield management is an attempt to match customers' purchase patterns and their demand for guest rooms with future occupancy forecasts. It is a method of measuring your hotel's marketing performance. It attempts to balance the demand of each market segment your hotel deals with and the supply of rooms made available to this segment by adjusting the major variable that you can most effectively control: the room rate.

The yield management system should match room rates to market demand, indicate how many rooms should be held for last-minute, high-rate customers, and indicate when room rates should be discounted to increase occupancy. You should not view yield management as a method of forcing customers to pay the highest rate, but rather as an attempt to bring room rates into line with normal economic forces. The foundation of a good yield management system is the accuracy and availability of the information that your hotel has about its customers' historic reservation patterns.

SIXTEEN

Budgeting

CONTROL PROCEDURES

In order to control any aspect of your hotel (such as its labor or operating supplies cost) you must follow these five steps:

1. Establish what you expect the hotel's performance standards to be (for example, what the labor cost percent should be).

2. Through your accounting system, collect the information that will allow you to measure actual results against the desired standard.

3. Compare the actual result with the standard, for example actual labor cost with standard labor cost.

4. Take corrective action, if necessary, to help ensure that during the next period the actual result is more in line with the performance standard desired. For example, if the actual labor cost were too high in comparison with the performance standard, then steps must be taken to reduce the actual labor cost by finding out where the problem lies and correcting it. This may require an investigative process and consideration of alternative operating procedures along with the impact those alternative procedures will have on actual results.

5. At the end of the next review period, evaluate the result of any corrective action taken to see if it was appropriate.

Planning Process

A common control technique that considers all aspects of your hotel's operation (rather than, for example, labor cost in isolation) is budgeting. Budgeting is a planning process, and your budget is a profit plan. In order to be successful and to make meaningful decisions about the future, you must look ahead.

One way to look ahead is to prepare budget forecasts. A forecast may be very simple. It may be no more than estimating tomorrow's occupancy in your hotel so that sufficient employees can be notified today that they are required to work tomorrow, and for how many hours. On the other hand, a forecast of cash flow for a proposed new hotel may be calculated for as far as five years or more ahead.

Purposes of Budgeting

The main purposes of budgeting are to provide:

- Organized estimates of such matters as future sales, expenses, labor requirements, and fixture and equipment needs—broken down by time period.
- A coordinated long-term and short-term management policy, expressed primarily in an accounting format.
- A method of control so that actual results can be evaluated against budget plans and adjustment can be made if necessary. In other words, the standard of performance planned for in the budget can be measured against actual results.

Advantages of Budgeting

Although there are some obvious disadvantages to budgeting, such as the time and cost involved and the difficulty in predicting the future, most successful hotel operators agree that the advantages far outweigh the disadvantages. Some of these advantages are:

- If key employees in the business are involved in budget preparation, it encourages motivation and improves communication. These key employees can then better identify with your hotel's plans and objectives.
- Those involved in budget preparation are required to consider alternative courses of action. (For example, what if the sales forecast does not reach the budgeted level?)
- Since operating budgets outline in advance the sales to be achieved and the costs involved with achieving those sales, at the end of each budget period actual results can be compared with the budget. In other words, you have a predetermined standard against which actual results can be evaluated.
- Budgeting forces those involved to look ahead. This does not mean that what happened in the past is not important for budget preparation. However, budgets are aimed at the future and require you to consider possibilities such as room rate changes, increasing labor and other costs, and what the competition is doing.

- Budgeting requires those involved to consider both internal and external factors. Internal factors include such matters as room rates, occupancies, and employee productivity. External factors include such matters as the competition, the local economic environment, and the general trend of inflation.

PREPARING THE BUDGET

Budgets can be either long-term or short-term. Long-term budgets are sometimes referred to as strategic budgets and are for periods of more than one year and up to five years ahead. These budgets concern matters such as hotel expansion, creation of a new market, and financing. From long-term plans evolve policies concerning the day-to-day operations of your hotel, and thus the short-term budgets.

Short-term budgets could be for a day, a week, a quarter, or a year, or for any period less than a year. Short-term budgets involve using your hotel's resources to meet the objectives of the long-term plans.

Although there are several different types of long-term and short-term budgets, this chapter deals only with the short-term operating budget (income statement) for periods up to one year ahead. The operating budget is concerned with projections of sales and expenses, that is, items that affect the income statement.

Who Prepares the Budget?

In a small hotel the owner prepares the budget. The owner might just have a plan in his mind about where he wants to go and operates from day to day to achieve his objective, or come as close to it as possible. If it were a formal budget, the help of an accountant might be useful in putting figures onto paper and refining them until the budget seems realistic.

In a large hotel, a number of individuals (department heads) might be involved in budget preparation. These department heads might well, in turn, discuss the budget figures with employees within their own departments.

Short-term operating budgets are generally prepared annually, with monthly projections. Each month, budgets for the remaining months of the year should be revised to adjust for any changed circumstances.

BUDGETED INCOME STATEMENT

The first step in preparation of the budgeted income statement is to establish attainable sales goals or objectives.

Establishing Attainable Sales Goals or Objectives

In setting goals, what would be the most desirable situation must be realistic. In other words, if there are any factors that limit your sales to a certain maximum level, these factors must not be ignored. An obvious example is that a hotel cannot have more than a 100 percent occupancy at any one time. If a hotel were operating at 100 percent of capacity, sales can only be increased in the short run by room rate increases. But because few hotels operate at 100 percent year-round, it would be unwise (desirable as it might be) to use 100 percent as the budgeted capacity on an annual basis.

Another limiting factor might be a lack of skilled labor or skilled supervisory personnel. Well-trained employees or employees who could be trained are often not available. Similarly, supervisory personnel who could train others are not always available.

Your management policy can also be a limiting consideration. For example, your front office manager may suggest that catering to bus tour groups would help increase sales. But if you feel that such groups would be too disruptive to the regular clientele, then this market for increasing sales is not available.

Another limiting factor might be in the area of increasing costs. You might find you are restricted in your ability to pass on increasing costs by way of higher room rates.

Finally, customer demand and competition must be kept in mind when budgeting. In the short run there is usually only so much business to go around.

Preparing Income Statements

The starting point in the income statement budget is an estimate of your sales, keeping the limiting factors in mind. Trend analysis of past performance (discussed in Chapter 10) is useful in this process. Even though budgeted income statements are generally prepared for one year ahead, each annual budget should be broken down into 12 monthly budgets because of the seasonal nature of the hotel business and so that comparison with actual results can be made each month. If you compare budget and actual figures only on a yearly basis, any required corrective action might then be eleven months too late.

So how do you prepare a sales forecast for a hotel? If you are already in business, you look first at past actual sales and trends for the same month for which you are presently forecasting. If you were forecasting for the month of January, you would look at sales levels for January for the past two or three years and observe the trend.

Note the effect of any special events in your area (such as sports events, conventions, holidays, and so forth) as well as weather and seasonal changes and the effect they have had on your sales.

External Factors.   In making your sales forecast you might also need to consider the following external factors:

- Population changes
- Political events
- Strikes
- Inflation and similar economic factors
- Consumer earnings
- Competition

Internal Factors.   Also, there are internal factors that you should consider such as:

- Additional advertising and promotion
- Changes in policies (such as accepting credit cards)
- Housekeeping quality changes
- Room rate changes
- Working capital problems
- Labor problems.

Of course, it is impossible to build all of these factors into precise forecasts of your sales, but this list should alert you to the many factors that you must consider so that you use the most critical or likely ones to refine your sales budget.

An Example.   For example, suppose your hotel's sales for the past three years for the month of January were:

Year 1 $30,000
Year 2 $36,000
Year 3 $40,000

It is now December in year 3 and you are finalizing your budget for year 4, commencing with January. The increase in sales for year 2 over year 1 was 20 percent ($6,000 divided by $30,000). The year 3 increase over year 2 was approximately 11 percent ($4,000 divided by $36,000). These increases were caused almost entirely by increases in demand for rooms.

Your room rates have not changed in the past three years. No expansion of your hotel will occur in year 4. Because a new competitive hotel is opening close by, you do not anticipate your occupancy to increase in January of year 4, but neither do you expect to lose any of your current customers. Because of economic trends, you are forced to meet rising costs by increasing room rates by 10 percent commencing in January of year 4. The budgeted sales for January of year 4 would therefore be:

$$\$40,000 + (10\% \times \$40,000) = \$44,000$$

The same type of reasoning would be applied for each of the other eleven months of year 4.

Deduct Expenses. Once forecast sales have been calculated, operating expenses that generally depend on sales (that is, your variable costs) can be calculated and deducted.

Historic accounting records will generally show that these variable costs vary within narrow limits as a percentage of sales. The appropriate percentage of expense to sales can therefore be applied to the budgeted sales in order to calculate the dollar amount of the expense. For example, if laundry cost varies between 4.5 and 5.5 percent of sales (an average of 5 percent), and sales are expected to be $44,000 for that period, budgeted laundry cost would be

$$5\% \times \$44,000 = \$2,200$$

There is a risk with this approach, however, in that it may be perpetuating a situation where the percent applied is higher than it really should be unless an analysis has been carried out to determine that it is the right one.

Similar calculations would be made for all other variable expenses. As you can now see, a breakdown of costs into their fixed and variable elements as discussed in Chapter 12 can be very useful in budgeting. Once variable expenses have been calculated and deducted from sales, your undistributed and fixed expenses can then be deducted to complete the income statement.

Usually, these expenses are estimated on an annual basis (unlike sales and variable expenses, which are generally calculated monthly). The simplest method of allocating these fixed expenses by month is to show one twelfth of the annual expense as a monthly cost.

Note that, in budgeting, some of these undistributed and fixed expenses will vary at your discretion. For example, you may decide that a special allocation will be added to the advertising budget during the coming year; or that a particular item of expensive maintenance can be deferred for a year.

Compare Budget with Actual Results

Comparing actual results with those planned or budgeted is probably the most important and advantageous step in the budgeting process. Comparing actual with budget allows you to ask questions such as: Actual sales for January were $40,000 instead of the budgeted $44,000; was the $4,000 difference caused by a reduction in number of rooms sold? If so, is there an explanation? (For example, are higher room rates keeping customers away, or did a competitive nearby hotel reduce its rates and take away some of our business?)

These are examples of the questions that can be asked (and for which you should seek answers) in analyzing differences between budgeted and actual performance. The budget is, then, a monitor of the actual performance of your hotel. It allows you to

- Compare your actual performance with budget expectations
- Analyze your hotel and track causes of variances
- Act to solve problems.

Variances.   Obviously, your budget and actual performance will not correspond exactly for any month. There are bound to be variances. The question is, when are those variances significant? It is up to you to set limits on allowable variances in both dollars and percentages.

Percentage variances are calculated by dividing the dollar variance by the budgeted figure for that item. For example, if the budgeted figure were $100 and the variance $10, the percentage variance is

$$\frac{\$10}{\$100} \times 100 = 10\%$$

It is unlikely that any revenue or controllable expense item will not have a variance because, even with comprehensive information available during the budgeting process, budgeted figures are still estimates. The variances to be analyzed are those that show significant differences from budgeted amounts. What is important in this significance test is the amount of the variance in both dollar and percentage terms, and not just in one of them. If only one of them is used it might not provide information that the other does provide.

For example, dollar differences alone ignore the base or budgeted figure, and the dollar difference may not be significant when compared to the base figure. To illustrate, if the dollar difference in revenue is $5,000 (which seems significant) and the budgeted revenue were $5,000,000, the percentage variance is

$$\frac{\$5,000}{\$5,000,000} \times 100 = 0.1\%$$

which is quite insignificant. In other words, if the actual amount can be so close to the budget in percentage terms, this would be remarkably effective budgeting. However, this is not disclosed if only the dollar difference is considered.

Similarly, considering the percentage difference alone may not be useful. For example, if a particular expense for this same property were budgeted at $500, and the actual expense were $550, the variance of $50 represents 10 percent of the budget figure. Ten percent seems like a large variance, but is insignificant when the dollar figure is also considered. In other words, a variance of $50 is insignificant in a business with revenue of $5,000,000 and would not be worth anybody's time to investigate.

What is significant as a dollar and percentage variance depends entirely on the type and size of establishment. You need to establish in advance the variances allowed in both dollar figures and percentages for each revenue and expense item. At the end of each budget period, only those variances that exceed what is allowed in both dollar and percentage terms will be further analyzed and investigated.

Take Any Corrective Action Required

The next step in the budget process requires you to take corrective action (if necessary) because of unacceptable variances between budgeted and actual figures.

The cause of a variance could be the result of an unanticipated circumstance (for example, weather, a sudden change in economic conditions, a fire on the premises) and about which nothing can be done.

On the other hand, a difference could be caused by the fact that your room rates were not increased sufficiently to compensate for an inflationary rate of cost increases; or that your occupancy forecast was not sufficiently adjusted to compensate for the opening of a new, nearby, competitive hotel.

Whatever the cause of variance, the problem should be corrected if possible so that future budgets can more realistically predict planned operations.

Improve Budget Effectiveness

The final step in the budgeting process is to try continually to improve the budgeting process. The information provided from past budgets, and particularly the information provided from analyzing variances between actual and budgeted figures, will be helpful. By increasing the accuracy of your budgeting, the effectiveness of your hotel's operation is improved.

BUDGETING IN A NEW BUSINESS

Owners of new hotels will find it more difficult to budget in their early years because they have no internal historic information to serve as a base for forecasts. If a feasibility study (business plan) had been prepared prior to opening, it could serve as a base for budgeting. Alternatively, forecasts must be based on a combination of known facts and industry or market averages for that type and size of hotel. Some of the sources of information for a new hotel might be:

- Chamber of commerce or board of trade
- City or municipal hall
- Local (federal or state/provincial) government offices
- Local hotel association
- Trade publications
- Hotels in the neighborhood where you plan to locate
- Local trade suppliers to hotels

Once you have contacted as many likely sources as possible to obtain information about possible sales levels and cost information, you can then prepare your budgeted income statement.

For example, a proposed hotel could use the following equation for calculating its sales:

$$\begin{array}{c} \text{Forecast} \\ \text{occupancy} \\ \text{percent} \end{array} \times \begin{array}{c} \text{Average} \\ \text{room} \\ \text{rate} \end{array} \times \begin{array}{c} \text{Number} \\ \text{of rooms} \\ \text{available} \end{array} \times \begin{array}{c} \text{Days} \\ \text{in} \\ \text{month} \end{array} = \begin{array}{c} \text{Total} \\ \text{revenue} \\ \text{for month} \end{array}$$

Once sales have been forecast, estimated variable expenses can then be deducted, applying industry average percentage figures for each expense to the calculated budgeted revenue. Finally, estimated undistributed and fixed expenses can be deducted.

Using Equations in an Ongoing Operation

Note that the equation illustrated in this section is not limited to a new operation. It could also be used in an existing hotel. For example, instead of applying an estimated percentage of sales increase to last year's figure to obtain the current year's budget, it might be better to break down last year's sales figure into its various equation elements and adjust each of them individually (where necessary) to develop the new budget amount.

For example, last year rooms revenue for a hotel was $100,200 for June and is broken down as follows:

Actual occupancy	×	Average room	×	Number of rooms	×	Days in	=	Total revenue for
percent		rate		available		month		month
83.5%	×	$40.00	×	100	×	30	=	$100,200

We can then apply the budget year trends and information to last year's detailed figures. In the budget period, because of a new hotel in the area, we expect a slight drop in occupancy to 80 percent. This will be compensated for by an increase in our average room rates of 12 percent. Our budgeted revenue is therefore

Budgeted occupancy	×	Budgeted average	×	Number of	×	Days in	=	Budgeted monthly
percent		room		rooms		month		revenue
		rate		available				
80.0%	×	$44.80	×	100	×	30	=	$107,520

This approach to budgeting might require a little more work, but will probably provide you with budgeted figures that are more accurate and can be analyzed more meaningfully than would otherwise be the case.

SEVENTEEN

Working Capital and Cash Management

WORKING CAPITAL

You will remember from Chapter 2 where the balance sheet was discussed that, listed under the assets, is a section called current assets. This includes items such as cash, accounts receivable, marketable securities, inventories, and prepaid expenses.

On the other side of the balance sheet is a section for the current liabilities, including such items as accounts payable, accrued expenses, income tax payable, and the current portion of long-term mortgages. The difference between total current assets and total current liabilities is known as net working capital:

Current assets − Current liabilities = Net working capital

Even though this chapter is about cash management, it is not just about the management of cash but about management of working capital —that is, all the accounts that appear under the "current" sections of your balance sheet. In cash management, your objective should be to conserve cash, earn interest on it (one possibility), and thus maximize profits.

Money does not always come into a hotel at the same rate that it goes out. At times you will have excess cash on hand, at other times there will be shortages of cash. You need to anticipate both of these events so that shortages can be covered. In this way, your cash balance will be kept at its optimum level.

How Much Working Capital?

How much net working capital does your hotel need? This cannot be answered in general terms with an absolute dollar amount. For example, suppose it were a rule of thumb that a hotel should have a net working capital of $5,000. One hotel might find itself with the following:

Current assets	$15,000
Current liabilities	10,000
Working capital	$ 5,000

On the other hand, a large hotel would have to have larger amounts of cash, inventories, accounts receivable, and other items that are current assets. Also, it would probably have larger amounts in its various current liability accounts. Its balance sheet might therefore look like this:

Current assets	$100,000
Current liabilities	95,000
Working capital	$ 5,000

The smaller hotel is in much better financial shape than the larger one. It has $1.50 ($15,000 divided by $10,000) of current assets for every $1.00 of current liabilities—a comfortable cushion. The large hotel has just over $1.05 ($100,000 divided by $95,000) of current assets for each dollar of current liabilities—not so comfortable a cushion.

You will recall from the discussion of the current ratio in Chapter 11 that as a general rule a business should have at least $2.00 of current assets for each $1.00 of current liabilities. This means that its net working capital ($2.00 minus $1.00) is equivalent to its current liabilities.

However, this rule is primarily for companies (such as manufacturing, wholesaling, and some retailing organizations) that need to carry very large inventories that do not turn over very rapidly.

Hotels can often operate with a very low ratio of current assets to current liabilities—often as low as 1 to 1. In other words, for each $1.00 of current assets there is $1.00 of current liabilities. This means that the business has, in fact, no net working capital.

At certain times of the year, some hotels can even operate with negative working capital. In other words, current liabilities will exceed current assets. This might be typical of a seasonal operation. Such a hotel would have current assets vastly in excess of current liabilities during the peak season, but the reverse situation could prevail in the off season.

Let us have a look at some of the more important working capital items that constitute cash management.

Cash

Cash on hand (as distinguished from cash in the bank) is the money in circulation in your hotel. This could be cash used by cashiers as "floats" or "banks" for change-making purposes, petty cash, or just general cash in your office safe. The amount of cash on hand should only be sufficient for normal day-to-day operations. Any surplus cash should be deposited in your bank in savings accounts or term deposits so that it can earn interest. Preferably, each day's net cash receipts should be deposited in the bank as soon as possible the following day.

Cash in the bank in your current account should be sufficient to pay only current bills or current payroll. Any excess funds should be invested in short-term securities (making sure there is a good balance between maximizing the interest rate and the security and liquidity of the investment) or in savings or other special accounts that earn interest.

Accounts Receivable

In certain types of hotels, there may be extensive accounts receivable. For example, a hotel handling group business (such as conferences or bus tour groups) might request a deposit prior to handling a function, but after the event will invoice the hosting organization for any balance due—creating an account receivable. Similarly, many hotels today accept credit cards in payment of accounts—unpaid credit card amounts are accounts receivable until the cash is collected.

Attention to accounts receivable should be focused on two areas: ensuring that invoices are mailed out promptly and following up on delinquent accounts to have them collected. Money you have tied up in accounts receivable is money not earning a return.

Extension of credit to customers is an acknowledged form of business, but it should not be extended to the point of allowing payments to lag two or three months behind the mailing of the invoice.

Methods of controlling accounts receivable (such as accounts receivable turnover and days sales in receivables) were discussed in Chapter 11. Another way of keeping an eye on your accounts receivable is to prepare a monthly chart showing their age. The following illustrates such a chart:

Accounts Receivable Aging Chart

Age	May 31		June 30	
0–30 days	$59,000	79.5%	$56,400	74.2%
31–60 days	11,800	15.9	8,800	11.6
61–90 days	2,400	3.2	8,600	11.3
over 90 days	1,000	1.4	2,200	2.9
Totals	$74,200	100.0%	$76,000	100.0%

This particular chart shows that the accounts receivable outstanding situation has deteriorated from May to June. In May, 79.5 percent of total receivables were less than 30 days old. In June only 74.2 percent were less than 30 days outstanding. Similarly, the relative percentages in the 31–60 day category have increased from May to June. By contrast, in the 61–90 days bracket 11.3 percent of accounts receivable are outstanding in June, against only 3.2 percent in May.

This particular aging schedule shows that the accounts receivable are getting older. If this trend continues, collection procedures would need to be improved. If, after all possible collection procedures have been explored an account is deemed to be uncollectible (a bad debt), it should then be removed from the accounts receivable and be recorded as a bad debt expense on your income statement. The decision on its uncollectibility should only be made by you as owner or manager.

Marketable Securities

Generally, any surplus cash not needed for immediate purposes should be invested in some type of security. Investments could be for as short as one day, but are usually for longer periods, although seldom more than a year. If you had surplus cash for periods of a year or more, it might then be wise to seek out long-term investments, such as building a new hotel or expanding your present one, because the return on those investments over the long run could be expected to be greater than for investment in short-term securities.

Most hotels, particularly those that rely on much or all of their trade from seasonal tourists, have peaks and valleys in their cash flows. You should invest surplus cash from peak-season flows in short-term securities until it is necessary to liquidate them to take care of low or negative cash flows during the off season.

Sometimes it is necessary to build up surplus cash amounts to take care of periodic lump sum payments, such as quarterly tax or dividend payments. These surplus amounts could well be invested in marketable securities until they are needed for payment of these liabilities.

In times of high interest rates, many hotels find it profitable to invest all cash in excess of day-to-day needs in the most liquid of marketable securities—that is, those that can be converted into cash quickly if an unanticipated event requiring cash occurs.

You must consider two important factors when investing in marketable securities: risk and liquidity. A low risk generally goes hand in hand with a low interest rate. A more risky investment would have to offer a higher interest rate in order to attract investors.

Government securities have very low risk and usually guarantee that the investment can be cashed in at full face value at any time. Their interest rate, however, is also relatively low.

On the other hand, investments in long-term corporate bonds with a distant maturity date may offer a higher interest rate. This type of security is, however, subject to economic factors that make their buy–sell price more volatile. This volatility increases the risk and can reduce the profitability of investing in them if they have to be liquidated, or converted into cash, at an inappropriate time.

Inventories

Although most hotels carry little or no inventory, it is possible that you will have a considerable investment in inventory if you operate a gift and/or souvenir shop in your hotel. In that case, a useful inventory control measure is to calculate your inventory turnover periodically.

Inventory Turnover. The turnover rate is calculated as follows:

$$\frac{\text{Cost of sales for the month}}{\text{Average inventory during month}}$$

Cost of sales for the month is calculated as follows:

Beginning-of-the-month inventory
+ Purchases during month
− End-of-the-month inventory

Average inventory is calculated as follows:

Beginning-of-the-month inventory + End-of-the-month inventory ÷ 2

Assume you had the following figures:

Beginning-of-the-month inventory	$ 7,000
End-of-the-month inventory	8,000
Purchases during month	24,500

The inventory turnover rate is

$$\frac{\$7,000 + \$24,500 - \$8,000}{(\$7,000 + \$8,000) \div 2} = \frac{\$23,500}{\$7,500} = 3.1 \text{ times}$$

The inventory turnover could be calculated annually, but it is preferable that you do it monthly, particularly if monthly income statements are prepared. This is because if the turnover rate at the end of any month is out of line, corrective action can be taken then, instead of only at the year-end.

Turnover Trends.   Perhaps of more importance to your hotel is not what the actual turnover rate is, but whether or not there is a change in this turnover rate over time, and what the cause of the change is. For example, let us assume that the earlier figures of $23,500 for cost of sales and $7,500 for average inventory, giving a turnover rate of 3.1, were typical of the monthly figures for your operation. If you noticed that the figure for turnover changed to 2, this could mean that more money was being invested in inventory and not producing a return:

$$\frac{\$23,500}{\$11,750} = 2 \text{ times}$$

Alternatively, a change in the turnover rate to 4 could mean that too little was invested in inventory:

$$\frac{\$23,500}{\$ 5,875} = 4 \text{ times}$$

In some hotels, the turnover rate may be extremely low (less than 2). For example, a gift shop in a resort hotel in a remote location may only be able to obtain deliveries once a month. It is thus forced to carry a large inventory. On the other hand, a gift shop that receives daily delivery of its products from a local wholesaler and carries little inventory could conceivably have a turnover rate as high as 30 times a month. Each hotel should establish its own standards for turnover, and then watch for deviations from those standards.

Accounts Payable, Accrued Expenses, and Other Current Liabilities

The cash conservation objective with accounts payable, accrued expenses, and other current liabilities is to delay payment until payment is required. However, this does not mean delaying payment until it is delinquent. A hotel with a reputation for delinquency may find it has difficulty obtaining supplies and services on anything other than a cash basis.

If a discount for prompt payment is offered, the advantages of this should be considered. For example, a common discount rate is 2 percent off the invoice total if paid within ten days, otherwise it is payable without discount within 60 days. On a $1,000 purchase that you paid within ten days this would save $20. This may not seem like a lot of money, but multiplied many times over on all similar purchases made during a year it could amount to a large sum.

However, in the example cited you may have to borrow the money ($980) in order to make the payment within ten days. Let us assume you borrowed the money for 50 days at an 8 percent interest rate. The interest expense on this borrowed money would be

$$\frac{\$980 \times 50 \text{ days} \times 8\%}{365 \text{ days}} = \$10.74$$

It would still be advantageous to borrow the money, because the difference between the discount saving of $20.00 and the interest expense of $10.74 is still $9.26.

PROFIT IS NOT CASH

One of the most important facts you must remember in cash management and in analyzing income statements is that the net profit amount shown on the income statement is not the equivalent of cash. A reason for this is the accrual nature of the accounting process (discussed in Chapter 1). With accrual accounting, sales are recorded at the time the sale is made, even though you may not receive the cash until some time later.

Similarly, you can purchase supplies on credit. In other words, the goods are received and used but not paid for until 30 days or more later. However, as long as the goods are used during the income statement period they are recorded on the income statement as an expense.

Also, some expenses may be prepaid at the beginning of the year (for example, insurance expense), yet the total insurance cost is spread equally over each monthly income statement for the entire year. This means that, for example, in January $12,000 might be paid out for annual insurance, yet only $1,000 is recorded on the January income statement as an expense, and $1,000 will be shown as an expense for each of the next 11 months.

Another complicating factor is that some items (such as depreciation) are recorded as an expense on the income statement even though no cash is involved.

For these and other reasons, the net profit shown on your income statement cannot normally be equated with cash. If you wish to equate net income with cash (a good idea in most businesses), you must convert it to a cash basis, and one of the ways to do this is to prepare cash budgets. Cash budgets are a major aid in effective cash management.

Cash Budgeting

The starting point in cash budgeting is the budgeted income statement showing the anticipated (forecast) sales and expenses by month for as long a period as is required for cash budget preparation.

	April		May		June	
Sales		$18,000		$21,000		$24,000
Payroll and related expenses	$9,000		$10,500		$12,000	
Supplies and other expenses	1,500		1,750		2,000	
Utilities	500		750		1,000	
Rent	1,000		1,000		1,000	
Advertising	500	12,500	500	14,500	500	16,500
Income before depreciation		$ 5,500		$ 6,500		$ 7,500
Depreciation		2,000		2,000		2,000
Net income		$ 3,500		$ 4,500		$ 5,500

Figure 17.1 Illustration of budgeted income and expense statement.

In our case we will use a three-month period. Assume that the bud-geted income statements for Tracy's Trailer Park for the next three months are as in Figure 17.1. In order to prepare the cash budget from these statements, Tracy needs the following additional information:

- Accounting records show that, each month, approximately 60 per-cent of the sales are in the form of cash, and 40 percent are on credit and collected the following month.
- March sales were $16,000 (Tracy needs this information so that he can calculate the amount of cash that is going to be collected in April from sales made in March).
- Payroll, supplies, utilities, and rent are paid 100 percent cash during each current month.
- Advertising has been prepaid in January ($6,000 cash) for the entire year. In order not to show the full $6,000 as an expense in January (because the benefit of the advertising is for a full year), the income statements show $500 each month for this prepaid expense.
- The bank balance on April 1 is $10,200.

Tracy can now use the budgeted income statements (Figure 17.1) and the above information to calculate the amounts for his cash budget. The process is simple. His first cash budget month is April, and cash receipts and disbursements can be calculated as follows:

Cash Receipts.   The cash receipts for April are:

- Current month sales $18,000 × 60% cash = $10,800
- Accounts receivable collections:
  March sales $16,000 × 40% =   6,400

Cash Disbursements. The cash disbursements for April are:

- Payroll and related expense, 100% cash = 9,000
- Supplies and other expense, 100% cash = 1,500
- Utilities, 100% cash = 500
- Rent, 100% cash = 1,000
- Advertising — already paid in January (The $6,000 would have been shown as a cash disbursement for that month.) 0
- Depreciation — does not require a disbursement of cash; it is simply a write-down of the book value of the related assets 0

Tracy's completed cash budget for the month of April would then be as follows:

Opening bank balance		$10,200
Receipts:		
Cash sales	$10,800	
Collections on accounts receivable	6,400	17,200
Disbursements:		
Payroll and related expense	$ 9,000	
Supplies and other expenses	1,500	
Utilities	500	
Rent	1,000	(12,000)
Closing bank balance		$15,400

Note that the closing bank balance each month is calculated as follows:

Opening bank balance + Receipts − Disbursements

or for April

$$\$10,200 + \$17,200 - \$12,000 = \$15,400$$

Each month the closing bank balance becomes the opening bank balance of the following month. Tracy's completed cash budget for the three-month period would be as in Figure 17.2.

From this figure, Tracy can see that the bank account is expected to increase from $10,200 to $28,000 over the next three months. When his cash budget for the months of July, August, and September is prepared, it

	April	May	June
Opening bank balance	$10,200	$15,400	$21,200
Receipts			
Cash sales	10,800	12,600	14,400
Collection on accounts	6,400	7,200	8,400
Total	$27,400	$35,200	$44,000
Disbursements			
Payroll and related expenses	$ 9,000	$10,500	$12,000
Supplies and other expenses	1,500	1,750	2,000
Utilities	500	750	1,000
Rent	1,000	1,000	1,000
Total	$12,000	$14,000	$16,000
Closing bank balance	$15,400	$21,200	$28,000

Figure 17.2 Illustration of three-month cash budget.

will show whether or not the bank balance is going to continue to increase or start to decline.

Investing Surplus.   From Figure 17.2, it is obvious that Tracy is going to have a fairly healthy surplus of cash (as long as budget projections are reasonably accurate) that should not be left to accumulate at no or low interest in a bank account. In this particular situation, Tracy might decide to take $20,000 or $25,000 out of the bank account and invest it in high interest rate short-term (30-, 60-, or 90-day) securities.

Without preparing a cash budget, it would be difficult for Tracy to know that there were to be surplus funds on hand that could be used to advantage to further increase his net profit.

If the cash were taken out of his bank account and invested, the cash budget would have to show this at that time as a disbursement until the securities were cashed in and shown as a receipt.

Similarly, interest on loans, principal payments on loans, purchases of fixed assets, income tax payments, and dividend payouts or owner cash withdrawals would also be recorded on the cash budget as disbursements. If any fixed assets were sold for cash, the cash received would show as a receipt.

Negative Cash Budgets

Seasonal hotels may find that for some months of the year their disbursements exceed receipts to the point that they have negative cash budgets. By preparing a cash budget ahead of time, however, the hotel can show that it has anticipated the cash shortage and can plan to cover it, for example, by means of a short-term bank loan. Such a loan will be easier to obtain when your banker sees that good cash management is being practiced through the preparation of a cash budget.

Any loans received to cover cash shortages will be recorded as receipts on the cash budget at that time, and as disbursements when paid back.

The cash budget, particularly if prepared a year ahead, not only helps you in making decisions about investing excess funds and arranging to borrow funds to cover shortages, but also aids in making discretionary decisions concerning such things as major renovations, replacement of fixed assets, and payment of dividends (in an incorporated company) or cash withdrawals (in a proprietorship or partnership).

EIGHTEEN

Long-Term Investments

CAPITAL BUDGETING

This chapter concerns methods of evaluating investments in long-term assets. Investment in long-term assets is sometimes referred to as capital budgeting, but we are not so much concerned in this chapter with the budgeting process as we are with the decision about whether or not to make a specific investment, or with the decision about which of two or more investments would be preferable.

The largest long-term investment that a hotel may have is in its land and building. This is a one-time investment for each separate property. However, this chapter is primarily concerned about more frequent investment decisions for items such as equipment and furniture purchases and replacements.

Differences from Day-to-day Decisions

Long-term investment decisions differ from day-to-day decisions for a number of reasons. For example, long-term investment decisions concern assets that have a relatively long life. Day-to-day decisions concern assets that turn over frequently. A wrong decision about a piece of equipment can involve a time span stretching over many years. A wrong decision about operating supplies has only a short-run effect.

Also, day-to-day operating decisions do not usually involve large amounts of money for any individual item, whereas the purchase of a long-term asset requires the outlay of a large sum of money that can have a major effect if a wrong decision is made.

CAPITAL BUDGETING METHODS

Four methods of investment decision making will be discussed in this chapter. These are:

1. Average rate of return (ARR)

2. Payback period (PP)
3. Net present value (NPV)
4. Internal rate of return (IRR)

To set the scene for the average rate of return and the payback period methods, let us consider Molly's—a motel that is presently using a manual system for recording sales. Molly is considering installing an electronic front office sales register that will eliminate part of the present wage cost and save an estimated $4,000 a year. The register will cost $5,000 and is expected to have a 5-year life with no trade-in value. Depreciation is therefore $1,000 a year ($5,000 divided by 5). Saving and expense figures are:

Saving—employee wages	$4,000
Expenses:	
Maintenance	$ 350
Stationery	650
Depreciation	1,000
Total	$2,000
Saving before tax	$2,000
Income tax	1,000
Net annual saving	$1,000

Average Rate of Return

The average rate of return (ARR) method compares the average annual net profit (after income tax) resulting from the investment, with the average investment. The equation for ARR is:

$$\frac{\text{Net annual saving}}{\text{Average investment}}$$

Note that the average investment is simply initial investment divided by two. Using the information from above, Molly's ARR is

$$\frac{\$1,000}{\$(5,000 \div 2)} \times 100 = \frac{\$1,000}{\$2,500} \times 100 = 40.0\%$$

The advantage of the ARR method is its simplicity. It is frequently used to compare the anticipated return from a proposal with a minimum desired return. If the proposal's return is less than desired, it is rejected. If greater than desired, a more in-depth analysis using other investment techniques might then be used. The major disadvantage of the ARR is that it is based on net profit rather than on cash flow.

Payback Period

The payback period (PP) method overcomes the cash flow shortcoming of the ARR. The PP method measures the initial investment with the annual cash inflows. The equation is

$$\frac{\text{Initial investment}}{\text{Net annual cash saving}}$$

Since the information given earlier for Molly provides her with net annual saving, and not net annual cash saving, she must first convert the net annual saving figure to a cash basis. This is done by adding back the depreciation (an expense that does not require an outlay of cash). The cash saving figure is:

Net annual saving	$1,000
Add depreciation	1,000
Net annual cash saving	$2,000

Molly's payback period is then:

$$\frac{\$5,000}{\$2,000} = 2.5 \text{ years}$$

The PP method, although simple, does not really measure the merit of an investment, but only the speed with which the investment cost might be recovered. It is useful in evaluating a number of proposals so that only those that fall within a predetermined payback period will be considered for further evaluation using other investment techniques.

However, both the PP and the ARR methods still suffer from a common fault: they both ignore the time value of cash flows, or the concept that money now is worth more than the same amount of money at some time in the future. This concept will be discussed in the next section, after which we will explore the use of the net present value and internal rate of return methods.

Discounted Cash Flow

The concept of discounted cash flow can probably best be understood by looking first at an example of compound interest. Table 18.1 shows, year by year, what happens if you invest $100.00 at a 10 percent compound

TABLE 18.1

Compound Interest, $100 at 10 Percent

	Jan. 1 0001	Dec. 31 0001	Dec. 31 0002	Dec. 31 0003	Dec.31 0004
Balance forward	$100.00	$100.00	$110.00	$121.00	$133.10
Interest 10%		10.00	11.00	12.10	13.31
Investment value end of year		$110.00	$121.00	$133.10	$146.41

interest rate. At the end of four years, your investment would be worth $146.41.

Discounting is simply the reverse of compounding interest. In other words, at a 10 percent interest rate, what is $146.41 four years from now worth to you today? You could work out the solution manually or with a hand calculator, but it can much more easily be solved by using a table of discounted cash flow factors.

Table 18.2 illustrates such a table, and, if you go to the number (called a factor) that is opposite year 4 and under the 10 percent column, you will see that it is 0.6830. This factor tells us that $1.00 received at the end of year four is worth only $1.00 × 0.683 = $0.683 right now.

Indeed, this factor tells us that any amount of money at the end of four years from now at a 10 percent interest (discount) rate is worth only 68.3 percent of that amount right now. Let us prove this by taking our $146.41 amount at the end of year 0004 from Table 18.1 and discounting it back to the present:

$$\$146.41 \times 0.683 = \$99.99803 \text{ or } \$100.00$$

We know that $100 is the right answer because it is the amount we started with in our illustration of compounding interest in Table 18.1.

For a series of annual cash flows, you simply apply the related annual discount factor for that year to the cash inflow for that year. For example, a cash inflow of $1,000 a year for each of three years using a 10 percent factor will give you the following total discounted cash flow:

Year	Factor	Amount	Total
1	0.9091	$1,000	$ 909.10
2	0.8264	$1,000	826.40
3	0.7513	$1,000	751.30
			$2,486.80

TABLE 18.2
Table of Discounted Cash Flow Factors by Percentage

Period	5	6	7	8	9	10	11	12	13	14	15	16	17	18	19	20	25	30
1	0.9524	0.9434	0.9346	0.9259	0.9174	0.9091	0.9009	0.8929	0.8850	0.8772	0.8696	0.8621	0.8547	0.8475	0.8403	0.8333	0.8000	0.7692
2	0.9070	0.8900	0.8734	0.8573	0.8417	0.8264	0.8116	0.7972	0.7831	0.7695	0.7561	0.7432	0.7305	0.7182	0.7062	0.6944	0.6400	0.5917
3	0.8638	0.8396	0.8163	0.7938	0.7722	0.7513	0.7312	0.7118	0.6931	0.6750	0.6575	0.6407	0.6244	0.6086	0.5934	0.5787	0.5120	0.4552
4	0.8227	0.7921	0.7629	0.7350	0.7084	0.6830	0.6587	0.6355	0.6133	0.5921	0.5718	0.5523	0.5337	0.5158	0.4987	0.4823	0.4096	0.3501
5	0.7835	0.7473	0.7130	0.6806	0.6499	0.6209	0.5935	0.5674	0.5428	0.5194	0.4972	0.4761	0.4561	0.4371	0.4191	0.4019	0.3277	0.2693
6	0.7462	0.7050	0.6663	0.6302	0.5963	0.5645	0.5346	0.5066	0.4803	0.4556	0.4323	0.4104	0.3898	0.3704	0.3521	0.3349	0.2621	0.2072
7	0.7107	0.6651	0.6228	0.5835	0.5470	0.5132	0.4817	0.4524	0.4251	0.3996	0.3759	0.3538	0.3332	0.3139	0.2959	0.2791	0.2097	0.1594
8	0.6768	0.6274	0.5820	0.5403	0.5019	0.4665	0.4339	0.4039	0.3762	0.3506	0.3269	0.3050	0.2848	0.2660	0.2487	0.2326	0.1678	0.1226
9	0.6446	0.5919	0.5439	0.5003	0.4604	0.4241	0.3909	0.3606	0.3329	0.3075	0.2843	0.2630	0.2434	0.2255	0.2090	0.1938	0.1342	0.0943
10	0.6139	0.5584	0.5084	0.4632	0.4224	0.3855	0.3522	0.3220	0.2946	0.2697	0.2472	0.2267	0.2080	0.1911	0.1756	0.1615	0.1074	0.0725
11	0.5847	0.5268	0.4751	0.4289	0.3875	0.3505	0.3173	0.2875	0.2607	0.2366	0.2149	0.1954	0.1778	0.1619	0.1476	0.1346	0.0859	0.0558
12	0.5568	0.4970	0.4440	0.3971	0.3555	0.3186	0.2858	0.2567	0.2307	0.2076	0.1869	0.1685	0.1520	0.1372	0.1240	0.1122	0.0687	0.0429
13	0.5303	0.4688	0.4150	0.3677	0.3262	0.2897	0.2575	0.2292	0.2042	0.1821	0.1625	0.1452	0.1299	0.1163	0.1042	0.0935	0.0550	0.0330
14	0.5051	0.4423	0.3878	0.3405	0.2993	0.2633	0.2320	0.2046	0.1807	0.1597	0.1413	0.1252	0.1110	0.0986	0.0876	0.0779	0.0440	0.0254
15	0.4810	0.4173	0.3625	0.3152	0.2745	0.2394	0.2090	0.1827	0.1599	0.1401	0.1229	0.1079	0.0949	0.0835	0.0736	0.0649	0.0352	0.0195
16	0.4581	0.3937	0.3387	0.2919	0.2519	0.2176	0.1883	0.1631	0.1415	0.1229	0.1069	0.0930	0.0811	0.0708	0.0618	0.0541	0.0281	0.0150
17	0.4363	0.3714	0.3166	0.2703	0.2311	0.1978	0.1696	0.1456	0.1252	0.1078	0.0929	0.0802	0.0693	0.0600	0.0520	0.0451	0.0225	0.0116
18	0.4155	0.3503	0.2959	0.2503	0.2120	0.1799	0.1528	0.1300	0.1108	0.0946	0.0808	0.0691	0.0592	0.0508	0.0437	0.0376	0.0180	0.0089
19	0.3957	0.3305	0.2765	0.2317	0.1945	0.1635	0.1377	0.1161	0.0981	0.0829	0.0703	0.0596	0.0506	0.0431	0.0367	0.0313	0.0144	0.0068
20	0.3769	0.3118	0.2584	0.2146	0.1784	0.1486	0.1240	0.1037	0.0868	0.0728	0.0611	0.0514	0.0433	0.0365	0.0308	0.0261	0.0115	0.0053

Net Present Value

Discounted cash flow can be used with the net present value (NPV) method for evaluating investment proposals. For example, Table 18.3 gives projections of savings and costs for a new microcomputer for Robin's Resort. The computer costs $5,000 and will have a trade-in (scrap) value of $1,000 at the end of its five-year life.

The estimate of the future savings and costs is the most difficult part of the exercise. In Robin's case, he is forecasting for five years ahead. Obviously, the longer the period of time, the less accurate the estimates are likely to be. Note that depreciation is calculated as follows:

Initial cost	$5,000
Less: Trade-in	(1,000)
	$4,000
Depreciation (straight line)	$4,000 = $800/year
	5

TABLE 18.3

Calculation of Annual Net Cash Flow

	Year 1	Year 2	Year 3	Year 4	Year 5
	Microcomputer (Investment Cost $5,000)				
Saving (wages)	$4,000	$4,000	$4,000	$4,000	$4,000
Expenses					
Initial training cost	$3,500				
Maintenance contract	350	$ 350	$ 350	$ 350	$ 350
Special overhaul			250		
Stationery	650	650	650	650	650
Depreciation	800	800	800	800	800
Total expenses	$5,300	$1,800	$2,050	$1,800	$1,800
Saving less expenses	($1,300)	$2,200	$1,950	$2,200	$2,200
Income tax 50%	0	1,100	975	1,100	1,100
	($1,300)	$1,100	$ 975	$1,100	$1,100
Add back depreciation	800	800	800	800	800
					$1,900
Add scrap value					1,000
Net cash flow	($ 500)	$1,900	$1,775	$1,900	$2,900

Also note that depreciation is deductible as an expense for the calculation of income tax, but this expense does not require an outlay of cash year by year. Therefore, Robin must convert the annual net saving from the investment to a cash situation by adding back depreciation each year. Note also that there is a negative cash flow in year one, and that the trade-in value is a partial recovery of the initial investment and is therefore added as a positive cash flow at the end of year 5 in Table 18.3.

The data Robin is interested in from Table 18.3 are the initial investment and the annual net cash flow figures. These figures have been transferred to Table 18.4 and, using the relevant 10 percent discount factors from Table 18.2, have been converted to a net present value basis. Note how the negative cash flow has been handled. As you can see from Table 18.4, Robin's net present value figure from this proposed investment is positive.

It is possible for a net present value figure to be negative if the initial investment exceeds the sum of the individual years' present values. In the case of negative NPV, the investment should not be undertaken, because, assuming the accuracy of the figures, the investment will not produce the rate of return desired.

Finally, the discount rate actually used should be realistic. It is frequently the rate that a hotel's owners expect the business to earn, after taxes, on the equity investment.

Internal Rate of Return

As you have seen, the NPV method uses a specific discount rate to determine if proposals result in a net present value greater than zero. Those that do not are rejected.

TABLE 18.4

Conversion of Annual Cash Flows to Net Present Values

Year	Net Cash Flow	×	Discount Factor	=	Present Value
1	($ 500)		0.9091		($ 455)
2	1,900		0.8264		1,570
3	1,775		0.7513		1,333
4	1,900		0.6830		1,298
5	2,900		0.6209		1,801
Total present value					$5,547
Less: Initial investment					(5,000)
Net present value					$ 547

The internal rate of return (IRR) method also uses the discounted cash flow concept. However, this method's approach determines the interest (discount) rate that will make the total discounted cash inflows equal the initial investment.

For example, suppose you decided to investigate renting a motel adjacent to your hotel in order to increase sales. Your investigation showed that it would cost $100,000 to renovate and furnish the building with a guaranteed five-year lease. The projected cash flow (net profit after tax, with depreciation added back) for each of the five years is as follows:

Year	Cash flow
1	$ 18,000
2	20,000
3	22,000
4	25,000
5	30,000
	$115,000

In addition to the total of $115,000 cash recovery over the five years, it is estimated the furniture could be sold for $10,000 at the end of the lease period. Your total cash recovery is therefore $115,000 + $10,000 = $125,000, which is $25,000 more than the initial investment required of $100,000.

On the face of it, you would appear to be ahead. If the annual flows are discounted back to their net present value, however, a different picture emerges, as illustrated in Table 18.5. Table 18.5 shows that the future flows

TABLE 18.5
Annual Cash Flows Converted to Net Present Value

Year	Annual cash flow	× Discount factor 12%	= Present value
1	$18,000	0.8929	$ 16,072
2	20,000	0.7972	15,944
3	22,000	0.7118	15,660
4	25,000	0.6355	15,888
5	30,000	0.5674	17,022
Sale of equipment and furniture	10,000	0.5674	5,674
Total present value			$ 86,260
Less: Initial investment			(100,000)
Net present value (negative)			$(13,740)

of cash discounted back to today's values using a 12 percent rate are less than the initial investment by almost $14,000. Thus, you know that, if the projections about the venture are correct, there will not be a 12 percent cash return on your investment.

The IRR method can be used to determine the return that you will earn if the investment is made. From Table 18.5, you know that 12 percent is too high. By moving to a lower rate of interest, you will eventually, by trial and error, arrive at one where the NPV (the difference between total present value and initial investment) is virtually zero. This is illustrated in Table 18.6 with a 7 percent interest (discount) rate.

Table 18.6 tells you that the initial $100,000 investment will return the initial cash outlay except for $157 and earn 7 percent on your investment. Stated slightly differently, you would recover the full $100,000 but earn slightly less than 7 percent on your investment. If you are satisfied with a 7 percent cash return on the investment (note this is 7 percent after income tax), then you would proceed with the project.

Nonquantifiable Benefits

In this chapter we have looked at various methods of making investment decisions. We have ignored information that is not easily quantifiable but that might still be relevant to decision making. In practice, however, you should not ignore such factors as prestige, goodwill, reputation, employee or customer acceptance, and the social or environmental implications of your investment decisions.

For example, if you redecorate your lobby, what are the cash benefits? They may be difficult to quantify, but to retain customer goodwill, it may have to be redecorated. Similarly, how are the relative benefits to be assessed in spending $5,000 on lobby redecoration versus Christmas

TABLE 18.6

Discount Factor Arrived at by Trial and Error

Year	Annual cash flow	× Discount factor 7% =	Present value
1	$18,000	0.9346	$16,823
2	20,000	0.8734	17,468
3	22,000	0.8163	17,959
4	25,000	0.7629	19,073
5	30,000	0.7130	21,390
Sale of equipment and furniture	10,000	0.7130	7,130
Total present value			$99,843

bonuses for your employees? Personal judgment must play a major role in such decisions.

LEASING EQUIPMENT

We have had a look at various methods of decision making for purchase of assets such as furniture and equipment. Another method of obtaining your hotel's productive assets is to rent or lease, rather than own, them. A lease is a contractual arrangement where the owner of the asset (the lessor) grants you (the lessee) the right to the asset for a specified period of time in return for periodic lease payments.

Leasing of land and/or buildings has always been a common method used by hotel operators to minimize the investment costs of going into business. In recent years, leasing of furniture and equipment has also become more common. Some suppliers of furniture and equipment will lease directly. In other cases you lease from a company that specializes in leasing. In other words, the lessor is a company that has bought the furniture and equipment from the supplier and has gone into the business of leasing to others.

Advantages of Leasing

As a hotel operator there may be advantages to you to lease rather than to buy furniture and equipment and similar assets.

First, you can avoid the obsolescence that you might otherwise have if the assets are purchased outright. However, the lessor has probably considered the cost of obsolescence (a form of depreciation) and calculated it into his rental rates. However, a lease contract that allows you to replace obsolete equipment with newer equipment that comes on to the market can give you an advantage over your competitor.

Second, leasing allows you to obtain equipment that you might not otherwise be able to afford immediately, or can purchase only with costly financing. In other words, 100 percent "financing" of leased assets is possible because there is no down payment required, and no loan to be repaid with interest. Even if you had the cash available to purchase the assets you need, or a line of credit at your bank that allowed you to borrow sufficient funds, leasing could allow you to use this available cash for investment in more long-lived assets such as land and buildings that, over time, frequently appreciate in value, whereas furniture and equipment generally (if not invariably) depreciate.

Third, income tax can be a consideration. Because lease payments are generally tax deductible, the lease cost is not as demanding on cash flow as it may at first appear. For example, if you lease an item of equipment for $4,000 a year, and this $4,000 is tax deductible and your company is in a 50 percent tax bracket, the net cash cost of leasing is only $2,000.

	Item Leased	Item Not Leased
Profit before lease cost	$10,000	$10,000
Lease expense	4,000	0
Profit before tax	$ 6,000	$10,000
Income tax 50%	3,000	5,000
Net profit	$ 3,000	$ 5,000

As you can see by these figures, even though the lease cost is $4,000, the net profit with leasing is only $2,000 less than if the item is not leased.

However, this is an oversimplified situation because if you owned the asset you would be able to claim depreciation on it (rather than lease expense) as a tax deduction. Also, if you borrow any money to help finance the purchase of an asset, the interest on that borrowed money is also tax deductible.

Finally, even though with a lease the lessor is generally responsible for maintenance of the equipment while you use it, the lessor also owns any residual value in the asset at the end of the lease period. The lease contract may give you the right to purchase the asset at that time at a specified price, or you may have the option to renew the lease for a further specified period of time.

Because of these variables and the result that each lease arrangement is different, you would be wise to obtain all necessary financial information prior to making the decision to buy or lease any item.

One of the ways to help you to make that decision, once you have all the facts, is to use the concept of discounted cash flow, discussed earlier in the chapter, to narrow those facts down to a purely financial comparison.

To Own or to Lease?

Assume that Dino (the operator of Dino's Inn) is considering whether to buy or rent new furnishings for his hotel.

Purchase of the furniture will require a $125,000 loan from the bank. Cost of the furniture is $125,000. The bank loan will be repayable in four equal annual installments of principal ($31,250 per year) plus 8-percent interest. The furniture will be depreciated over five years at $25,000 per year. It is assumed to have no trade-in value at the end of that period. The

TABLE 18.7

Bank Repayment Schedule for $125,000

Year	Interest at 8%	Principal Amount	Balance
1	$10,000	$31,250	$93,750
2	7,500	31,250	62,500
3	5,000	31,250	31,250
4	2,500	31,250	0

income tax rate is 50 percent. Alternatively, the furniture can be leased for five years at a rental of $30,000 per year.

First, with the purchase plan, Dino must prepare a bank repayment schedule showing principal and interest payments for each of the four years (see Table 18.7).

Purchase Cash Outflow.   Next, under the purchase plan he must calculate the net cash outflow for each of the five years. This is shown in Table 18.8. In this table, note that because depreciation and interest expense are tax deductible and since the hotel is in a 50 percent tax bracket, there is an income tax saving equal to 50 percent of these expenses.

Thus, in year one the expenses of $35,000 are offset by the $17,500 tax saving. Dino's net cost after tax is therefore only $17,500. This $17,500 has to be increased by the principal repayment of $31,250 on the bank loan,

TABLE 18.8

Annual Net Cash Outflow With Purchase

	Year 1	Year 2	Year 3	Year 4	Year 5
Interest expense (from Table 18.7)	$10,000	$ 7,500	$ 5,000	$ 2,500	0
Depreciation expense	25,000	25,000	25,000	25,000	$25,000
Total tax deductible expense	$35,000	$32,500	$30,000	$27,500	$25,000
Income tax saving 50%	(17,500)	(16,250)	(15,000)	(13,750)	(12,500)
After-tax cost	$17,500	$16,250	$15,000	$13,750	$12,500
Add: principal payments	31,250	31,250	31,250	31,250	0
Deduct:					
depreciation expense	(25,000)	(25,000)	(25,000)	(25,000)	(25,000)
Net annual cash outflow (inflow)	$23,750	$22,500	$21,250	$20,000	($12,500)

and reduced by the depreciation expense of $25,000 because depreciation does not require an outlay of cash. In year one, the net cash outflow is thus $23,750.

Figures for the other years are calculated similarly. Note that in year 5, because there is no interest expense and bank loan payment to be made, the cash flow is positive rather than negative.

Rental Cash Outflow. Table 18.9 shows Dino's calculation of annual net cash outflows under the rental plan. Note that under the rental option there is no depreciation expense (because Dino's Inn does not own the furnishings), and no interest or principal payments because no money is to be borrowed.

Discounted Cash Flows. Finally, the net cash flow figures from Tables 18.8 and 18.9 have been transferred to Table 18.10 and discounted using the appropriate discount factors from Table 18.2. The discount rate used is 8 percent because it is Dino's current cost of borrowing money from the bank. Table 18.10 shows that from a present value point of view, Dino would be better to rent in this particular case because his total present value of cash outflows is lower by $4,450 ($64,339 − $59,889).

Other Considerations. In any buy-or-lease situation there could be other factors to be taken into the calculations. For example, in the purchase option, a hotel might use some of its own cash as a down payment and borrow less than the full purchase amount required. In such a case, the down payment is an additional cash outflow at the beginning of the first year.

Under a purchase plan there might also be a trade-in value at the end of the period. This trade-in amount would be handled in the calculations as a cash inflow at the end of the period.

In a rental plan the annual payment might be required at the beginning of each year rather than at the end, as was assumed in Dino's situation.

TABLE 18.9

Annual Net Cash Outflow With Rental

	Year 1	Year 2	Year 3	Year 4	Year 5
Rental expense	$30,000)	$30,000	$30,000	$30,000	$30,000
Income tax saving 50%	(15,000)	(15,000)	(15,000)	(15,000)	(15,000)
Net cash outflow	$15,000	$15,000	$15,000	$15,000	$15,000

TABLE 18.10

Total Present Value (Converted from Figures in Tables 18.8 and 18.9)

	Purchase			Rental		
Year	Annual Cash Outflow (Inflow)	Discount Factor 8%	Present Value	Annual Cash Outflow	Discount Factor 8%	Present Value
1	$23,750 ×	0.9259	= $21,990	$15,000 ×	0.9259	= $13,888
2	22,500 ×	0.8573	= 19,289	15,000 ×	0.8573	= 12,860
3	21,250 ×	0.7938	= 16,868	15,000 ×	0.7938	= 11,907
4	20,000 ×	0.7350	= 14,700	15,000 ×	0.7350	= 11,025
5	(12,500) ×	0.6806	= (8,508)	15,000 ×	0.6806	= 10,209
	Total present value		$64,339	Total present value		$59,889

This means that the first rental payment is at time zero, and each of the remaining annual payments is advanced by one year. Under a rental plan, there might also be a purchase option to the lessee at the end of the period. If the purchase is to be exercised it will create an additional cash outflow.

Further, terms on borrowed money can change from one situation to another and different depreciation rates and methods can be used. For example, the use of an accelerated depreciation method will give higher depreciation expense in the earlier years, thus reducing income tax and increasing the cash flow in those years.

Because of all these and other possibilities you must investigate each buy-or-lease situation on its own merits, taking all the known variables into consideration in the calculations before you make your decision.

Computers in Hospitality Management

Throughout most of this book manual systems of financial control have been discussed and demonstrated. Today, many hotels use computers in this area of management.

In the three decades or so since computers have been commercially produced, they have become a major factor in our lives. Despite this, they have been slow to impact the hospitality industry. Initially, this was so because of their high cost and space requirements. For that reason, only chain operations or quite large independent hotels used them.

More recently many hotels have been using computers in their reservation, guest history, registration, and guest accounting area, as well as in back office accounting. Also more recently, computers have been put to valuable use to remove much of the drudgery present in manual cost control systems such as budgeting and inventory control.

Today, the small and low-cost (but still very powerful) microcomputer or personal computer has made computers available to even the small independent hotel entrepreneur. These microcomputers are so low in price that a separate computer can be used cost-effectively by a single department within a hotel. An example of this might be for maintaining storeroom inventory records.

Computers no longer have to be expensive, take up otherwise valuable space, and require a highly skilled technical person to operate them. No longer is it necessary for them to be operated by specialist computer departments remote from day-to-day operations and decision making, producing voluminous reports long after the need for the information they provide is past.

The new, low-cost computers may dictate a change in the way that hotel managers behave on the job. Competitive survival may require managers to learn to use computer resources and the wealth of information they can provide effectively.

The main difference between a computerized and a manual system is the computer's speed and accuracy. Computerized systems, however, cannot do anything that cannot be done manually, and they do not relieve management from the responsibility of decision making once the information is produced.

TYPES OF COMPUTERS

Generally, computers can be categorized into three types.

Mainframe Computers

In the early days, computers were very large, requiring dedicated air-conditioned rooms and specialist personnel to operate them. They were often remote from the departments that needed the information that they could provide. Sometimes the main computer could be accessed by a terminal located in an individual department or by an individual operation that was part of a chain. This type of computer is often referred to today as a *mainframe computer*.

Minicomputers

With the introduction of *minicomputers* this situation changed. A minicomputer was smaller and cheaper than its mainframe predecessors. A chain organization could now afford to have a minicomputer in each separate operation and still be linked to the head office mainframe. Also, a number of users could be connected through terminals to the minicomputer at the same time. This is known as computer time-sharing.

As a timeshare user accesses the minicomputer, the computer locates that user's information, receives instructions from the user to manipulate or add to it, and then stores it again until the user next wants it. For a computer to do this with several users, it needs to be programmed so that information from different users is not mixed up and so that each user is treated in turn if several are using the computer at the same time.

The result is that time-shared computers (either mainframe or minicomputer) operate at only about 50 percent efficiency. As the computer gets busier from more users accessing it, it slows down. Its response time is also irregular, and a user may not know, if the computer does not respond promptly, whether the machine is slowed down because of heavy use or because the user has supplied information that the computer does not understand and cannot process.

A minicomputer may also need a complicated set of instructions and an expensive communication system, as well as extra levels of security with passwords and protected security levels, to link it with all its users and prevent unauthorized access to confidential information.

Finally, with a large time-shared mainframe or minicomputer, if the computer breaks down every user is out of business unless there is a backup computer linked to the first one.

Despite these shortcomings, mainframe and minicomputers have value where common information must be shared by several users. This might be the case in a hotel where guest reservation, registration, and accounting information can be accessed not only by front office personnel but also by accounting office, housekeeping, and marketing employees.

Microcomputers

The heart of a microcomputer is the microprocessor. The microprocessor is sometimes referred to as a microcomputer on a chip, but it is actually only a processing and controlling subsystem on an electronic chip (a very small part of the actual microcomputer).

Computer chips are so small that 20,000 of them can fit into a briefcase. When the microprocessor was introduced, it dramatically changed the accessibility of computer power and created a major reduction in the cost of this power. Today, a stand-alone microcomputer (or personal computer, as it is sometimes referred to) can cost as little as a few thousand dollars and can be easily placed on a manager's desk or small table. No specialist expertise is required to operate these computers. Indeed, it is no more necessary to know how a computer works in order to use it than it is to know how a car works in order to drive it.

The terms *microprocessor* and *microcomputer* are sometimes used interchangeably, but they do not mean the same thing. A microprocessor is the physical design and structure engraved on the chips that make a microcomputer function. Microcomputers are known as microcomputers because their systems are miniaturized.

A microcomputer could therefore be simply described as a small computer, although that can be misleading because today's microcomputers, small as they are, are as powerful as much larger computers were 20 years ago. Microcomputers are so independently versatile that it is often better (and cheaper) to buy an extra machine for a special type of job than it is to create a special mainframe or minicomputer time-sharing program that several users can access.

The major disadvantage of microcomputers is their somewhat limited storage capacity, which means that some of the more complex programs that a hotel operator wishes to use may not run on them.

Microcomputers can be operated independently but can also be linked together to access the same common information that all their users need from time to time (such as reservation information). The linking of several independent computers is known as networking. As networking capability is further advanced, it may soon be possible for a hotel operation to have its purchasing needs transmitted by its microcomputer to a network of suppliers' computers.

Also in the future may be electronic funds transfer, in which sales terminals in a hotel are connected directly to a computer at a local bank, which, in turn, is networked to terminals at other banks. If hospitality industry customers pay their bills by bank credit card or check, the card or check can be verified by the local bank's computer, which then issues instructions that are transmitted to the customer's bank so that the funds are immediately transferred to the hotel operation's local bank account. The advantage of this to the hotel operator is the time saving of one or more days (and the resulting increase in interest income) that occurs and the reduction of losses from dishonored credit cards or not sufficient funds (NSF) checks.

HARDWARE VERSUS SOFTWARE

The *hardware* of a computer system is the physical equipment that follows a predetermined set of instructions in a self-directed fashion. Instructions are developed by programmers. Once a program (or set of instructions) is placed in the hardware, the computer can carry out those instructions without any operator intervention. Any intelligence that a computer has must be programmed into it, and any weaknesses in that intelligence are the fault of the program.

Software

A computer may be able to operate with many different programs for different jobs. Each program is copied into the computer when it is needed. When a new program is fed in (loaded), the previous program is replaced. When the machine is switched off, any program currently in the machine is lost to it. Thus, because of the temporary nature in the computer of each program, programs are known as *software*. Software is generally stored on tape or on disks, and when it is loaded into the machine it is not removed from the tape or disk but only copied.

Once stored on tape or disk, this storage medium can be used with any other computer of the same type. The information on the disk or tape is read by the computer scanning the magnetic surface and copying the encoded data into the computer's temporary memory (sometimes referred to as random access memory or RAM). Once the data are in the computer they can be amended, added to, or removed if they are no longer wanted before they are stored again on the disk or tape. In other words, software storage tapes or disks are the permanent record of a program.

Good hardware is not hard to find, but good software is the key to a computer system's performance. Software has to be written (contain instructions) in a language, or set of codes, that the computer understands, and it then usually has to convert these instructions into another internal language of its own before it can actually carry out the instructions. There are more than 2,000 different computer languages available to programmers today, and each of these languages may have several dialects of its own.

System Software

Sometimes the term *firmware* or *system software* is used. Firmware is a piece of software that is built into the computer by its manufacturer. In other words, it is a piece of hardware that behaves like a piece of software. It generally comprises some circuits that load certain instructions into the computer immediately when it is switched on. For example, firmware might contain some identification codes for security purposes so that only users who properly identify themselves can use the computer or use some of its applications, depending on who they are. Firmware is also used for diagnostic purposes, such as detection of user errors (for example, using an inappropriate code that the computer does not understand).

Hardware Systems

Computer hardware systems usually comprise a number of components. Even a microcomputer cannot do much without the aid of some other hardware, or peripheral equipment. The main part of the computer where all the work or manipulation is carried out is sometimes referred to as the *central processing unit* (CPU). The CPU is often referred to as the brain of a hardware system because it controls all other hardware devices.

The CPU has its own set of built-in instructions in its memory chips that cannot be altered by the user. These instructions are known as *read-only memory* (ROM) which the user can access and "read" but cannot change. These instructions are specified by the computer manufacturer by its own codes. Because different manufacturers use different codes, programs from one manufacturer often do not work on competitor computers.

In order to load user programs or instructions into the CPU, another hardware device is required. For microcomputers that operate from programs on disks, that input device is known as a *disk drive*. With some microcomputers the disk drive (or drives, if there is more than one) may be built into the CPU.

Also needed is another input device so that the user can interact with the CPU as work is in process. This input device is a *keyboard*, much like a typewriter keyboard. Again, this keyboard is sometimes built into the CPU instead of being a separate item of hardware linked to it.

Another hardware item is the *monitor*, also known as a screen, cathode ray tube (CRT), or video display unit (VDU). The monitor displays prompts to the user from the CPU, what is input from the keyboard by the user, and the result of the work that is being done. With some computers, the monitor may be built in and be part of the CPU. The keyboard and monitor together are sometimes referred to as input/output (I/O) devices.

Finally, for most work performed a printer is needed. The printer is invariably a separate piece of equipment attached by cable to the CPU. When work performed by the user is printed out, the printed material is often received as "hard copy" to differentiate it from "soft copy," or work that is only viewed on the monitor and might still have further work done on it before a hard copy is needed.

For example, when a guest is staying in a hotel that has a computerized system, the front office cashier can view the soft copy of the guest's account on the monitor during the course of the stay and add charges to it during that stay. When the guest indicates he wishes to check out and pay, the final copy of the guest account can be viewed on the monitor prior to printing out the hard copy (guest account) for presentation to the guest.

Obviously, with all these various pieces of hardware comprising a computer system there has to be a high degree of compatibility among them. In addition to compatibility of hardware, the software that is used must also have language compatibility with each item of hardware.

Canned Software

The question sometimes arises whether it is better to have software specifically written for an individual hospitality operation's needs or to buy an already written software package (known as canned software). Specifically written software is far more expensive than canned programs. Also, most hospitality operations are small businesses that do not have the resources necessary to carry out the systems analysis and program design work necessary to develop their own computer software.

Canned programs normally have been widely tested and any errors (bugs) in them generally have been detected and corrected. Demonstrations of canned software can usually be viewed before the purchase decision is made. The cost to buy, install, and train employees can also be determined in advance, and any compromises that need to be made between an operation's needs and the software's capabilities can be adjusted for. A successful canned software package thus represents a proven product obtainable at much less cost than a custom-designed one.

Obviously, the benefits of using off-the-shelf software have to be considered against its disadvantages. A software package written for broad hospitality requirements may not be as easy to use, or as fast, as one that is custom designed.

Interactive Programs

Software programs can be either interactive or noninteractive. An interactive program prompts the user sequentially step by step. It is thus easier to use because it helps ensure that no information that should be entered by the user is omitted.

A noninteractive program provides no prompts. Thus the user must know exactly what information to enter in correct sequence line by line and in a predetermined format. This requires more user skill (and thus an added training cost). The advantage is that the program is much faster.

Integrated Software Systems

In a hospitality operation, some information is used for more than one purpose. The name of a guest registering in a hotel is an example of information that might be used for room reservation, registration, guest history, housekeeping, and accounting purposes.

With a computer system it is feasible, sensible, and advantageous to use software that is integrated. In integrated software systems, the objective is to record an item of data only once and then to use it in every possible way to provide information for planning and control purposes. If the item of data had to be entered into the computer each time it was wanted, errors could be made. Correcting errors costs time and money.

One could consider a hospitality operation as an entire system and have a completely integrated package of computer software to control and plan every single aspect of its operation. However, a completely integrated software package to handle all this would be costly and complex, would probably incur high training costs because of its complexity, and would create severe maintenance and data security problems. Further, if one part of the system failed it would create difficulties in all departments or areas. For these reasons, a small property would find justifying a completely integrated system financially difficult.

Application-oriented Software Systems

At the other extreme is a software system that is oriented to a single application. If software is application-oriented, it is generally designed to handle one specific type of job and does not allow much integration. An example is a payroll system that is not integrated with labor cost budgeting.

Because of their relative simplicity, application-oriented software systems can be easily evaluated to see whether they will perform precisely the limited jobs that they are to carry out. These systems are inexpensive to buy and install and can be introduced into an operation over time as finances allow. An ideal situation is to move from a piecemeal stand-alone set of application systems to an integrated system over time as long as each part can be made compatible with others. In this type of in-house network, each computer system is able to operate on a stand-alone basis but can integrate with all others for transmission of certain data.

Obviously, the more narrow an application-oriented system is, the easier it is to develop and the lower will be its cost. It will also be more efficient and reliable because it controls fewer functions. However, the narrower an application system becomes, the less effective it may be as far as overall control is concerned. For example, if a guest accounting system has to be supported by a separate reservation system, then two packages of software are required, two different computer hardware systems may be needed, and two sets of user/operator systems have to be learned.

Initially, most microcomputer applications in the hospitality industry were stand-alone applications. But as the power and memory capacity of microcomputers have improved, the software packages available have become less stand-alone and more integrated.

Three common application-oriented software packages are word processing, data base managers, and spreadsheets.

Word Processing

Word processing refers to software that is programmed to manipulate words (text). Any small computer can be programmed to handle word processing. Surprisingly, many people do not think that machines that are only used to do word processing are true computers. But if they can be programmed to do word processing, then they can be programmed to do other things as well.

The purchase of a low-cost microcomputer to be used primarily for word processing is a good way to introduce computers into a business. Word processors can be very useful when a large amount of standard correspondence is handled, as in a hotel reservation department where a form letter is used to confirm reservations.

The main purpose of a word processor is to facilitate text creation and editing, and the ease with which this may be done is a major factor in selection of word-processing software. One of the major advantages of using computers rather than typewriters for word processing is that documents can be printed more attractively. For example, with some computer printers a variety of typestyles can be used in the same document.

As well as allowing text editing, more sophisticated word-processing software contains spelling checkers with a dictionary of as many as 30,000 words. If a word is typed that is not in the dictionary, it will be highlighted on the monitor. If it is a technical word not found in the regular dictionary, that word can be added to the dictionary so that it will not be highlighted the next time it is used.

Some word-processing software also has graphics capabilities, meaning that bar or pie charts can be used to highlight certain types of information, such as departmental expense trends.

Data Base Manager

A *data base manager* is a collection of records such as addresses of regular customers or personnel data. These are records that form a data base. A data base manager allows quick access to and ready manipulation of the records that are in that data base. In other words, it is much like an office filing system where records (files) can be randomly accessed, used as required, and then restored in the same order or rearranged in some other order before storing.

It may be useful to purchase a software package that includes both word processing and a data base. For example, it may be necessary for a hotel to send out a standard form letter to all the travel agencies it regularly does business with advising them of a change in room prices or commission rates. The computer can be programmed to take each travel agency's address in turn from the data base, type it on the hotel's letterhead, type in the letter from the word processor, then move to the next address and letter on a new page until all addresses have been used. All of this can be completed without any user intervention once the process has been started.

A data base manager can be particularly useful in yield management (see Chapter 15) because it can be used to store guest history information and reservation patterns.

Spreadsheet

Spreadsheet software is basically a large electronic sheet with rows down the side and columns across the top, much like a work sheet for preparing a budget. Most managers have struggled with budgets using pencils and column pads and have become frustrated when they wish to see what happens, for example, if the labor cost to sales ratio is altered over a twelve-month annual budget. The changes that have to be made to labor cost, total expenses, and net profit require 36 alterations, considerable erasing and correcting, and a risk that one or more errors will occur. A properly programmed electronic spreadsheet will allow a manager to answer this type of "What if?" question in seconds and print out the results. Indeed, multiple "What if?" changes can be made at the same time at rapid speed.

Spreadsheets lend themselves not only to budgeting but also to forecasting. For example, a spreadsheet could have in its memory all the various room types a hotel offers, including how many of each are sold on average by day of the week for each specific month. The spreadsheet can then forecast for the current month, on the basis of past performance, how many of each will be sold each day next month. Spreadsheets also lend themselves well to the following applications:

- Scheduling employees for improved labor cost control.
- Preparing depreciation schedules.
- Calculating percentages (given the dollar amounts) for common-size financial statement analysis.
- Converting budgeted income statements (given appropriate ratios) to cash flow budgets.
- Using NPV and IRR analysis for long-term investments.
- Preparing budget variance analyses.
- Using CVP analysis for various types of decisions.

Integrated Work Stations

As far as planning and control are concerned, word processing, data base manager, and spreadsheet software are closely related. A computer ought to be able to pass data from its data base manager to a spreadsheet and then in turn pass the results to a word processor for addition of text and final printing of a report, including graphics where valuable. Indeed, for many microcomputers today, single software packages that include all three of these software systems on one disk are available. These are known as integrated work stations.

ACCOUNTING PACKAGES

Another area that lends itself well to an integrated software package is general accounting. Most businesses with a manual system of accounting use an integrated approach for their general ledger, sales, accounts receivable, purchases, accounts payable, payroll, and inventory control. Hotel front office, reservations, registration, and guest accounting can also be integrated into this system. Today, there are integrated software packages —commonly known as property management systems (PMS)—available for computerization of this work. In some situations it may not be feasible or practical to integrate each of these subsystems on the mainframe computer. For example, it may be useful to separate inventory control so that a specialized software package that will do many more things than a general accounting system's inventory control subsystem will do can be purchased.

Similarly, it may not be practical for a hotel to computerize its payroll. One of the reasons is that the expense of maintaining computerized payroll software is comparatively high. Each time the laws relating to employment change (such as for minimum wage rates, tax deduction rates, and unemployment insurance rates), the software must be rewritten to accommodate those changes. For this reason, many hotels contract out their payroll preparation to a computer service company that specializes in this kind of work.

INVENTORY CONTROL

Computers can be very valuable as a tool in inventory control. Computers can

- Prepare purchase orders for suppliers. It is now also possible for the computer, through networking, to place orders automatically with approved suppliers who submit the best price for the items and quantities needed.
- Prepare lists of items to be received from each supplier so that receiving employees can compare what is delivered with what should be delivered.
- Compare information against purchase orders and specifications for those items as products are received and product information is recorded in the computer from invoices.
- Issue appropriate credit memoranda for goods short-shipped or returned to suppliers.
- Produce receiving reports for products delivered.
- Maintain a record of all storeroom purchases from information entered from invoices and update the perpetual inventory of each storeroom item.
- Record all issues from the storeroom from information entered from requisitions, use this information to adjust the perpetual inventory of

each item, and calculate the total cost of all items issued each day to aid in the calculation of a daily and monthly cost.

- Calculate the cost of items requisitioned by any individual department for any period of time.
- Compare requisition signatures (using a scanner) with a record of those signatures stored in the computer to ensure they are authentic.
- Compare at any time quantity information of actual inventory for any specific item with what the computer-maintained perpetual inventory record is and print out variance reports.
- Let both management and purchaser know when quantities purchased exceed prescribed limits for storeroom stock.
- Provide each month a list of all items that were short-stocked during that period.
- Issue monthly dead-stock reports showing items that have not moved in a stipulated period, such as 30, 60, or 90 days.
- List how many units of each item were purchased from any one supplier and whether that purchase was made at the best quoted price.
- Verify supplier month-end statements against receiving invoices and/or receiving reports, and issue checks in payment of those statements.

A sophisticated inventory control computer program can also adjust the volume of storeroom inventory required according to the level of business. Thus, instead of leaving it to management to establish a fixed minimum and maximum level of stock for each storeroom item, the computer can adjust the reorder point and the order quantity to the actual usage or sales (which may change over time or by season) for that item. Each day, the computer prints out a list of items to be ordered, the quantities needed, and the economic order quantity (if this is built into the system). In cases where particular suppliers are under contract to provide specific storeroom items at contracted prices, the actual purchase orders can be prepared for those suppliers.

Bar Codes

One of the recent advances in inventory control is the use of bar codes on product containers. The *bar code* is a series of parallel black bars of varying width on a white background. The scanners that read the code can be counter-level models (such as those found at check-out stands in supermarkets) or hand-held wands (the type most useful in hospitality industry receiving so that heavy cases do not have to be lifted to pass over the scanner).

A common bar code is the ten-digit Universal Product Code (UPC) system, in which the first five digits identify the manufacturer or processor and the second five digits provide information about the product. The bar code information read and recorded by the computer can include the product's name, container size, item quantity (from which inventory records can be adjusted), and other desired information. For example, part of the bar code can represent specifications for each product.

The UPC has also been advantageous to suppliers who may have dozens of different qualities and container sizes of a particular product, each of which can be quickly identified by reading its bar code and matching it with the purchaser's purchase order specification.

Where bar coding is used by a hospitality operation, it offers the following advantages:

- Fast order processing.
- Reduction in purchasing time.
- Reduction in specification misunderstandings between purchaser and seller.
- More accurate purchasing, ordering, receiving, and inventory records.
- Improved supplies cost control.
- Improved supplier delivery schedules and performance.
- Simplification of receiving procedures.
- Improved inventory and issuing control (as items are issued they can again be passed over the scanner so that each item's perpetual inventory count will be adjusted and proper cost information recorded on requisitions).

Note that bar codes do not contain price information because they are placed on products by the manufacturer, who usually does not know what the end price of the product will be after it has gone through various distribution levels. Thus, pricing information has to be entered into the hotel's computer from invoices received from suppliers.

FRONT OFFICE SYSTEMS

The main objective of a front office system for a hotel is maximization of revenue or sales. For this reason, most front office computer systems are revenue rather than cost control oriented and are based on the reservation, registration, and guest accounting needs of the property.

However, front office systems can provide cost control in certain areas. For example, front office computers can be linked to the telephone system to monitor calls from guest rooms and add to guest accounts charges for both local and long distance calls, so that the hotel is not paying for telephone costs not recovered through charges on guest accounts.

The front office system can also provide constantly updated information to other departments (such as housekeeping) relating to rooms occupancy and guest counts, so that adequate staffing can be arranged and so that departments are not overstaffed.

Finally, front office computers can prepare and print rooms department operating ratios such as occupancy and double occupancy percentages, average daily rates, and the daily yield statistic. In this latter regard, front office computer systems can be immensely useful in maximizing yield by providing information to form a data base of guest history and reservation patterns by type of guest for yield management.

Security Control

More recently, front office systems have been keyed to security control. A computer can be programmed to allow certain keys to open doors during limited periods each day. This might mean that housekeeping staff can only have access to rooms during the room makeup period.

The system can also issue "keys" to guests. These keys are simply plastic cards (about the size of a credit card) that have data encoded on them on magnetic strips or have a series of holes punched through them. The guest room door has on it a device that reads the card and allows the door to be opened.

As they register, the computer issues new guests a "key" card with a unique code on it for each guest and for each specific room. At the same time, the computer erases the old code for that room in the device on the guest room door (so that a departed guest can not reuse his card) and creates a new code corresponding to the arriving guest's card. Departing guests do not even have to turn in their "keys" on leaving. They can be discarded. In cases of emergency, the guest room card reader device can be overridden by a conventional key used by authorized hotel personnel. The plastic key cards can also be used as internal credit/ID cards so that guests can charge to their room accounts food or beverages consumed in the hotel's dining room/bar areas.

For small hotels and motels there is now available computerized equipment located at the front office that can be operated by an arriving guest. The computer accepts specified credit cards that automatically charge the amount for that room to the credit card, print a "paid" invoice for the guest, and issue a plastic key coded to let the guest open the door of the assigned room. No longer is an all-night employee required to register late-arriving guests or check out early-departing ones!

Glossary

Absolute changes: the amount of change in dollars of an item on the income statement from one period to the next.

Accelerated depreciation: a method of depreciation that gives greater amounts of depreciation expense in the earlier years of an asset's life. See also *Depreciation*.

Account: a record in which the current status (or balance) of each type of asset, liability, owners' equity, sale (revenue), and expense is kept.

Accounting equation: assets = liabilities + owners' equity.

Accounting period: the time period covered by the financial statements.

Accounts payable: amounts due to suppliers (creditors); a debt or a liability.

Accounts receivable: amounts due from customers or guests (debtors); an asset. See also *City ledger* and *House account*.

Accounts receivable aging: preparing a schedule classifying receivables in terms of time left unpaid.

Accounts receivable average collection period: the number of days the average receivable remains unpaid.

Accounts receivable turnover: annual sales divided by average accounts receivable.

Accrual accounting: as opposed to cash accounting, a method of accounting whereby transactions are recorded as they occur and not when cash is exchanged; the matching of sales and expenses on income statements regardless of when cash is received or disbursed.

Accrued expenses: expenses that have been incurred but not paid at the balance sheet date; a liability.

Accumulated depreciation: the total depreciation that has been shown as an expense on the income statements since the related assets were purchased. See also *Depreciation*.

Acid test ratio: see *Quick ratio*.

Adjustments: entries made at the end of each accounting period in journals and then in the accounts so that the accounts have correct balances under the accrual accounting method.

Allowance for doubtful accounts (bad debts):   an amount established to cover the likelihood that not all accounts receivable outstanding at the balance sheet date will be collected.

Amortization: a method of writing down the cost of certain intangible assets (such as franchises or goodwill) in the same way that depreciation is used to write down the cost of tangible fixed, or long-term, assets.

Asset: an item, a property, or a resource owned by a business.

Audit tape: a continuous chronological record of each transaction recorded in a cash or sales register (such as front office guest account equipment). The tape can usually be removed only at the end of each day by an authorized person.

Average rate of return (ARR):   a method of measuring the value of a long-term investment. The equation is net annual saving divided by average investment.

Average rate per guest: room revenue divided by number of guests accommodated for a period of time.

Average rate per room occupied: room revenue divided by number of rooms occupied for a period of time.

Bad debt: an account receivable considered or known to be uncollectable. See also *Allowance for doubtful accounts.*

Balance: the amount of an account at a point in time.

Balance sheet: a statement showing that assets = liabilities + owners' equity. A balance sheet shows the financial position of a company at a point in time.

Balance sheet equation: assets equals liabilities plus owners' equity.

Bank: see *Float.*

Bank reconciliation: a monthly or periodic procedure to ensure that the company's bank account balance amount agrees with the bank's statement figure.

Blind receiving: a method of receiving goods without an accompanying invoice so that the receiver is forced to weigh or count all products delivered.

Book value: initial cost of an asset or assets less related accumulated depreciation.

Break-even analysis: an analysis of fixed and variable costs in relation to sales as an aid in decision making.

Break-even equation or formula: an equation useful in making business decisions concerning sales levels and fixed and variable costs.

Break-even point: the level of sales at which a company will make neither an income nor a loss.

Budget: a business plan, usually expressed in monetary terms.

Budget cycle: the sequence of events covered by a budget period from initial budget preparation through to comparison of actual results with budgeted estimates.

Call sheet buying: see *Competitive buying.*

Capital asset: see *Fixed assets.*

Capital budget: a budget concerning long-term, or fixed, assets.

Cash accounting: a method of accounting (as opposed to accrual accounting) whereby transactions are only recorded at the time cash is received or disbursed.

Cash budget: a budget concerned with cash inflows and cash outflows.

Cash disbursements: money paid by cash or by check for the purchase of goods or services.

Cash management: cash conservation and the management of other working capital accounts to maximize the effectiveness of the business's use of cash.

Cash receipts: cash or checks received in payment for sale of products or services.

City ledger: the accounts receivable of guests who have left the hotel and charged their accounts.

Collusion: two or more people working together for fraudulent purposes.

Common shares: a form of stock or share issued by an incorporated business to raise money.

Comparative/common-size statement analysis: two or more financial statements presented with all data in both dollar and percentage figures.

Comparative statement analysis: financial statements for two or more periods presented so that the change in each account balance from one period to the next is shown in both dollar and percentage terms.

Competitive buying: a method of purchasing in which a number of suppliers are contacted to quote prices before the decision is made to buy from the supplier who offers the best price.

Contribution margin: the difference between sales and variable costs or expenses.

Contribution statement: a form of income statement presentation where variable costs are deducted from sales to show contribution margin, and fixed costs are then deducted from contribution margin to arrive at profit.

Controllable cost or expense: a cost that is controllable by an individual (such as a department head).

Cooperative buying: a method of purchasing in which a number of hotels coordinate their purchases in order to receive a lower price as a result of bulk buying.

Cost: the price paid to purchase an asset or to pay for the purchase of goods or services. Also frequently used as a synonym for expense.

Cost management: an awareness of the various types of cost and the effect that the relevant ones have on individual business decisions.

Cost of sales: calculated by adding beginning of the accounting period inventory to purchases during the period, and deducting end of the period inventory.

Cost-plus buying: a method of purchasing in which the purchaser arranges with a supplier to purchase all requirements for a product or products at a specific percentage markup over the supplier's cost for a future fixed period of time.

Credit: 1. an entry on the right-hand side of an account; 2. to extend credit or to allow a person to consume goods or services and pay at a later date.

Credit invoice: an invoice prepared by a supplier showing, for example, that goods delivered to a company have been returned as unacceptable.

Credit memorandum: a dummy credit invoice made out by a company prior to receipt of a credit invoice from the supplier.

Creditor: a person, or company, to whom a business owes money.

Current assets: cash or other assets likely to be turned into cash within a year.

Current dollars: historic (previous periods') dollars converted to terms of today's dollars for purposes of comparison.

Current liabilities: debts that are due to be paid within one year.

Current liquidity ratios: ratios that indicate a company's ability to meet its short-term debts.

Current ratio: the ratio of current assets to current liabilities.

Day rate: the rate charged by a hotel for the use of a room for a portion of the day and not overnight.

Debit: an entry in the left-hand side of an account.

Debt: money owed to a person or organization; an obligation.

Debt to equity ratio: the amount of debt (liabilities) expressed as a ratio of owners' equity.

Declining balance depreciation: a method of accelerated depreciation where higher amounts of depreciation expense are recorded in the earlier years of an asset's life.

Demand, elasticity of: see *Elasticity of demand.*

Department budget: an operating budget prepared for an individual department in a multidepartment organization.

Departmental income: the income of an individual department after direct expenses have been deducted from sales; sometimes referred to as contributory income.

Dependent variable: an item that is affected by what happens to another item. For example, labor cost is affected by the level of sales; labor is the dependent variable.

Depreciation: a method of allocating the cost of a fixed asset over the anticipated life of the asset, showing a portion of the cost, for each accounting period of the life, as an expense on the income statement.

Direct cost or expense: an expense that can be distributed directly to an operating department and is generally controllable by that department.

Discount: a reduction of the amount paid on a purchase because of prompt payment.

Discounted cash flow: a method of converting future inflows and/or outflows of cash to the value of today's dollars.

Discount grid: a table that shows the additional hotel room occupancy required to compensate when rack rates are discounted at various percentages.

Discretionary cost or expense: one that could be incurred but does not have to be at the present time.

Dividend: an amount paid out of profit after tax to shareholders as a return on their investment in the company.

Double-entry accounting: an accounting procedure that requires equal debit and credit entries in the accounts for each business transaction to ensure the accounting equation is kept in balance.

Double occupancy percent: the percentage of rooms occupied in a hotel that are occupied by more than one person.

Drawings: see *Withdrawals.*

Earnings statement: see *Income statement.*

Elasticity of demand: the effect that a change in price has on demand for a product or service.

Employee orientation: a formalized procedure of introducing each new employee hired to his or her job.

Employee turnover: the loss and replacement of an employee.

Exit interview: a procedure of meeting with each employee who leaves employment to try to determine the reason he or she is leaving.

Expenditure: payment in cash for purchase of a product or service, or incurrence of a liability for purchase of a product or service.

Expense: products or services consumed or used in operating a business.

Financial leverage: a method of financing where the amount of debt (liability) is increased in proportion to equity (owners' investment).

Financial position: the financial condition of a business as indicated by its balance sheet.

Financial statements: a balance sheet and an income statement and, where appropriate, a statement of retained earnings and other supporting information.

Fiscal period: an annual accounting period that may not coincide with the calendar year.

Fixed assets: assets of a long-term or capital nature that will be depreciated over a number of years.

Fixed cost or expense: a cost that does not change in the short run with changes in volume of business.

Float (or Bank): an amount of money advanced to an employee for change-making purposes.

Folio: see *Guest account.*

Franchise fee or cost: the cost to purchase the right to use the name and/or services of another organization.

Goodwill: the value of an established business, based on its name or reputation, above the value of its tangible assets.

Gross profit: sales less cost of sales.

Guest account: the account of a guest staying in a hotel; the account is usually kept at the front office until it is paid.

Historic cost: the cost of something at the time it was paid for, not adjusted to current cost.

Horizontal statement analysis: see *Comparative statement analysis.*

House account: 1. the account of a guest still registered and staying at the hotel. See also *City ledger.* 2. a hotel that purchases from a supplier (usually by telephone) without the supplier's having a sales representative regularly calling at the hotel.

Income and expense statement: see *Income statement.*

Income statement: a financial statement showing money earned from sales of products and services for a period of time, less the expenses incurred to earn those sales; sometimes referred to as the profit and loss statement.

Incorporated company: a legal form of business operation that differentiates it from a proprietorship or partnership.

Independent variable: an item that is not affected by what happens to another item. For example, room sales are not affected by the labor cost; sales are the independent variable.

Indirect cost or expense: a cost not allocated directly to a department. See also *Direct cost.*

Interest earned ratio: profit before interest and income tax divided by interest expense.

Internal control: a system of procedures and forms established in a business to safeguard its assets and help ensure the accuracy of the information provided by its accounting system.

Internal rate of return (IRR): a method of measuring the value of a long-term investment using discounted cash flow. See also *Discounted cash flow.*

Inventory: products purchased but not yet used to generate sales. See also *Physical inventory.*

Inventory turnover: cost of sales for a period of time divided by the average inventory for that period.

Invoice: document prepared to record the sale of products or services and giving details about the transaction and the total value of the sale.

Job description: a description of what a job entails, the tasks that must be performed, and when those tasks must be performed. See also *Task procedures.*

Job rotation: training employees at different jobs so that they can easily be moved from one job to another when the need arises.

Joint cost or expense: one that is shared by more than one department.

Journal: accounting record summarizing business transactions as they occur prior to posting the information to the individual accounts.

Kickback: cash or merchandise given to a purchaser by a supplier to encourage the purchaser to favor that supplier.

Labor cost percent: labor cost divided by sales and multiplied by 100.

Labor productivity standard: a predetermined level of employee productivity, such as the number of guest rooms a maid should clean during a standard shift.

Lapping: a method of fraud that can occur when an employee has complete control of accounts receivable and payments received on these accounts.

Leasehold improvements: architectural and/or interior design changes made to rented (leased) premises.

Ledger: a book of accounts in which business transactions are entered after having been recorded in journals.

Leverage: see *Financial leverage* and/or *Operating leverage.*

Liability: a debt or an obligation owed by a business.

Liquidation: the closing of a business by selling its assets and paying off its liabilities.

Liquidity: the financial strength of a business in terms of its ability to pay off its short-term or current liabilities without difficulty; a healthy working capital position; a good current ratio.

Loan: an amount borrowed; a debt; a liability.

Loan principal: the repayment of the initial amount borrowed on a loan is a principal payment as distinct from interest that is in addition to principal payments.

Long-term assets: see *Fixed assets.*

Long-term budget: a budget for a period of time generally in excess of one year.

Long-term liability: a debt or obligation to be paid off more than one year hence.

Loss: an excess of expenses over revenue.

Lowballing: a supplier's practice of quoting low prices for products in order to obtain the purchaser's business, then gradually increasing the price.

Marketable securities: investments in government bonds or similar securities that can be readily converted into cash.

Market quotation sheet: a form used to record suppliers' quotes so that prices for products to be purchased can be compared.

Market quote buying: see *Competitive buying.*

Market value: the current value of an asset, sometimes known as its replacement value.

Mark-up: the difference between the cost of an item and its selling price.

Matching principle: a principle of accrual accounting relating expenses to the revenue earned during a period regardless of when the cash was received or the expenses paid.

Memorandum invoice: a temporary, dummy invoice prepared in the absence of a proper invoice.

Mortgage: a long-term debt or liability generally secured by using long-term assets (such as land and/or building) as collateral.

Net assets: see *Net worth.*

Net book value: see *Book value.*

Net income: total revenue from sales and other income less total expenses.

Net present value (NPV): a method of measuring the value of a long-term investment using discounted cash flow. See also *Discounted cash flow.*

Net working capital: current assets less current liabilities.

Net worth: total assets less total liabilities; owners' equity.

Night auditor: the front office employee who completes the daily night transcript.

Noncontrollable cost or expense: costs or expenses that are generally fixed in nature in the short run, such as rent or interest.

Note payable: a liability documented by a written promise to pay at a specified time.

Occupancy percentage: the ratio of rooms occupied to rooms available expressed in percentage terms.

One-stop buying: a method of purchasing in which all items of a particular type (such as paper or cleaning supplies) are purchased from one supplier.

Open-market buying: see *Competitive buying.*

Operating budget: a budget concerned with revenue and/or expenses.

Operating cost: see *Expense.*

Operating leverage: the relationship between fixed and variable expenses; high fixed expenses compared to variable expenses indicate high operating leverage.

Outstanding check: a check issued in payment of a debt that has not yet been cashed in by the payee, or has been cashed in but has not yet been deducted from the payer's bank account.

Owners' equity: total assets minus total liabilities; net worth.

Paid out: 1. an amount paid out of cash for a minor purchase. 2. an amount paid out for a purchase for a guest that is then added to the guest's account.

Par stock: the maximum amount of stock that should be on hand at any time for each inventory item.

Partnership: an unincorporated business owned by two or more persons.

Payback period: the time it takes to recover an investment; initial investment divided by net annual cash saving.

Perpetual inventory card: a form that is used to record the movement of all items in and out of storage rooms. One card is used for each item.

Petty cash: a fund of money controlled by an individual from which minor purchases of products or services can be paid.

Physical inventory: the actual counting, recording, and pricing of assets.

Preferred shares: a form of stock or share issued by an incorporated business to raise money, generally ranking before common shares with reference to dividends.

Prepaid expense: an expense paid for and shown as an asset until it is matched up with related revenue and shown as an expense. See *Matching principle.*

Present value: see *Discounted cash flow.*

Prime vendor buying: see *One-stop buying.*

Product differentiation: a method of presenting a product or service in a different way from competitors, for example by creating a unique ambiance or providing superior service.

Productivity standard: see *Labor productivity standard.*

Profit: see *Net income.*

Profit and loss statement: see *Income statement.*

Profit margin: see *Profit to sales ratio.*

Profit to sales ratio: Profit divided by sales and multiplied by 100. Also known as profit margin.

Proprietorship: an unincorporated business owned by a single individual.

Purchase order: a form prepared by a purchaser authorizing a supplier to deliver needed goods or services to a hotel.

Quick ratio: the ratio of quick assets to current liabilities.

Quotation buying: see *Competitive buying.*

Rack rate: the normal maximum rate charged for a hotel guest room.

Rate spread: the difference between the rate for single occupancy of a guest room and double occupancy of that room.

Ratio: the relationship of one item to another. For example, $2,000 of current assets to $1,000 of current liabilities would be a 2:1 ratio.

Ratio analysis: the use of various ratios to monitor the ongoing progress of a business.

Receiving stamp: a stamp placed on each invoice and initialled in the appropriate place by each person responsible for control procedures for products received.

Registration card: the form on which a guest records necessary information when checking into a hotel.

Relative change: the change for each item on an income statement from one period to the next expressed in percentage terms.

Relevant cost or expense: one that is important and to be considered in a particular business decision.

Requisition: a form completed by an authorized person requesting that needed items be issued from the storeroom.

Retained earnings statement: a financial statement used by an incorporated business to show accumulated net incomes less accumulated losses less any dividends paid since the business began. See also *Statement of capital.*

Return on owners' equity: profit after income tax divided by owners' equity.

Revenue: money earned from sales and/or income received in exchange for products or services.

Riding the market: see *Competitive buying.*

Sales: see *Revenue.*

Scrap value: see *Trade-in value.*

Sealed-bid buying: a formalized method of competitive purchasing where potential suppliers provide information, including a quoted price, on a bid form.

Semifixed or semivariable cost or expense: one that has both fixed and variable elements and is neither entirely fixed nor entirely variable in relation to sales.

Share: see *Common shares* and *Preferred shares.*

Shift schedule: see *Stacked schedule.*

Short-term budget: a budget prepared for a period of time generally less than a year.

Short-term liability: see *Current liabilities.*

Single-source buying: a method of purchasing used when a specific supplier is the only one who can supply a needed product.

Skip: a guest who has stayed in a hotel and left without paying the account.

Solvency: the ability of a company to meet its debts as they become due.

Specification: a detailed description of a product that needs to be purchased.

Stacked schedule: a stacked, or shift, schedule is an employee schedule used in departments where groups of employees arrive on the job at the same time and then leave together at the end of their shift. See also *Staff schedule* and *Staggered schedule.*

Staff schedule: a schedule, usually prepared in advance week by week, showing which employees will be on duty each day, and the hours each one will be working. See also *Stacked schedule* and *Staggered schedule.*

Staffing guide: a form developed for each department showing the number of employees, by job category, that should be on duty to meet various possible levels of business volume.

Staggered schedule: a staff schedule used when individual employees in a department arrive on the job at various times and leave at various times at the end of their shift. See also *Stacked schedule* and *Staff schedule.*

Standard cost or expense: what the cost should be for a particular level of sales or revenue.

Statement of capital: statement used by a partnership or proprietorship to show the status of each owner's investment in the business. See also *Statement of retained earnings.*

Statement of operations: see *Income statement.*

Statement of retained earnings: a statement used by an incorporated company showing previous balance sheet figure, plus net income for the period, less any dividends paid during the period, to arrive at current period-end retained earnings.

Stockholder: an investor who owns common and/or preferred shares (stock) in an incorporated business.

Stockholders' equity: see *Owners' equity.*

Stockless buying: see *Volume buying and warehousing.*

Straight-line depreciation: a method of depreciation where equal portions of the amount paid for an asset are shown as an expense during each accounting period of the life of the asset.

Strategic budget: a long-term budget for periods of time generally in excess of one year.

Sunk cost or expense: a cost incurred that is no longer relevant and cannot affect any future decisions.

T-account: a simplified form of account in the shape of a T, with account title on top, debit on the left, and credit on the right.

Task procedures: detailed, step-by-step procedures, preferably in writing, of how a particular task is to be performed.

Trade-in value: the scrap or cash value of an asset at the time its useful life is over or when it is exchanged with cash for a new asset.

Transaction: a business event requiring an entry in the accounting records.

Transcript: a document completed daily that summarizes the charges to and payments made on guest accounts and ensures that each account is properly balanced.

Trend index: in a series of periods of operating results, the result for the first (base) period is given the value of 100. Subsequent period results are then given a number higher or lower than 100 to better reflect each period's change relative to the base year.

Trend results: business operating results compared for a number of sequential periods.

Turnover ratios: ratios that measure the activity of an asset during an accounting period, such as inventory turnover.

Units of production depreciation: a method of depreciation basing depreciation expense on the number of units used or produced by the asset during an accounting period.

Variable cost or expense: one that increases or decreases in direct or linear fashion with increases or decreases in the related sales or revenue.

Vertical statement analysis: see *Comparative/common-size statement analysis.*

Volume: level of sales expressed in dollars or units.

Volume buying and warehousing: a method of purchasing in which large quantities of a product are purchased, stored either at the seller's premises or elsewhere, and shipped to the hotel as needed.

Voucher: a document supporting a business transaction.

Walk-in guest: a hotel guest who arrives and registers without having made a prior reservation.

Withdrawals: monies taken out of a business by individual owners in a proprietorship or partnership (similar to dividends in an incorporated company).

Working capital: current assets less current liabilities.

Working capital management: see *Cash management.*

Yield management: a method of matching customers' rooms reservation patterns and demand for rooms to derive more precise occupancy forecasts and develop appropriate room rates to maximize revenue.

Yield statistic: actual total room revenue for a period of time divided by potential revenue for that period and multiplied by 100.

Index